T0275061

City on the Edge

For decades, Hong Kong has maintained precarious freedom at the edge of competing world powers. In *City on the Edge*, Ho-fung Hung offers a timely and engaging account of Hong Kong's development from precolonial times to the present, with particular focus on the post-1997 handover period. Through careful analysis of vast economic data, a myriad of political events, and intricate networks of actors and ideas, Hung offers readers insight into the fraught economic, political, and social forces that led to the 2019 uprising, while situating the protests in the context of global finance and the geopolitics of the US–China rivalry. A provocative contribution to the discussion on Hong Kong's position in today's world, *City on the Edge* demonstrates that the resistance and repression of 2019–2020 do not spell the end of Hong Kong but the beginning of a long conflict with global repercussions.

Ho-fung Hung is the Henry M. and Elizabeth P. Wiesenfeld Professor in Political Economy at Johns Hopkins University. The author of the award-winning *The Protest with Chinese Characteristics* (2011) and *The China Boom* (2015), he has been featured or cited in media outlets including the *New York Times*, the *Wall Street Journal*, *BBC News*, *The Guardian*, and the *South China Morning Post*.

City on the Edge
Hong Kong under Chinese Rule

Ho-fung Hung

CAMBRIDGE
UNIVERSITY PRESS

CAMBRIDGE
UNIVERSITY PRESS

University Printing House, Cambridge CB2 8BS, United Kingdom

One Liberty Plaza, 20th Floor, New York, NY 10006, USA

477 Williamstown Road, Port Melbourne, VIC 3207, Australia

314–321, 3rd Floor, Plot 3, Splendor Forum, Jasola District Centre, New Delhi – 110025, India

103 Penang Road, #05–06/07, Visioncrest Commercial, Singapore 238467

Cambridge University Press is part of the University of Cambridge.

It furthers the University's mission by disseminating knowledge in the pursuit of education, learning, and research at the highest international levels of excellence.

www.cambridge.org
Information on this title: www.cambridge.org/9781108840330
DOI: 10.1017/9781108885690

© Ho-fung Hung 2022

First published 2022

Printed in the United Kingdom by TJ Books Limited, Padstow Cornwall

A catalogue record for this publication is available from the British Library.

Library of Congress Cataloging-in-Publication Data
NAMES: Hung, Ho-fung, author.
TITLE: City on the edge : Hong Kong under Chinese rule / Ho-fung Hung.
DESCRIPTION: Cambridge ; New York, NY : Cambridge University Press, 2022. | Includes bibliographical references and index.
IDENTIFIERS: LCCN 2021049213 (print) | LCCN 2021049214 (ebook) | ISBN 9781108840330 (hardback) | ISBN 9781108885690 (ebook)
SUBJECTS: LCSH: Economic development – China – Hong Kong – History. | Hong Kong (China) – Economic conditions. | Hong Kong (China) – Politics and government. | Hong Kong (China) – Social conditions. | China – Foreign economic relations – United States. | United States – Foreign economic relations – China.
CLASSIFICATION: LCC HC470.3 .H69 2022 (print) | LCC HC470.3 (ebook) | DDC 330.95125–dc23/eng/20211206
LC record available at https://lccn.loc.gov/2021049213
LC ebook record available at https://lccn.loc.gov/2021049214

ISBN 978-1-108-84033-0 Hardback

Pessimism of the Intellect, Optimism of the Will

CONTENTS

FIGURES

TABLES

PREFACE

I have for years been thinking about writing a book on Hong Kong, looking at how long-term, large-scale global processes interacted with local social forces to make it the unique place I grew up in and how they led it into the crisis today. But besides observing and documenting the dramatic political conflicts unfolding in the city from afar and offering occasional commentary for the media and certain public-intellectual venues, I keep delaying this project. It is a difficult book to write. I have always believed that a social scientist is best at studying a subject from which he or she could maintain a certain critical distance. With the typically intense love–hate relationship with one's hometown, maintaining such critical distance from Hong Kong is challenging.

When I was pursuing a master's degree in sociology in Hong Kong about a quarter of a century ago, I embarked on different sociological–historical projects on the state building and the making of modern Hong Kong society in the 1950s and 1960s. I focused on the rural society that has been marginalized in most urban-centric accounts of Hong Kong's past. The time and place under scrutiny were alien to me, as I grew up in the urban part of Hong Kong in the 1980s. I was surprised how much of the forces of the distant past (well, not so distant from a longer historical perspective, in which I was schooled later) and the forgotten quarters in the countryside were still core to shaping Hong Kong's contemporary development. This reckoning was vindicated in the 2000s when social conflicts centered on rural land development flared up and unleashed a chain reaction that contributed to the upheavals in the 2010s.

I left for the US to pursue a Ph.D. in the very summer when the British handed over Hong Kong's sovereignty to China. Since then, I have been attracted to the study of world capitalism and nation-state formation from the vantage point of the *longue durée*. Over the last two decades, I delved into the centuries-long trajectory of state building and protest in China, the shifting pattern of global economic inequality, the fall and resurgence of China in the world economy since the sixteenth century, and the politics of money and inflation in rich postwar democracies. While I was absorbed in the study of slow-moving structural forces in global capitalism, Hong Kong was always on my mind. As a member of the Hong Kong diaspora, I could not but anxiously watch the fast-paced transformation of Hong Kong's economy and politics, as well as the precipitation of a general crisis that threatens the city's existence as we know it.

Any Hong Kong observer would notice how swiftly and fundamentally the social equilibrium underlining the relative political stability of pre-1997 Hong Kong unraveled under Chinese rule. Growing up in Hong Kong in the 1980s, we watched the speedy political opening in Taiwan and South Korea fostered by dramatic mass movements and street battles. In contrast, protest actions in Hong Kong never went beyond polite petitions or candlelight vigils, though the inequality and power monopoly in Hong Kong was no less outrageous than those in its East Asian neighbors. In any protests or political debates in Hong Kong, crossing a police line or using foul language was regarded as so unforgivable that most fellow protesters and movement leaders would immediately denounce and disown anyone doing so. Many social scientists in Hong Kong have devoted their careers to explaining this apparent stability and conservatism. But this stability and conservatism rapidly gave way to increasingly confrontational protest and abrasive political discourse after the sovereignty handover.

The explosion of conflicts – on the street and within elite circles – culminated in the 2019 uprising. When the uprising began in the early summer, correspondence with Cambridge University Press editor Lucy Rhymer, who was looking for someone to write a book on post-sovereignty-handover Hong Kong, encouraged me that it was the right time to start my book.

Amidst the summer heat of 2019, firebombs and bloodshed in the fall, and the mass arrests and the National Security Law in 2020, the Hong Kong crisis developed at lightning speed. In the short span of fewer than two years, the change in the political consciousness of the Hong Kong people and the policy shift of Beijing and other great powers toward Hong Kong were far greater than the total changes that transpired in the preceding twenty-three years. This makes the writing of the book as challenging as it is necessary.

To understand the dynamics underlying seismic activities that happen in seconds, one has to look at processes measured in geological time of millions of years. As I was writing, the Hong Kong crisis unfolded and media around the world overwhelmed us with a saturation of images of dramatic clashes resembling war zones. It became imperative that I not let my train of thought be carried away by this torrent. I had to stay on course to explicate the slow rupture of local social fabrics and the buildup of global tectonic stress around Hong Kong over the past two decades. Only by understanding the historical origins of the present can we better understand what lies ahead for Hong Kong and the different scenarios' implications for China and the world.

As a keen observer and commentator on Hong Kong, I have amassed a wealth of materials on Hong Kong's economy, politics, and society over the years. From my years as a student activist to my scholarly career in the US, I have been privileged to benefit from countless dialogues and arguments with scholars and political practitioners from a wide spectrum of stances and perspectives. This book is the culmination of this long-accumulated knowledge and insight, for which I have so many to thank. In particular, I owe much to my mentors and peers from my formative years as a sociologist and political economist at the undergraduate and master's programs in the Chinese University of Hong Kong from 1991 to 1997. That was a time when a vibrant community of young intellectuals strived through engaged scholarship to understand the past and to shape the future of Hong Kong at its watershed moment. I was lucky to be involved in the reading groups, research projects, and aimless but inspiring conversations about all sorts of topics over meals and snacks with them. After more than two decades, I realized how much of my convictions and perspectives I owe to these memorable few years of my life. For this, I am indebted to Stephen Chiu, Lui Tai-lok, Lee Ching-kwan, Chan Kin-man, Hui Po-keung, Ip Iam-chong, Law Wing-sang, Lo Sze-ping, Ngo Tak-wing, Tam Man-kei, Thomas Tse, and Wu Kaming.

Throughout my Ph.D. journey in the US, a group of social scientists, including Giovanni Arrighi, Mark Selden, Beverly Silver, Dale Tomich, and Immanuel Wallerstein, opened my eyes. Their heroic defense of grand theory and large-scale, long-term perspectives prevents us from ever losing sight of the forest at a time when everyone else is obsessed with the minutest details of individual trees. The rigorous training in this school of thought ensured that I could anchor whatever subject I studied into the solid foundation of comparative and world-historical perspectives.

While I moved on to research Chinese and global political economy, I continued to have occasional opportunities to engage with the community of scholars of Hong Kong studies. The energy and intellectual integrity of Alvin So, Ray Yep, Brian Fong, Max Wong, Edmond Cheng, Suzanne Choi, Kwong Kin-ming, Ma Ngok, Simon Shen, Eric Tsui, Sebastian Veg, and many others that I experienced firsthand in various joint projects and activities keep me optimistic about the continuous growth in size and rigor of the field. I learned something new in every conversation with each of them. Engagement with a few friends always reminds me of the blind spots of my perspectives. Evans Chan's sensibility that always leads us to reflect upon our personal dilemmas in the historical milieu, Angelina Chin's insights into the memories and legacies of Hong Kong's colonial and Cold War past, and Priscilla Tse's fascinating research on the vernacular culture and sexuality represent the facets of Hong Kong that are still not adequately addressed, if at all, in this book. It is why this book is not the end but the beginning of a new journey.

I conducted additional research when finishing the book, collecting economic data throughout 2019 and 2020. I also did library research in Hong Kong during the winter break of 2019. For that research, Fang Zhicao offered meticulous research assistance. Stephen Chu helped me access the library collections and news archive at the University of Hong Kong, entry to which was heavily restricted in the aftermath of the 2019 unrest. Rachel Blaifeder and Lucy Rhymer at Cambridge University Press guided the conception and fruition of this project every step of the way. Sasha Milonova copyedited the manuscript before it went to production. If this book succeeds in reaching a wide general audience without compromising its academic rigor, credits should go to the comments and suggestions from the two anonymous reviewers at the press.

As always, I have the deepest gratitude to my parents and sister, whose tolerance of my venturing away from their expectations offered me the freedom to chart my path. My mother is my model for stamina and perseverance, which prepared me well for the many frustrations and hurdles in my academic journey. Her family's passion for knowledge and books, despite governmental persecution amidst suffocating anti-intellectualism in the Mao era, ensures that I never take my freedom of thought and expression for granted. When I was younger, I did not appreciate my father's carefree attitude toward life enough, but the older I get, the more I value his sarcasm and sense of humor, his wit about little things, and his love of good food. These are not the qualities that drive you to work hard and think big, but they can keep you upbeat and sane in the face of grave difficulties in this increasingly ridiculous world.

Most of the book's writing happened in the surreal year of 2020, when I was locked down at home and when Beijing was doubling down on its efforts to destroy Hong Kong as we know it. The patience and companionship of my family, including Huei-ying, Henry, Helia, and Penny (the feline who arrived right when the lockdown began), made this endeavor more bearable and at times even enjoyable. I will consider my efforts not wasted if Henry and Helia could learn what happened to their father's hometown through the book. It will be even better if the book can make the slightest contribution to the eventual restoration and advancement of freedom and justice in Hong Kong. If nothing else, may it give us a glimpse into what lies ahead for the city.

ABBREVIATIONS

CCP	Chinese Communist Party
CE	chief executive
CEO	chief executive officer
CEPA	Closer Economic Partnership Arrangement
CFO	chief financial officer
CICC	China International Capital Corporation
CP	Civic Party
DAB	Democratic Alliance for the Betterment and Progress of Hong Kong
ECOSOC	Economic and Social Council
ExCo	Executive Council
FC	Functional Constituency
FDI	foreign direct investment
FSDC	Financial Services Development Council
FTZ	free-trade zone
HKASPDMC	Hong Kong Alliance in Support of Patriotic Democratic Movements in China
HKEX	Hong Kong Exchanges and Clearing
HKFS	Hong Kong Federation of Students
HKSAR	Hong Kong Special Administrative Region
HKTDC	Hong Kong Trade Development Council
HYK	Heung Yee Kuk
IMF	International Monetary Fund
IPO	initial public offering
KMT	Kuomintang
LegCo	Legislative Council
LGBT	lesbian, gay, bisexual, and transgender
LSD	League of Social Democrats

NPCSC	National People's Congress Standing Committee
PLA	People's Liberation Army
PRC	People's Republic of China
RMB	renminbi
SDR	special drawing rights
TARPC	Tibet Autonomous Region Preparatory Committee
TCP	Tibetan Communist Party
TVE	township and village enterprise
SOE	state-owned enterprise
UN	United Nations
USD	United States dollar
WTO	World Trade Organization

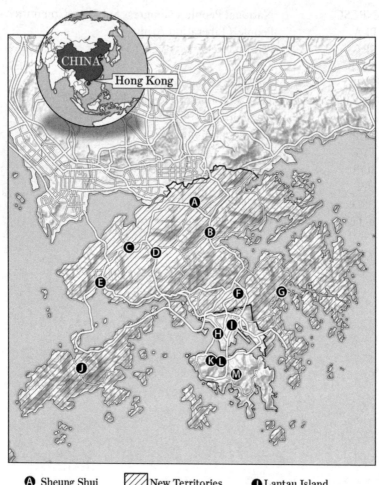

1 INTRODUCTION

On the night of November 17, 2019, the Polytechnic University campus in Hong Kong became a war zone. Heavily armed police encircled the campus. Inside the campus were more than a thousand militant pro-democracy protesters, who used the campus's access to the cross-harbor tunnel to throw roadblocks and paralyze traffic for more than a week. It was part of the protesters' efforts to seize control of campuses sitting on strategic chokepoints of the city's transportation network to halt the city's activities and put pressure on the government.[1]

According to journalists stationed on the campus, protesters were mostly youngsters in their twenties, with some in their teens. That night, the police issued an ultimatum for occupiers inside to surrender, or they would invade with real bullets. The whole world was watching in real time, anticipating a bloodbath. The police attempted to storm the campus, but it proved futile. First, they tried to use armored and water cannon vehicles to storm through the road leading into the main building, but they were blocked by obstacles that the protesters laid on the road. Then, protesters attacked the vehicles with a hail of firebombs that they made from chemicals seized from the campus laboratories. The armored vehicles were completely destroyed. When squads of police officers tried to storm through the foot entrance, a burning barricade and a barrage of firebombs stopped their advance.

After several failed attempts, the police gave up on storming the campus. They tightened the siege and tried to starve the protesters into surrender. The next night, tens of thousands of Hong Kong citizens, many of them middle-aged and middle-class citizens, took to the streets near the campus to try to deliver supplies to the campus and break open a path for the besieged protesters to escape. Skirmishes between police and protesters involving barricades and firebombs broke out in several spots throughout the night.

In the chaos of street battles surrounding the campus, a team of motorcyclists managed to rescue a few dozen besieged protesters, who climbed down ropes hanging from a blocked flyover footbridge. Another group of a few dozen protesters broke out by climbing into the underground sewage system and were fetched by vehicles waiting outside. The rescue operation underground was aided by a group of civil engineers who had a copy of the underground sewage system map. They also closely monitored the system's tidal level to determine when the waterway was open. In the end, only about a hundred protesters remained on the campus. On November 22, nearly a week after the siege began, the last of the protesters surrendered to the police. It was believed that the protesters trapped in the Polytechnic University were among the most militant participants in the movement, with specialists in the making of firebombs and catapults, and the use of archery. The massive rescue efforts throughout the siege showed that these militants commanded broad-based support among Hong Kong citizens.

About a week before the siege of Polytechnic, the campus of the Chinese University of Hong Kong was in a similar situation. On November 11 and 12, protesters occupied a bridge extending from the campus over the Toto Highway. Millions of commuters rely on this route every day, as it connects most of the suburban area in the Eastern New Territories suburbs to downtown Kowloon and the Hong Kong Island. From that bridge, protesters threw furniture and other obstacles to form a barricade and disrupt traffic.[2]

Throughout both days, police with full riot gear entered the campus and tried to clear the bridge. A fight broke out with intense exchanges of firebombs, tear gas, and rubber bullets. At the height of the fight on the night of the 12th, the president of the university, a group of administrators, and a group of notable alumni tried to broker a truce between the students and the police. Others flooded in to defend the campus against the police. Unable to break the resistance and retake the bridge, the police retreated before dawn. After regrouping, the police tried again to storm the occupiers on the 13th. This time, with dwindling numbers, the protesters decided not to defend their position and fled before the police arrived. Many militants who left the Chinese University campus moved on to Polytechnic, and this was how the battle in Polytechnic began.

Beginning in June, the protests were against the government's attempt to amend a law in Hong Kong that would allow the transfer of suspects allegedly violating mainland Chinese law to be tried in mainland courts. The plan evoked an outcry in Hong Kong and the international community. With the recent cases of cross-border kidnapping of dissident booksellers and Chinese business tycoons at odds with the Chinese government, many feared that the amendment would dissolve the insulation of Hong Kong's legal system, which has maintained its common-law tradition under the "One Country, Two Systems" arrangement, from the Chinese legal system, which is tightly controlled by the Communist Party. Many perceived the amendment as the last straw of Hong Kong's local autonomy, which had been eroded for years despite Beijing's promise to protect it when it took Hong Kong from the British in 1997.

The protest movement started with the peaceful Million March on June 9, followed by a violent clash between protesters and riot police outside the Legislative Council (LegCo) on June 12, when the vote on the law was scheduled in the chamber. The conflict paralyzed the traffic surrounding the Legislative Council. The government called off the meeting and announced it would suspend the vote. The government's reluctance to withdraw the bill altogether, and the draconian force that the police used against protesters on June 12, motivated the protesters to fight on. Every weekend after the June 12 clash, protests erupted in different parts of the city and grew in size and militancy. Protesters asked for a complete withdrawal of the law and an independent investigation of police violence during the protests. The government's intransigence and escalation in the use of force by police in dealing with the weekly protests continued to fuel public anger. The protests continued over the summer. Protesters' tactics escalated from barricades to flying rocks to fire-bombs, as well as vandalism and arson against symbols of the government and pro-establishment businesses.[3]

On July 1, during the anniversary of Hong Kong's sovereignty handover, a group of several hundred protesters successfully broke into the Legislative Council building. They sprayed the meeting chamber with graffiti and slogans, and defaced the emblem of the Hong Kong Special Administrative Region (HKSAR), established on July 1, 1997, when the British handed Hong Kong's sovereignty to China. They fled before the police arrived. On July 21, protesters encircled the Central Government Liaison Office, the de facto Chinese Communist Party (CCP) headquarters in Hong Kong, and vandalized the national emblem with a dirt bomb at the main entrance. On many other occasions, the national flags in highly symbolic places were pulled down and either burned or thrown into the sea. By the end of the summer, the protesters' goals had crystallized into the "Five Demands": full withdrawal of the extradition bill, retraction of the characterization of the June 12 protests as "riots," release and exoneration of arrested protesters, establishment of an independent commission of inquiry into police violence, and universal suffrage for Hong Kongers to vote for the Legislative Council and the Chief Executive. They declared that they would not yield until all five demands were met.

In the course of the protest, the slogan "Liberate Hong Kong, revolution of our times" (*gwong fuk heung gong si doi gak ming*), which originated from a pro-independence group whose leaders were either in prison or in exile after an incident of violent conflict with the police in 2016, became the slogan most protesters chanted in nearly all gatherings. The protest song that included the slogan as its main theme, "Glory to Hong Kong," became a big hit. It was dubbed the "national anthem" of Hong Kong.[4] Protesters also consciously drew on slogans from the independence movement in Taiwan and Catalonia to create their versions, like "Hong Kong is not China" (after the slogan "Catalonia is not Spain" in the Catalan independence movement) and "We save our own Hong Kong" (after the slogan "We save our own Taiwan" in Taiwan's Sunflower movement). The momentum of the protests did not wane even after the government finally yielded and declared a formal withdrawal of the extradition law on September 5. The government still adamantly refused an independent investigation of police brutality.

The Puzzling Broad Social Base of a Radical Uprising

The protesters' militant actions that defied heavily armed riot police, as well as their overt cry for Hong Kong independence, surprised many observers of Hong Kong. Ever since the sovereignty handover, Hong Kong had been rife with protests, but the overwhelming majority of these protests had been nonconfrontational and involved no more than peaceful marches or rallies. Very few, if any, of their demands involved anything beyond piecemeal changes. These mild protests fit the cliché image that Hong Kong people are conservative and practical, never venturing too far away from money-making activities. The scenes of fire and blood on university campuses as was witnessed at Polytechnic and Chinese Universities in November 2019 was not something most Hong Kongers had ever seen or expected to see in Hong Kong.

Yet the most surprising part about the 2019 protests, especially for the authorities, was that, despite the militancy and radical consciousness it manifested, the movement garnered solid support from the wider population. The demographic of protesters, reflected in those arrested, was mostly young students, but there were also professionals, including medical doctors, airline pilots, accountants, artists, and older middle-class professionals caught in action on the front line.[5] Since its inception, the Chinese University of Hong Kong's School of Journalism and other organizations have conducted regular polling to gauge public opinion of the protests. It found that even after a long summer of turmoil, most of Hong Kong's population still supported the protesters. They blamed the government for the escalation of conflict.[6]

The broad support of the protesters was once again confirmed in the district council election on November 24, just a few days after the university battle ended. This grassroots election has always been about mundane neighborhood issues like road construction projects and sewage maintenance. Pro-government candidates always won the majority of the seats through its patron–client networks in the neighborhood. But in the 2019 election, democratic candidates, including many newbies explicitly supportive of the protest, won a landslide victory that the HKSAR had never seen before.[7] This caught Beijing by surprise, as it had been waiting for the "silent majority" to tire of the protests and deal a blow to the increasingly radical opposition in the election.

Resistance to the extradition bill and widespread sympathy for the resulting movement are not limited to ordinary citizens, but also quite explicit among the conservative business elite of the city.

Even before the resistance gathered momentum, Joseph Lau Luen Hung, a real-estate billionaire, filed a judicial review against the extradition law and spearheaded the elite's opposition to the law. Afterward, a handful of influential Beijing allies, including Charles Ho Tsu-kwok, a second-generation tycoon and a member of the National Committee of the Chinese People's Political Consultative Conference, also spoke out against the extradition law. He remarked on March 26, 2019, in his speech at an elite business social event, that many of his friends "were afraid of being arrested and transferred [to the mainland]," and that the extradition amendment would severely damage Hong Kong's common-law practice, which is "the most essential [aspect of] the One Country, Two Systems" and "Hong Kong's business environment."[8] Many other pro-Beijing representatives of business associations and political groups also expressed their opposition or doubt about the amendment.[9]

When the protests were in full force during the summer, Beijing tried to mobilize its wealthy elite allies to denounce the protesters and express support for the government's efforts to restore law and order, as it has always done. But the response was lukewarm. Li Ka-shing, the richest man in Hong Kong and Asia for many years, and Beijing's long-term ally in securing Hong Kong's smooth transition from British to Chinese rule, published a full front-page ad in various newspapers – according to most interpretations, it denounced violence on both sides, not only the protesters but also the police. He was later criticized openly by the official Chinese media for being suspiciously unenthusiastic in denouncing the protesters.[10] A wide range of establishment business and professional elites stepped forward to call for further government compromise, such as establishing an independent inquiry commission into the police violence, as the only way to quell the unrest.[11] They appeared to put more blame on the government than on the protesters for perpetuating the unrest.

More surprisingly, even some mainland Chinese tycoons in Hong Kong were against the extradition law. In late May, on the eve of the eruption of protest, a group of wealthy, powerful elites from mainland China with residency in Hong Kong joined a dinner party with Hong Kong's chief executive, Carrie Lam Cheng Yuet-ngor. At the dinner, they lobbied Lam for scrapping the legislation and expressed their worry about the law.[12] The fear of being extradited to mainland China concerned not only democratic activists but also many businesspeople. Likewise, most business organizations representing foreign business interests in Hong Kong, including the American Chamber of Commerce in Hong Kong and the International Chamber of Commerce – Hong Kong, spoke out against the law.[13]

This massive mobilization across the population of Hong Kong against the law, coupled with the apparent sympathy and neutrality of the establishment elite, would have been unthinkable in the HKSAR's early days. Radical, confrontational activists had been a minority in Hong Kong's opposition movement, which had always been dominated by moderates who sought dialog and compromise with Beijing. For years, most Hong Kongers had been known for their conservatism and pragmatism, if not apathy toward politics. One has to ask: what happened to Hong Kong since the sovereignty handover that made this massive mobilization of society in defiance of Beijing possible? Why did even the business elite, whose alliance with Beijing brought them huge privileges and benefits, become hesitant to support the Hong Kong government and Beijing during the unrest?

Besides the changes within Hong Kong, we also need to ask what changes occurred in the geopolitical and global economic environments of Hong Kong that helped make the 2019 movement possible. One key feature of the 2019 protest movement is that protesters consciously developed an international front that joined hands with the Hong Kong diaspora to lobby parliaments and governments worldwide, most of all in the UK and the US, to support the movement.[14] This international lobbying contributed to the passage of the Hong Kong Human Rights and Democracy Act in the US Congress in November 2019. The international attention centered on Hong Kong as one of the most contentious issues that intensified confrontation in US–China relations.

With the heavy-handed imposition of the National Security Law from Beijing on Hong Kong in July 2020 and the widespread arrests that followed, the earthquake that shocked Hong Kong in 2019 seems to have subsided. But resistance elsewhere, as with the aftermath of Hong Kong's 2014 Umbrella Movement, clearly shows that such tranquility could only be temporary. Tensions along the fault line continued to grow, and another tremor in the future is certain. Underlying the 2019 movement is a major tectonic shift in local society and the global political economy. To discern the scale and dynamics of that tectonic shift, we have to consult and move beyond the existing studies of the colonial and post-handover development of Hong Kong.

Perspectives on a City That Refuses to Die

In 1968, the British writer Richard Hughes published *Borrowed Place, Borrowed Time*, in which he characterized Hong Kong:

> [a] borrowed place living on borrowed time, Hong Kong is an impudent capitalist survival on China's communist derrière ... There is work and profit today. There will be work, and there may be profit, tomorrow – if tomorrow is allowed to come. That is Hong Kong's credo.[15]

To Hughes, the whole existence of Hong Kong as a free-as-the-Wild-West city was transient. It was destined to die at some point and be absorbed into China. Everything was temporary. This notion of "borrowed place, borrowed time" became a dominant theme, even a cliché, in the discussion of Hong Kong in literature, culture, and academic studies. This notion of "borrowed place, borrowed time" does capture the reality of Hong Kong before the 1997 handover. Some would argue that the "One Country, Two Systems" that Beijing promised Hong Kong after the handover was an extension of this transient state of Hong Kong's existence.[16]

After the founding of the People's Republic of China in 1949, the British were well aware that the city was indefensible if Beijing decided to invade. Politically, the continuation of British colonial rule was at the mercy of Beijing and could end at any time. It rang ever truer amidst the waves of decolonization in other parts of the British Empire. The democratic movement in Hong Kong also accepted Hong Kong's existence as an entity separate from China as temporary. It saw Hong Kong's democratization as part of China's larger democratic movement in the tradition of the May 4 student movement in 1919 and the Tiananmen movement in 1989. The democratization of Hong Kong was not significant in its own right. Instead, many saw and continue to see it as little more than the

Chinese democratic movement temporarily in exile in Hong Kong as an offshore space.[17] Many activists in the movement believe that "One Country, Two Systems" would not be necessary if China became democratic. They dream that Hong Kong's democratization will pioneer the democratization of China at large. For them, the Hong Kong democratic movement's ultimate goal is Hong Kong's absorption into a democratic China.[18]

Economically, Hong Kong's prosperity has historically hinged on China's exclusion from the world economy. Hong Kong has been a gateway or a proxy for China into international markets. The rise of Hong Kong as an industrial powerhouse in the 1950s through the 1970s was fueled by Chinese capitalists and working-class migrants who fled mainland China after the Communist takeover. The rise of Hong Kong as a trading and financial center connecting China and the world after the 1970s was also based on China's closure from free trade and capital flows. It is often assumed that these economic functions of Hong Kong would dissipate as China continued opening up.[19]

Students of Hong Kong culture notice that hybridity is a defining characteristic of Hong Kong identity. Hong Kong has been a capital of China's diaspora worldwide, with high concentrations of cultural institutions and influences from the US, the UK, and other Western countries. Hong Kong saw the coexistence of various discourses of Chinese nationalism, first from Taiwan's Nationalist Party (Kuomintang, KMT) and then from the CCP.[20] Some characterize Hong Kong culture as a "cultural supermarket" or "kaleidoscope" consisting of a plurality of cultural idioms from which Hong Kong dwellers choose to assemble their own hybrid identities.[21] Whether and how this "cultural supermarket" or "kaleidoscope" of Hong Kong identity will perpetuate itself or be absorbed by a singular Chinese nationalist identity emanating from Beijing has been a point of contention.

The signing of the Sino-British Joint Declaration in 1984 and the finalization of the Basic Law, the mini-constitution governing post-handover Hong Kong, in 1990 warranted the continuation of Hong Kong's pre-existing politico-legal system, economic institutions, and the so-called "Hong Kong way of life" beyond 1997 for at least another five decades. Despite that, the notion that Hong Kong was dying was so prominent that cultural studies scholar Ackbar Abbas asserted on the eve of the handover that the cultural politics of

Hong Kong was a "politics of disappearance."[22] Journalistic coverage of Hong Kong around the handover did not shy away from predicting the "death of Hong Kong."[23] The common perception was that Hong Kong was gradually dissipating, on its way to being absorbed into the fabric of the Chinese state, the Chinese economy, and the Chinese identity. This perception was reinforced in many official Chinese publications on Hong Kong. They uniformly saw Hong Kong's development, after deviating from the main current of the Chinese nation-state's development because of British colonial rule, finally returned to the main current after 1997. Hong Kong became an organic part of the "great revival of the Chinese nation."[24]

A casual search of English-language academic publications on Hong Kong shows that after a peak in publications in the wake of the sovereignty handover, there was a respite. During that peak, most publications look back on Hong Kong's colonial past as if they were elegiac, concluding a bygone era.[25] The number of English-language publications on Hong Kong declined right after the year 2000. Among the post-handover publications, many are about Hong Kong's new role in the context of the economic rise of China, how Hong Kong was overshadowed by other Chinese global cities like Shanghai, the merging of Hong Kong with the great Pearl river delta economy, and so on.[26]

On the other hand, the literature on the political and cultural development of Hong Kong after 1997 started to notice the resilience of Hong Kong politics and society. An increasing number of works on Hong Kong politics saw the intensifying struggle between the democratic movement, which was striving to actualize universal suffrage in the local legislature and the chief executive, as promised in the Basic Law, and Beijing's attempt to tighten its political control of the city by denying genuine universal suffrage to the city.[27] Despite increasing political control by Beijing, Hong Kong's democratic movement did not fade away. Instead, it became ever more lively with the injection of a new wave of social movements.[28]

This new wave of movements, to be sure, is in part a continuation of the traditional social movements connected to the broader quest for Chinese democratization. The annual June 4 vigil in commemoration of the 1989 massacre, protests that asked for the release of Liu Xiaobo, protests against human rights abuse during the Olympic torch relay in Hong Kong in 2008, and others were prominent examples of this type of contentious politics in post-handover Hong Kong.[29] But there were also many more locally grown protest movements not connected to China. They were about preserving local communities and historical buildings, movements against the dissolution of the Hong Kong–China border, and protests against various forms of local injustice and everyday-life encroachment by China. These movements, disconnected from the theme of China's democratization, became the new source of energy for the Hong Kong opposition movement.[30] At the same time, Hong Kong citizens have been increasingly active in defending the independent judiciary, which continued to operate under the common-law tradition, separate from the Chinese legal system, despite the creeping political pressure from Beijing. Legal activism that challenged the authorities through litigation was on the rise in post-handover Hong Kong.[31]

Corresponding to this rise of local social movements was a renewed search for a local Hong Kong identity that was not only distinct from the Chinese national identity, but also more locally grounded than the previous mosaic notion of Hong Kong's culture and identity. How this emerging local identity conflicted and negotiated with the encroaching Chinese national identity in the realm of the media, the arts, and education became the focus of many works on Hong Kong culture published after 1997.[32]

These works suggest that the tension between Hong Kong's continuous global connectedness, the expanding economic and political presence of the Chinese nation, and the emerging quest for a local identity underlie the dynamics of conflict in Hong Kong after 1997. This literature offers us precious insights into the tectonic shifts of Hong Kong's economy, politics, and cultural identity underneath the superficial tranquility and apparent "death" of the city as a distinct entity. Nevertheless, few works so far offer a comprehensive examination of these tectonic shifts in their own right, or look at how these shifts are interconnected with one another. With a sharp focus on a particular issue in Hong Kong, many of these studies offer blurry, if any, images of China and the global economy. Some recurrently resort to the generic notion of the "rise of China" and "globalization" to contextualize Hong Kong developments. As the fault lines underlying Hong Kong's development are always linked to the larger fault lines driving and straining the dynamic changes in the Chinese and global political economy, any full understanding of the Hong Kong crisis today has to take into account the global and regional contexts in their full complexity.

As a city-state, Hong Kong's story and its struggles for autonomy are far from unique in the history of nation-state formation. Beijing has never viewed this project of absorbing Hong Kong into the PRC's economic, political, and cultural fabrics as unique. It often draws on the playbook of its absorption of other ethnic frontiers in its early days in deliberating its strategy on Hong Kong. The Hong Kong question has often been discussed in connection with the Tibet and Xinjiang questions in many texts published in the PRC about China's territorial integrity.[33] Beijing has also long seen Hong Kong as a precursor to the solution to the Taiwan question.[34]

To be sure, Hong Kong managed to hold out longer against a full absorption than Tibet, Xinjiang, and other ethnic minority areas in the early days of the PRC, despite the fact that China is a much stronger power in the world than it was in the 1950s. This staying power of Hong Kong has something to do with Hong Kong's connectedness to the global flow of capital and the involvement of the US, as well as of the international community, in maintaining Hong Kong's autonomy. The latter's influences were, until recently, significant in deterring a full obliteration of Hong Kong's autonomy for the sake of the interests of global businesses in the city.

Cities and States in World Capitalism

The continuing autonomy of a city-state or a small political entity that thrived on international trade and finance at the interstices of great powers is common throughout world history. The capitalist world economy, at its inception in early modern times, was stitched together by a global network of commercial and financial city-states. The Italian city-states and Hanseatic League in the spaces between declining and rising empires, and the port city-states of Oman and Malacca at the intersections of rising Western colonial powers and Asian empires are cases in point.[35] The emergence of the international system of sovereign nation-states – either in the form of kingdoms or in the form of republics – fomented intensifying conflicts between centralizing states and wealthy cities with distinct histories and identities. The long transformation of the capitalist world economy from a network of cities to a patchwork of national economies was largely a history of incorporation and subjugation of autonomous cities by territorial national states.[36]

The question of how larger territorial powers could absorb and subjugate a city and its citizens, who are used to autonomy and freedom, has occupied centralizing rulers since the Renaissance and early modern times. Machiavelli devoted a section in *The Prince* to discussing the pros and cons of different strategies that the ruler of a kingdom could employ to hold on to a free, wealthy city that he had just conquered.[37] The strategies he discussed include giving a free hand to the locals for self-governance, erecting a trusted oligarchy to rule on the prince's behalf, and completely annihilating local customs and ruling directly with an iron hand. These are exactly the different modes of governance with which Beijing has been experimenting in Hong Kong over the years. China's incorporating of British Hong Kong into its sovereignty is by no means unique in the twentieth century. The challenge of incorporating and ruling city-regions that had enjoyed self-governance or had been ruled by other powers was common to postcolonial nation formations. India's seizure of Goa from Portugal in the 1960s, Indonesian incorporation of Portuguese East Timor in the 1970s, Argentina's futile attempt to capture the British Falklands and the Spanish ordeal to absorb British Gibraltar are all well-known cases.

The Hong Kong question for Beijing goes beyond this perennial question of how a centralizing state exerts political control over a newly incorporated city. Neoliberal globalization in the late twentieth century fostered the rise of a global economy connected by a hierarchical network of global cities or world cities. Globally connected cities re-emerged to replace nation-states as the forefront of economic development, somehow returning to the early modern world economy with cities instead of national economies as its foundational units.[38] In this new context of development, many global cities gained new regulatory and political autonomy vis-à-vis the nation-state they were embedded in. Some go as far as becoming political actors pursuing city-to-city diplomacy and independent policies addressing significant global issues, such as climate change and financial (de)regulation, sometimes at odds with their national governments.[39]

In the new global economy, many nation-states that strive to maintain the integrity, security, and regulation of the national economic system while benefiting from free trade and free capital flow in the global economy find it beneficial to create autonomous city-regions at their borders in the form of special economic zones or free-trade zones, which enjoy the suspension of many national regulations and a much more porous interface with the global economy. In most cases, like the Subic Special Economic and Freeport Zone in the Philippines, the free-trade zone on the US–Mexican border, various export-processing zones in India, and Shenzhen in China, such special zones were created from scratch.⁴⁰ In all these cases, the special zones' management is always about balancing national economic security and economic openness, creating a dilemma between local autonomy and central control. This dilemma sometimes leads to political conflict between the national states and the autonomous local governments.

From this perspective, Hong Kong after 1997 is a super special economic/free-trade zone in China. Its global connectedness and its economic freedom do not need to be created from scratch. They were inherited from more than a century of British rule and are recognized formally by international treaties and law from the very beginning of the establishment of the HKSAR. This super special free-trade zone is of utmost importance to China's state capitalism under the ever-tightening authoritarian control of the CCP and the continued dominance of state enterprises. The CCP aspires to develop China's economy by benefiting from global free trade and global capital, but it still jealously guards its regulatory and monopoly power over the national economy. Hong Kong offers a solution to the CCP's dilemma. But it also creates tension between the need to maintain a special economic/free-trade zone and the imperative of establishing total political control over a newly absorbed, culturally and institutionally distinct city. This tension created an increasingly explosive situation for Beijing, Hong Kong citizens, and anyone holding a stake in Hong Kong. The contentious relation between Hong Kong and Beijing after 1997 results from two questions at the same time: the age-old question of how a territorial ruler could establish effective control over a newly incorporated city that had developed its own identity and autonomy, and the twenty-first-century question of how a closed or semi-closed economic system could benefit from a globally connected autonomous and open city without losing control of it.

While the first question drives Beijing to follow its playbook over Tibet and Xinjiang to move toward direct rule over Hong Kong, the second question restrains Beijing from going too far. The result is a tug of war between two opposite tendencies that creates a space of indeterminacy for human actions to shape outcomes. Hong Kong is a city constantly on the edge. It is on the edge of great powers, on the edge of being annihilated, and on the edge of breaking free.

Method and Outline: Capital, Empire, and Resistance

In all of the cases of autonomous city-regions ruled by larger states mentioned in the last section, the ebbs and flows of autonomy and fortunes of the regions are not determined by local forces alone, but also by global economic and geopolitical shifts. To understand the long-term development of these autonomous entities fully, we need to develop an in-depth understanding of the interactions of the global and local forces involved. Hong Kong is no exception. We cannot make sense of its post-handover development unless we have a thorough understanding of such larger trends as the financialization of the global economy, the restructuring of the global division of labor, the China boom and its faltering, and the shift of US–China relations from amity to rivalry.

With the explosion of violence witnessed in 2019–2020, we can now benefit from hindsight to examine in full the seismic shifts underneath Hong Kong that unleashed the earthquake. This book attempts to build on and move beyond previous works on post-handover Hong Kong to reassess the political economy of the city-state and its resistance movement under Chinese rule. Aided by systematic analysis of original data, thick description of key events, and interrogations of larger fluxes in the global economy and geopolitics, this book looks at how the social and political fault lines in Hong Kong that originated in colonial times transformed and intensified after 1997. It will exposit how these local fault lines are linked to the global system of fault lines. This book will look at what new possibilities and new perils the 2019 turmoil – and its suppression – have generated for the future of Hong Kong.

Social-scientific studies of protests and politics have been divided between analyses that focus on structures, long-term trends, and inevitability and those emphasizing actors' choice, events, and contingency.[41] In this regard, Marx's "Eighteenth Brumaire" is still the classic that showcases how to combine both a structural and an eventful approach with reference to the unfolding of an epochal political struggle – the mobilization and countermobilization of different French political forces that led to the destruction of a constrained liberal democracy established after the 1848 Revolution and its replacement with the dictatorship of Emperor Napoleon III in 1851.[42] Many have valued that the text highlights the relative autonomy of the political and transgressed Marx's (and Marxians') historicism and structuralism in other works that emphasize inevitable and predetermined structural trends.[43]

"The Eighteenth Brumaire" encompasses the analysis of the balance of forces among different classes, class factions, and the state bureaucracy that had developed with French capitalism over long periods and had been shaped by the state of world capitalism at that moment. Built upon this mapping of French social formations is a careful examination of the strategies and tactics of, and the dynamic interactions between, the political representatives of these social forces. It resembles an analysis of a key battle in a war that does not lose sight of either the structural determinants – the logistics, organization, training, equipment, and size of different forces engaged in the battle – or the contingencies – such as the strategy and tactics chosen by different sides and the weather on the battlefield – that shape the battle's outcome. After all, it is from "The Eighteenth Brumaire" that Marx's oft-cited quote originated – "Men make their own history, but they do not make it just as they please; they do not make it under circumstances chosen by themselves, but under circumstances directly found, given and transmitted from the past."[44]

In this book, I follow the spirit of "The Eighteenth Brumaire" to trace the historical structures within and surrounding Hong Kong and key players' actions in the contexts of such structures. The substantive analysis of the book is divided into three parts. In the first part, "Capital," I look into Hong Kong's economic connection with mainland China and the resulting change in the balance of power between different factions of global and local capital. The second part, "Empire," focuses on Hong Kong's place in the development of the nation- and empire-building projects of the Communist party-state throughout the CCP's hundred-year history. In the third part, "Resistance," I examine the evolving class politics and political consciousness underlining the democratic and social movements in Hong Kong from colonial times to the present.

The structural and historical analysis in this book is based on a large amount of original statistical data and a rich secondary literature. Mapping the economic, political, and social formations within and around Hong Kong is just a starting point. I also rely on news accounts available in journalistic sources, aided by the insights I gained from my decades-long interaction with scholars and political practitioners from different camps in Hong Kong, to reconstruct the unfolding of contingent social and political struggles after the sovereignty handover in 1997. This historical, structural, and eventful study will lead us to understand the origins, outcome, and future prospect of the present crisis in Hong Kong.

This book is centered on Hong Kong under Chinese rule after 1997. But all social and political forces at play after 1997 had deep roots in local and global history. For millennia, Hong Kong's history has been shaped by its unchanging geo-location at the interface of a land-based power and a maritime civilization. Contrary to British colonial historiography, Hong Kong was far from a "barren rock" before the British came in the mid-nineteenth century. As far back as at least the twelfth century, present-day Hong Kong hosted modest-sized settlements and markets. Throughout its history, the Hong Kong area has been at the edge of the Chinese empire, bordering an oceanic world. Access to the sea and the imperial center's remoteness made Hong Kong a space of outcasts and rebels. Over centuries, layers of settlements repeatedly relived the tug of war between the imperial state and the defiant fishing, agrarian or commercial communities. Hong Kong's geo-location at the edge of empire did not end with the British, who established Hong Kong as its most distant colony. From then on, Hong Kong became the periphery of multiple political powers from the British to the US and the People's Republic of China. The power and resistance in post-handover Hong Kong are, in many ways, a continuation of this geo-history of Hong Kong in the long run. Any serious analysis of Hong Kong at the present, therefore, has to start with the deep history of the major sociopolitical groups and institutions of Hong Kong today.

Chapter 2 starts by outlining the colorful history of power and resistance in pre-British Hong Kong. Many communities involved in this part of Hong Kong's history continued to play a part in the colonial and postcolonial struggles. The chapter also discusses how the rise of Hong Kong as an industrial and financial center fomented different social groups that were mobilized in the struggle for Hong Kong's future by competing political forces at the height of the Cold War. Most significant is the rise of a new middle class in tandem with the transformation of Hong Kong's economy into a finance- and service-centered one in the 1970s and the 1980s. This new middle class, combined with the plurality of grassroots social movements, charted a course for the locally rooted democratic movement that continued to grow after the sovereignty handover, constituting the backbone of the resistance in its quest of greater autonomy for Hong Kong under Beijing's rule.

Chapter 3 addresses Hong Kong's economic function for China after 1997. Beijing's challenge has been to perpetuate Hong Kong's role as China's offshore financial and trading center after the sovereignty handover. After 1997, the US–Hong Kong Policy Act allowed the US and the international community to continue treating Hong Kong as an independent trading entity separate from mainland China. Hong Kong maintained its separate membership in international organizations like the World Trade Organization (WTO), even after China joined those organizations. This continuous special status, conditional upon Hong Kong's autonomy from Beijing under "One Country, Two Systems," made Hong Kong a conduit and stepping-stone for Chinese capital and the elite who sought access to global capital or relocation to other parts of the world. It is also a key to Beijing's plan to internationalize the Chinese currency, renminbi (RMB), without making RMB fully convertible in mainland China. Hong Kong's unique offshore financial-center role for China led to increasing Chinese capital's domination in Hong Kong.

Chapter 4 looks at how Hong Kong's local business elite and foreign businesses were gradually squeezed out from center stage of the financial market in Hong Kong by Chinese companies and the Chinese business elite. While local tycoons worked closely with the CCP to defend the city's undemocratic status quo and advance their

business interests on the mainland, they valued the legal and institutional autonomy of Hong Kong as safeguards of their wealth.
Chinese tycoons with Hong Kong residency, some of whom are
publicly known as CCP members, also value such autonomy and
legal protection of their private wealth, though many see themselves
as caretakers of Beijing's interests in Hong Kong. The business elites'
contradictory character manifests itself amidst the fight over the
extradition bill, when many local and mainland Chinese tycoons
explicitly or implicitly acted against the bill. The US–China trade
war that began in 2017, superimposed on the elite conflict in
Hong Kong, cast a shadow on the offshore financial-center role of
Hong Kong.

   One cannot fully understand Beijing's long strategy over
Hong Kong without considering China's imperial legacy of stepwise
absorption and assimilation of its ethnic frontiers and the history of
the CCP's struggle to control these frontiers in the early years of the
PRC. Chapter 5 outlines the development of the ideas and experi-
ments of "One Country, Two Systems" before Hong Kong, analyz-
ing the CCP's attempt to absorb and assimilate its ethnic frontiers
such as Tibet since the 1950s. Beijing's leadership explicitly refer-
enced these histories, in particular the history of Tibet in 1951–1959,
when they first devised and promoted the "One Country, Two
Systems" formula for Hong Kong in the early 1980s.

   Chapter 6 looks at how the design and implementation of
the Hong Kong version of "One Country, Two Systems" codified
and reproduced pre-existing socio-political divisions in Hong Kong
and generated new ones via the Sino-British Joint Declaration in
1984 and the Basic Law adopted in 1990. The Basic Law guarantees
some fundamental rights and freedoms for Hong Kong's residents. It
promises eventual universal suffrage of the chief executive and all of
the legislative councilors. But an alliance of Beijing and the local
business elite in Hong Kong prevented it from specifying the exact
form and timetable for universal suffrage. It also contains a clause
about the necessity of antisubversion legislation to protect China's
national security. Such a clause posed an unprecedented threat to the
rights and freedoms that Hong Kong had been enjoying under British
rule. These contradictions and ambiguities of the Basic Law sowed
the seeds of political conflicts after 1997. These conflicts, coupled
with the rising monopoly of Chinese capital in Hong Kong,

stimulated Beijing's urge to forfeit indirect rule and move to a radical assimilationist politics and direct rule. Beijing's urge has been articulated systematically by a group of official scholars who advocated the revival of the Chinese empire and saw Beijing's governance of Hong Kong as a rehearsal of its power projection farther abroad. Beijing's premature crackdown on Hong Kong's autonomy unleashed escalating resistance that culminated in the great clash of 2019.

Chapter 7 discusses the evolution of the opposition movements seeking Hong Kong's democracy and autonomy before and after the handover. The mainstream democratic opposition in Hong Kong grew out of the anticolonial and Chinese nationalist movement in the 1970s and 1980s. Their moderate, nonconfrontational approach to gradual democratic reform made some gains in the first fifteen years of China's rule. Simultaneously, the increasing aggressiveness of Beijing's crackdown on Hong Kong's autonomy and freedom, coupled with the rising social polarization caused by the influx of Chinese capital, fueled the growth of more radical, confrontational social and opposition movements.

Chapter 8 discusses how the rise of the radical wings of the democratic movement reverberated with the rise of localist, or even separatist, consciousness among the younger generation. For a long time, the ambiguous Hong Kong local identity had been no more than a cultural identity. Most social and opposition movements had been imbued with the Chinese nationalist discourse and saw Hong Kong's democratic movements as part of China's. But as a reaction to rising interclass and intergenerational inequality driven by Chinese capital and Beijing's tightening direct rule over Hong Kong, the consciousness that Hong Kong constitutes a political community separate from China's emerged, and after about 2010 became mainstream among the younger generation of activists. Corresponding to this politicization of the Hong Kong identity was the germination of the demand for self-determination or even for Hong Kong independence within the democratic movement. The localist turn of political demands and increasingly confrontational tactics of protest underlined the escalating conflicts, starting from the anti-National Education Curriculum mobilization in 2012, to the Umbrella Movement in 2014, and to the 2019 uprising.

The concluding chapter discusses the ramifications of Beijing's response to the 2019 protests through the imposition of the National Security Law on Hong Kong in June 2020, as well as the US reaction through decertifying Hong Kong's autonomy vis-à-vis mainland China, in light of the complicated system of fault lines that underlie these developments. Many see an endgame for Hong Kong and the full absorption of Hong Kong into China under a "One Country, One System" arrangement like Tibet after the 1950s, well in advance of the official expiry date of the "One Country, Two Systems" arrangement, set to end in 2047.

While the end of Hong Kong is a possible outcome, it is still too early to tell whether this will be its fate. As the vibrant social forces of resistance unleashed in 2019 have proved to have staying power in one form or another, Beijing is still far from establishing total control of the self-mobilized and defiant society. Undoubtedly, the National Security Law is intimidating Hong Kong society into more egregious self-censorship. Nonetheless, the continuous financial and commercial connectedness of Hong Kong with the global economy, together with China's increasing reliance on Hong Kong's function as an offshore financial center amidst China's deepening economic woes and the tightening US sanctions on China, could make the National Security Law more difficult to enforce without damaging China's financial interests. The host of countries, including the US, the UK, Taiwan, and Australia, accepting escapees from Hong Kong could help keep the resistance in Hong Kong alive. The National Security Law further unifies democratic countries in confronting China on various other issues, intensifying China's rivalry with the US and its allies. It will only make the road ahead for Hong Kong more uncertain. Hong Kong's fate is far from sealed.

2 AT EMPIRES' EDGE, 1197–1997

The cliché has long held that Hong Kong transformed from a "fishing village" before British colonization into a modern metropolis upon the handover of its sovereignty to China in the twentieth century.[1] This textbook representation of Hong Kong's history focuses on Hong Kong's economy and misses all the complex political and social processes and actors involved in the making of modern Hong Kong. What has become today's Hong Kong had a long and colorful history before colonial times.

Today, what is known as Hong Kong constituted three-fifths of Xin'an county under the imperial administration of the Qing dynasty.[2] Under the Nanjing Treaty of 1842, the Qing court ceded today's Hong Kong Island to the British. British territory was extended to the Kowloon peninsula in 1860. Then, the British took advantage of the weakness of the Qing government after its defeat in the Sino-Japanese War of 1894–1895 to pressure the Qing to lease a vast area north of the original Hong Kong colony, plus the outlying islands of the region, to the British in 1898 for ninety-nine years. These areas became the New Territories of today's Hong Kong region.

Resembling any other agrarian communities in late imperial China, precolonial Xin'an county was governed by a bureaucratic gentry class. This gentry class based their power on their control of cultivable land and local markets, local militia organizations, monopolization of land-tax farming, and their familial and other social connections with local government officials. The county was located at the mouth of the Pearl river, with abundant marine resources. Fisher communities also thrived along the coastal area.

Since at least the Tang dynasty in the seventh to tenth centuries, Tuen Mun in today's western New Territories was a customs checkpoint, guarded by an imperial garrison, for merchants from Southeast Asia, India, and the Arab world to lay over before entering the Pearl river on the way to Guangzhou (Canton). Tuen Mun was the first place named in today's Hong Kong in Chinese historical documents.[3] Elaborate towns with significant commercial and nonagricultural activities developed in today's Kowloon area during Song times in the tenth to thirteenth centuries.[4] Escaping from the invading Mongols, the Song court temporarily relocated to Hong Kong before the last Song emperor, Zhao Bing, committed suicide by jumping into the sea in 1279. In today's Hong Kong, gods in many local temples originated from the legendary generals and aristocrats who accompanied the last Song emperor to Hong Kong.[5]

The British colonial rule of Hong Kong was founded on the many pre-existing communities in the region. Mainland Chinese immigrants attracted by the new economic activities brought by the British moved to the city. They built new communities and outnumbered the original inhabitants. This brought new conflicts among the new arrivals, as well as between the new and old communities. This pattern of settlement and contention recurred throughout Hong Kong's history, reproducing Hong Kong as an economically vibrant but politically contentious space at the edge of empires – first the Chinese empire, then the British Empire, and more recently the reviving Chinese nation that has started to project its power overseas like an empire.

James Scott describes Zomia, the mountain regions of inland Southeast Asia where diverse ethnic minority communities settled, as a periphery of state space. It constituted a zone of refuge and resistance where populations evaded incorporation and subordination by the imperial, colonial, and national states located in the lowland.[6] Hong Kong, located at the edge of the Chinese landmass and cut off from the political and economic centers of the Chinese empire or nation by mountains, constituted a comparable space of refuge and resistance of peoples escaping from repression and turmoil in the core regions controlled by the Chinese state in various epochs.

From the mid-nineteenth century, Hong Kong was on the geographical periphery of the Chinese empire and of the British oceanic empire centered in London. Colonial Hong Kong thrived on this double periphery at the interstices of the British Empire and the Chinese empire – both the old Chinese empire that vanished in 1911 and the new one in the making in the early twenty-first century. Prasenjit Duara aptly characterizes Hong Kong as a global "liminal space" and "contact zone" between China and the Western world, as well as within maritime Asia.[7] In this space, communities settled, thrived, or rebelled against the dominating political powers throughout the long history of Hong Kong.

Fishers and Empires

Tanka fishers were among the first human settlers in early Hong Kong. Their communities dotted the coastline of the region when the British came. Tanka people are not a homogeneous ethnic group. "Tanka" refers to those who reside in fishing boats and make a living by fishing. It is more an occupation-caste category than an ethnic one. The Tankas in different places share a similar language (the Tanka dialects), folk religions (worship of Tin Hau and Hung Shing), as well as customs and lifestyles. The Tanka in Xin'an county, among the earliest "settlers," never really settled ashore as the late-coming agrarian cultivators did. Their origins are unknown. It is believed that they come from diverse sources, including pirates from Southeast Asia, Han Chinese banished by the state, and indigenous Austronesian people marginalized by agrarian Han Chinese migrants from the north.[8]

In imperial China, the Tanka were ranked as one of the most inferior classes. They were sometimes referred to in Chinese historical writings as subhuman.[9] For a long time, the imperial state forbade the Tanka people to settle ashore, marry Hans, own land, or participate in imperial examinations. They were stripped of all political rights enjoyed by the landed population. On the other hand, they had many obligations to the imperial state. Many times the fishers were forced to labor in state-run salt pans or were conscripted into the imperial army. They were obliged to pay taxes. Their marine-resources-based livelihood rendered them incapable of attaining self-subsistence as most agrarian communities do. They had to trade with Han merchants for agricultural products, usually on unfavorable terms of trade.[10]

During the 1120s, the Song state was at war with the Jurchens on the empire's northern border. The embattled imperial state redoubled its conscription. It recruited a large number of fishers from today's Lantau island in Hong Kong into the military. In exchange, the government loosened the salt monopoly and allowed fisher households to produce and trade salt privately. The impoverished fishers grasped this rare opportunity to profit from the salt business. But in the 1190s, when the Southern Song economy was crumbling and the state's fiscal crisis deteriorated, the imperial government re-established its salt monopoly as a revenue source. The fishers-turned-salt-makers in Lantau resisted. They joined hands with soldiers in the local garrisons to fight the state's agents and loot trading vessels passing through the Pearl river delta. In 1197, imperial troops were dispatched to Lantau to confiscate the privately produced salt. This intervention triggered an all-out rebellion.[11]

The fishers stopped the troops from seizing their salt pans by blocking their coastline with wooden sticks. They turned their fishing vessels into warships and sailed north along the Pearl river to attack Guangzhou. The insurgency brought panic and chaos to the city, but it also led to a government massacre of the rebellious fishers and salt makers in Lantau. Additional troops were stationed in Lantau in the aftermath of the unrest.[12]

The Tanka fishers' communities survived and continued to grow in the Hong Kong region as in other South China coastal areas through the Ming and Qing periods. In 1729, the Yongzheng Emperor issued an edict to emancipate all low-status social groups such as indentured household bondservants. He ensured they enjoyed the same rights to landownership and other rights granted to all imperial subjects. The Tankas were included in this emancipatory edict, but they continued to face economic hardship and discrimination from the landed population. Unable to afford to own land, many of them settled in shack villages along the shoreline.[13]

After the British established a colonial port in Hong Kong in 1842, many Tankas found an economic opportunity transporting cargo for foreign traders on their boats. The British merchant houses actively recruited Tankas as guides and go-betweens. A student of earlier compradors in Hong Kong regarded the co-opted Tanka as one of the essential foundations of colonial rule and the rapid development of the infant colony, as they "provided British naval and merchant vessels with fuel and other supplies" and the British "rewarded the Tankas with land in the new town of Hong Kong."[14]

Many Tankas became newly rich through their business with the British. For example, Loo Aqui and Kwok Acheong (Kwok Chung) were Tanka-turned-compradors who became the wealthiest Chinese residents in early Hong Kong. The former was an opium farmer and the leader of a triad society. He became the wealthiest Chinese landowner in the colony. The latter was the owner of a fleet of steamships and the third-largest taxpayer in the colony at the time.[15] Over the twentieth century, many water transportation businesses originating from Tanka fishing families thrived. One of the best-known examples is Henry Fok Ying Tung. He inherited his family's transportation business and helped the People's Republic of China break the international embargo during the Korean War (1950–1953) by smuggling strategic supplies into China. He later became a real-estate developer and a leading pro-Beijing tycoon under the watchful eyes of the British during the Cold War. He was one of the most important power brokers in Hong Kong's transition to Chinese rule, and his heirs continue to be key players in the ruling elite circle of Hong Kong since 1997.[16]

While the Tanka-turned-compradors became wealthy in the early colonial period, most Tanka fishers remained poor. During Hong Kong's post-World War II industrial takeoff, the government started to regulate the fishing industry and eventually brought about the demise of the fishing communities in Hong Kong. The fishers had maintained the ecological balance and a steady fish supply in the Pearl river delta for centuries. In the 1950s, the government was determined to guarantee cheap marine products for the rapidly expanding industrial workforce. The government promoted and sponsored the mechanization of the fishing industry through technical advice and low-interest loans. It also organized fishers into cooperatives that pooled financial resources in order to upgrade their fishing vessels. Mechanization enabled the Tanka to boost their yield at a lower cost, but it also caused overfishing.[17]

Mechanized fishing guaranteed the supply of marine products to urban Hong Kong in the 1950s. The proportion of local production over local consumption of fishes rose from 50 percent to 90 percent during industrial takeoff. However, since the late 1950s, the nearshore marine resources in Hong Kong have depleted rapidly.[18] Fishers with means were able to survive by upgrading their fishing vessels and fishing on the high seas. Most poor fishers, on the other hand, ended up bankrupt. Some of them went to work for the rich Tankas as wage laborers on their boats, whereas others found jobs in urban areas. All Tanka communities in Hong Kong have experienced a demographic decline since the 1960s.[19]

By the 1970s, most families in the Tanka communities had quit fishing. They became reliant on urban industrial jobs, even though many of them still lived on boats docked in typhoon shelters and shacks along the shore in deteriorating sanitary conditions. With intervention from social activists and university students, some of these communities started to mobilize to demand housing rights and requested relocation to public housing developments in the late 1970s. This right-to-housing movement turned into one of the most significant social movements of the time, drawing the support of idealistic students and the attention of the media.

Many university students participating in this housing-rights movement were radicals influenced by Maoist ideology in one way or another. One such student was Carrie Lam. Lam was also active in working with Chinese officials to organize student tours to mainland China to learn about the "socialist motherland development."[20] After graduation, she joined the British colonial government as an administrative officer and continued to climb the government bureaucracy ladder after the sovereignty handover. She eventually became Beijing's handpicked chief executive of the HKSAR in 2017. It was she who introduced the extradition amendment bill that triggered the 2019 uprising. Other students in the housing rights movement turned to political activism and became scholars or career opposition politicians in the 1980s through the 2010s. The final decline of the longest-lasting indigenous communities in Hong Kong and the rise of the new Hong Kong – including both the post-1997 ruling bloc and its challengers – crossed paths with the social movements of the 1970s.

Agrarian Conflicts from Manchu to British Rule

Most inland areas of Xin'an county were barren until the ancestors of the Tangs came to settle in the northwestern region (the

Kam Tin area of today) during the Song Dynasty in 973 AD.[21] Then came the Haus and Pangs in Southern Song in the twelfth century, the Lius in the late Yuan in the fourteenth century, and the Mans in the early Ming dynasty in the fourteenth century. They were branches of established lineages in Guangdong and spoke Cantonese. They were known as the "five great clans." Later, Hakka families from further north flocked into the county and established their villages, mostly in the nineteenth century. The "five great clans," especially the Tangs, held hegemonic power in the region. The great clans were commonly known as the Punti (Cantonese local) of Xin'an.[22]

Settling in the territories from the Song through the Ming dynasty as loyal subjects of the imperial state, many villagers from the five great clans participated in the resistance against the Manchu invasion in the seventeenth century. Some of them secretly traded with the last Ming loyalist regime based in Taiwan in the 1660s through the 1680s, just as many other coastal south China lineages did. The Qing government forcefully resettled these big clans further inland to depopulate the coastal area in order to cut off the supply line for the Taiwan regime. Because of its proximity to the sea, all of Xin'an county was evacuated. After the fall of Taiwan in 1683, the Qing government allowed the resettled lineages to move back to Xin'an. They became loyal subjects of the Qing.[23]

The Tangs occupied the most fertile land in the northwestern plain of today's Hong Kong. The Haus and Lius settled in the northern region with lands of moderate fertility. The Pangs were the poorest of all and farmed at the fringes of the Sheung Shui area, which frequently flooded.[24] The clans did not only own the lands around their villages – much of the cultivable regions of the eastern New Territories, Hong Kong Island, and even the outlying islands were granted to the Tangs by imperial decree when they settled in the Hong Kong area.

In contrast, land owned by other clans was usually not very far from their core settlements.[25] The Hakkas, who came after the five great clans, could only establish their villages on the hilly and infertile lands with inadequate water supply. The ownership of their farmlands was mostly claimed by the great clans, above all the Tangs, who appropriated a portion of their harvest as rent.[26]

Armed rent collection teams, organized by the Tangs, traveled around the county during the harvest months. Having arrived at a tenant village, they usually stayed for several weeks to collect rent, household by household. Villagers were obliged to provide the team with splendid meals during their stay. Over time, many Hakka villages organized themselves into local alliances or *yuek* for self-defense against the bullying collection teams. There were occasions when bloody rent resistance broke out to expel the rent collectors. The martyrs of these resistances are still worshipped in the temples of some Hakka villages, such as those in Lam Tsuen.[27] The Tangs and other great clans also charged trading peasants in the market towns under their control. They extracted a portion of the land tax submitted by weaker lineages and extorted protection fees. The great clans' hegemony was guaranteed by the local magistracy, which was largely staffed by members of the Tangs and other great clans.[28]

With the British arrival in 1842, many Hakka villagers, attracted by the opportunities of urban Hong Kong, moved to the city and worked as coolies and stonecutters. Some of them started businesses and became wealthy. The growth of urban Hong Kong also attracted more Hakka farmers from the rest of the crumbling Qing empire to establish villages in Xin'an. Between 1819 and 1899, more than 300 Hakka villages were founded in the area. The Taiping Rebellion in the mainland redoubled the influx of Hakka into the territories in 1850–1864. With their increasing wealth and population, the Hakkas consolidated their alliance against the Tang landlords, and the frequency of rent resistance increased.[29]

Once the British took over Hong Kong in 1842, they identified the Puntis as enemies and the Hakka and Tanka as allies; as a secretary to Governor Hennessy wrote in 1882, the Hakkas were "friends, purveyors, commissariat and transport coolies of the foreigners," and the Tankas "provided boatmen and pilots for the foreign trade."[30] Before World War II, the *raison d'être* of the Crown colony of Hong Kong was trade rather than agrarian or primary-resource extraction. The rural New Territories put under British rule in 1898 had no immediate economic significance to the British – they were little more than a buffer zone with mainland China. However, the British did establish a colonial administration in the New Territories and restructured land relations there to check the power of the great clans.[31]

When the British first seized control of the New Territories in 1899, they faced an armed uprising by the great clans led by the

Tangs, who feared the British would confiscate their landholdings.[32] After defeating the rebellion, the British administration started to curtail the Tang landlords' power by reforming the agrarian economy's landownership and tax system. Between June 1900 and June 1903, the colonial government conducted an extensive land survey in the New Territories by summoning the villagers to submit their land deeds to colonial officials and issued a block Crown lease. Any non-registered land was converted into Crown land. To dismantle the great clans' power over the Hakkas, the British granted most agricultural landownership to the Hakka tenants cultivating it. As such, the British deprived the great clans of most of their landholdings. This de facto land reform freed the Hakka tenant farmers from the Tang landlords. The Hakka cultivators became peasants working their own land.[33]

The British administration also abolished tax farming by the Tangs in the New Territories. It instituted a monetary land tax to be collected directly from individual landowners. In rural as in urban areas throughout the colony, the colonial government maintained a low tax rate on property, as the government's main revenue came from selling Crown land for private development. This revenue model driven by government land sales persisted and continued well beyond the sovereignty handover. Four district offices were founded in four administrative regions in the New Territories. They performed such functions as arbitrating disputes between villagers, collecting information about village life, informing the villagers of government policies, and collecting taxes.[34] The British reshaped the power structure of agrarian Hong Kong by replacing the pre-existing hegemony of the great clans and imposing their own authority.

Having lost their hegemony in the region, the Tangs and other great clans were left to send humble petition letters to the colonial government expressing their opinions when issues arose. They also tried to organize themselves into voluntary associations acceptable to the colonial state. In 1926, leaders from the great clans gathered to form the Heung Yee Kuk (literally "rural deliberation council," also known as the HYK or the Kuk). New Territories people were allowed to join the Kuk if they donated a certain amount of money. This made the Kuk an association of wealthy villagers, and it was dominated by the great clans, especially the Tangs, who still profited from their control of market towns.[35] The Kuk constituted itself as an organization focused on local charitable work and on redressing local grievances among original inhabitants – a residential category that the British authorities bestowed upon members of the lineages in the New Territories pre-dating British rule.[36]

In the 1950s, Hong Kong transformed itself from an entrepôt to a labor-intensive manufacturing center. The expanding urban industrial population urged the state's deeper involvement in agrarian communities. The government appropriated lands from villagers for building reservoirs, new industrial towns, highways, and other projects.[37] The government also started to regulate agricultural production to secure stable supplies and prices.[38] To achieve these ends, the colonial government expanded and reorganized its administrative apparatus in the New Territories. This included the forceful reconstitution of the HYK and the establishment of local co-operatives and the Vegetable Marketing Organization.[39]

From the end of World War II to the late 1950s, the Tangs and other great clans continued to control the HYK, which became a territory-wide rural organization representing the interests of its original inhabitants. While the Hakka rural elite, who had been allies of the colonial administration, welcomed government-initiated development projects that brought new cash income and compensation for land appropriation, elites from the Tangs and other great clans were often resistant to these projects, as the projects would further erode their influence. The domination of the HYK by the great clans made it a platform to mobilize villagers against government-initiated land appropriation and development through protest and sabotage. British intelligence detected infiltration from the CCP in the HYK.[40]

To stop the growth of the HYK into a center of opposition to the colonial government, the authorities imposed a Heung Yee Kuk Bill in 1958 to restructure the HYK, making it an organization made up of government-appointed rural elites and representatives elected from rural districts. The number of representatives from each district was proportional to the local population. After the reconstitution, the great clans' hold on the HYK gave way to domination by the Hakka elites, who came from areas experiencing rapid urbanization and population growth. After the 1950s, voices of opposition to development projects dissipated in the HYK, which became a mediator in development projects, negotiating with the government over compensation on behalf of the villagers.[41]

From the 1950s, the government policy was to encourage a shift from rice (which was increasingly imported from Southeast Asia) to vegetable cultivation in the New Territories to keep down the prices of foodstuffs for the expanding urban population. The colonial government established a monopoly over wholesale vegetable produce in the colony through the Vegetable Marketing Organization founded in 1946. Government-sponsored co-operatives were established in each village to facilitate the production and sale of agricultural and husbandry products. These co-operatives were active in providing credit and technical advice to farmers. They also organized the construction of public works in the villages.[42]

While most mainland Chinese immigrants settled in the urban areas and became industrial workers in the 1950s and 1960s, a significant number of them settled in the New Territories and rented land from Hakka or Punti landlords. As such, rural Hong Kong was split into two worlds. On one side, Punti and Hakka landlords left the agrarian economy and eagerly pursued monetary interests by renting or selling their lands. They enjoyed the exclusive right of negotiating with the colonial government through the HYK. On the other side, immigrant tenant farmers were excluded from the HYK structure and did not enjoy any institutional representation. Whenever the government appropriated land for development, only the original inhabitant landholders obtained compensation. Immigrant farmers would face expulsion with meager, if any, compensation.[43]

After the sovereignty handover, development in the New Territories, particularly the areas bordering the rapidly expanding Shenzhen and areas covered by the high-speed rail project, led to more frequent land appropriation. Protests by the immigrant farmers and their offspring still working or residing on the land they rented from original inhabitants flared up. This resistance converged with young urban activists to shape a new wave of radical community and opposition movements culminating in the protest against the high-speed rail in 2010. Veteran participants and activists in these movements were the foundation of the rise of localist movements that paved the way for the 2019 uprising. On the other hand, the Punti and Hakka landowners, tamed and co-opted by the British colonial administration and forming part of the land development machine, transferred their loyalty to Beijing on the eve of the sovereignty handover, like many of the business elites. In the 2019 uprising, some of these original inhabitants, who maintained their lineage militias and were involved in mobster organizations over the years, became the primary suppliers of pro-establishment thugs that the authorities unleashed to attack the young rebels and escalate the conflict.[44]

Urban Industrial Class Formation

The British took Hong Kong to turn it into an entrepôt that connected trade between China and other parts of Asia and Europe. The intention was to take away trading activities from the traditional port city of Guangzhou. The British-built Victoria Harbor was a port where seafaring vessels docked, loaded, and unloaded. It became the center of commercial activities that attracted European and Chinese merchants. It also attracted peasants-turned-laborers to work in the expanding construction and transportation sectors. Transshipment business thrived after the completion of the Kowloon–Canton railway in 1910 that connected the Victoria Harbor to Guangzhou along the vast agrarian hinterland of the eastern shore of the Pearl river.

While Europeans resided mostly at the top and middle of Victoria Peak on Hong Kong Island, Chinese settlement developed at the mountain's foot. It soon turned into slum areas with contagious diseases and all kinds of social malaise, from gambling to a large orphan population, and was generally associated with poverty. Chinese business elites, following the tradition of Confucianist philanthropic merchants, coalesced to form the Tung Wah Hospital to provide health and other social services to the general Chinese community. Soon, the Tung Wah Hospital leaders became representatives of the Chinese communities in the eyes of the British. The colonial authorities started to co-opt these Chinese leaders as agents of indirect rule to facilitate the governance of the Chinese settlements.[45]

Hong Kong's entrepôt business grew at Guangzhou's expense, which had been the only port open for foreign trade in China before the Opium War of 1839–1842. In 1925–1926, the nascent CCP and the KMT, which established a united-front nationalist revolutionary government in Guangzhou with Soviet support, initiated an anti-British general strike in Hong Kong to paralyze the port city. The strike was in the name of protesting the British authorities' killing of Chinese anti-imperialist protesters in the Shanghai International Settlement on May 30, 1925. Seeing the rise of Hong Kong and Guangzhou's eclipse as a symbol of the imperialist subordination of China, the KMT–CCP government hoped to decimate Hong Kong's status as a global trading center and revive Guangzhou through the strike.[46]

To defend Hong Kong's business interests and defeat the strike, Chinese business leaders in Hong Kong worked with British support to devise plans to subvert the Guangzhou government. They also raised funds to recruit workers to replace strikers. With the labor union's financial resources running low and fearing military intervention by the British, the Guangzhou government and KMT-affiliated unions ended the strike in the fall of 1926. The CCP had no choice but to follow. After commercial activities resumed in full force, Hong Kong's rise as a global nexus in the intra-Asia and Asia–Europe–America trade continued.[47]

Besides the dominant commercial sector, at the turn of the twentieth century Hong Kong saw the rise of industry, such as oil refineries and shipyards operated by British companies. From the 1930s onward, the world economy disintegrated into imperial spheres of influence separated by tariffs, and Hong Kong fell into the British tariff blocs. It attracted many Chinese manufacturers to relocate to Hong Kong so that their products could be marketed freely in the rest of the British Empire. This resulted in the rise of Chinese industrialists specializing in textiles, preserved food, machinery, tools, and other products in Hong Kong. However, these industrialists were not integrated with the predominantly Cantonese-speaking Chinese merchants in the Tung Wah circle. They found themselves outside the colonial collaborative power structure.[48]

All these developments were interrupted by the Japanese invasion and occupation of Hong Kong during World War II from December 1941 to August 1945. In this period, most British and European elites escaped Hong Kong or were imprisoned. Some Chinese elites collaborated with the Japanese, while others escaped to southwest China, which was the base of the Chinese resistance at the time. After Japan surrendered in 1945, British colonial rule resumed, and many of the prewar elites and Chinese settlers returned.[49]

While the British rebuilt their prewar colonial institutions based on indirect rule and collaboration between the British and Chinese mercantile elite, the CCP–KMT civil war in China from 1945 to 1949, followed by the founding of Communist China in 1949, led to an influx of Chinese refugees, including laborers and Shanghai or Guangdong industrialists evading the Communist takeover. Equipped with an ample supply of Chinese capital and workers from the mainland, Hong Kong embarked on an industrial takeoff in the 1950s.

While some Chinese business elites, having relocated to Hong Kong, established themselves in shipping (such as the Tung family, whose heir, Tung Chee-hwa, became the first chief executive of Hong Kong after the handover of sovereignty), more continued their businesses as industrialists, such as the Tang family (its heir, Henry Tang Ying-yen, became a close ally of Beijing in posthandover Hong Kong and a one-time chief executive hopeful). Another example is Li Ka-shing from Chaozhou, Guangdong, who started his plastic factory in 1950 and later moved to real-estate development, utilities, energy, retail, and other businesses, creating one of the most powerful business empires in Asia and the world. The Chinese industrialists built their factories near the spontaneously formed squatter areas where most of the poor refugees from China resided. When the international blockade of Communist China upon the outbreak of the Korean War in 1950 stifled the entrepôt trade of Hong Kong, the colony transformed itself into an export-oriented industrial economy.[50]

In the early postwar era, the colonial regime continued the prewar structure of co-option. The British business elite, including financiers and prominent merchant house representatives, participated in the Executive Council (or ExCo, where the colonial governor and top bureaucrats made critical decisions in consultation with appointed elites from the community) and the LegCo, which comprised government officials and appointed elites. A handful of Chinese mercantile elites from the Tung Wah circle participated in the LegCo as the governor's appointees. The emerging industrialists, newly relocated from mainland China, were excluded from the colonial power structure at the outset. Industrial development obtained minimal assistance from the colonial government because of opposition to such assistance from the commercial and financial business elite, who worried about elevated government expenditures and taxes.[51] Cast out from the colonial power structure, Chinese manufacturers established associations to support one another. Some built on pre-existing ethnic networks like the Chaozhou Chamber of Commerce, which such Chaozhou industrialists as Li Ka-shing counted on. Some were closer to the KMT network, linked to the KMT government that fled to Taiwan after the Communist takeover of mainland China. Some were part of the United Front of the CCP underground in Hong Kong, as represented by the Chinese General Chamber of Commerce and its "red capitalist" leaders such as Henry Fok, the Tanka boatman mentioned earlier, whose business thrived as a result of helping China break the embargo during the Korean War.[52]

Under the tacit agreement between the British and the new-born Communist government in Beijing, China would not reclaim Hong Kong in exchange for British tolerance of underground CCP activity in the colony. Under the British watch, the CCP covertly maintained its system of banks, schools, cinemas, Cantonese opera troupes, publishers, newspapers, business associations, and labor unions. In Hong Kong, the New China News Agency acted as the de facto representative of the People's Republic of China government in the British colony.[53]

Besides organizing a united front with intellectuals and a segment of the Chinese industrialists, the CCP organized the expanding working class through labor unions and grassroots community organizations. CCP organizations provided social services to the residents in the growing and crowded squatter areas neglected by the colonial administration. Support for the CCP amongst grassroots communities and intellectuals of Hong Kong grew in the 1950s and early 1960s. CCP-affiliated filmmakers made some of the most popular movies. "Red capitalist" Henry Fok owned one of the hottest football (soccer) clubs in the colony. The CCP unions successfully launched a few labor strikes that brought the city to a standstill to obtain employers' concessions on wages and benefits.[54]

The British administration was mindful that the CCP's expanding popularity posed a threat to its governance. It admitted in a famous report about the state of Hong Kong in 1956 that "seeds of discontent would remain" in the "predominantly immigrant settlements" and that the "Communist Government of China was rapidly establishing itself and it lost no time in trying to win over the whole-hearted allegiance of overseas Chinese [in Hong Kong] ... with some success."[55] The British administration was aware of the need to be more interventionist in providing basic social services to the expanding working-class population to counteract the expanding influence of the Communists. However, the politically dominant financial and mercantile elite in the colony, afraid of the new tax burden on them, kept any attempts to increase public expenditure in check. It left the ground fertile to Communist organizing that turned the impoverished workers in the city into challengers to the colonial status quo.[56]

This plausibility of Hong Kong becoming a Communist hotbed alarmed the US, which harnessed various leverage points to pressure the British to be more proactive in catering to the needs of lower-class residents. Its pressure yielded some successes in the 1950s and 1960s. The US threatened to raise the issue of the miserable living conditions of Chinese refugees in Hong Kong to the United Nations as a humanitarian problem. The Hong Kong government, fearing embarrassment at the UN, took the initiative to improve immigrants' living conditions by starting a public housing program, which resettled residents from the squatter areas to public housing estates with better sanitation and facilities. The clearance of squatter areas broke up the organizational networks that the CCP had built in those communities.[57]

Besides the public housing program, government provision of education and other social services and assistance remained minimal in the 1960s, continuing the story of class polarization and alienation. Worsening social antagonism exploded in uprisings in 1966 and 1967. The 1966 unrest was spontaneous, triggered by an increase in ferry fares. The 1967 uprising started with an ordinary dispute between workers and management in a plastics factory. The labor dispute intensified when police intervened to break up the protesting workers. Having received the order from radicals in Beijing to instigate an uprising as part of the Cultural Revolution in

China, the Communist labor unions tried to turn the dispute into a full-scale, protracted anti-British insurgency in the spring of 1967.[58]

The uprising involved mass rallies that besieged the colonial governor's mansion, as well as mobilization for a general strike, roadside bombs, the assassination of anti-Communist intellectuals, and a militia gun battle with police near the Hong Kong–China border. The fear of the spread of the Cultural Revolution to Hong Kong turned the majority of the Hong Kong population against CCP organizations. After Chinese premier Zhou Enlai guaranteed that China had no intention of invading Hong Kong and entered a truce with the British in the summer of 1967, the Hong Kong authorities, with the support of public opinion in the Chinese community, took the offensive to round up Communist organizers and root out any antigovernment activities. By the spring of 1968, the turmoil had died down entirely.[59]

Though the Communist insurgency was repressed, the spontaneous support that it garnered from young people in its initial phase, together with the 1966 unrest that had no Communist involvement, revealed genuine discontent that the colonial authorities needed to address. In the aftermath of the unrest, the colonial government started many social reforms, such as a public assistance program as a social safety net. The program gestated before the insurgency but was vetoed by the financial–commercial elite in the establishment. The government was able to overcome the business elite's resistance only after the riots showed the urgency of the problem of poverty and social polarization. The beginning of the governorship of Lord MacLehose, a British diplomat with a Labor Party background, in 1971 contributed to a new level of activism of the colonial government, which implemented a wide range of reforms during the 1970s. The reforms included expansion of free education, public housing, government health care, infrastructure construction projects, and the powerful Independent Commission against Corruption that successfully rooted out corruption in the police force and the civil service.[60]

Concurrent with the colonial reforms was a transformation of the colony's economy. While Hong Kong had established itself as an export-oriented industrial powerhouse by the early 1970s, China's normalization of relations with the US and its Cold War allies after

Nixon's visit in 1972 restarted China's trade with the capitalist bloc of the world. Most of this trade went through Hong Kong. In cooperation with the Hong Kong business elite, American companies in Hong Kong started to participate in the annual Canton Trade Fair in Guangzhou and to seek investment and trade opportunities with China. Hong Kong once again became an entrepôt of China's trade. This revival of entrepôt business fostered the rise of business and financial services of Hong Kong in the 1970s.[61]

The colonial reform and transformation of the Hong Kong economy brought profound restructuring of Hong Kong society. The social reform fomented expansion of the public sector, including education, health care, and social services. These, in turn, brought the rise of new professionals in these sectors – teachers, health care workers, and social workers. The thriving of business and financial services led to the expansion of the managerial class. These highly educated professionals in the private and public sectors, and the expanding student body in tertiary education getting ready to enter the upskilled workforce, constituted an ascendant new middle class in Hong Kong.[62]

This new middle class, particularly those in the public sector, drove a wave of social movements in the 1970s. These included a grassroots housing-rights movement organized by professional social workers, the expansion of teacher and independent trade unionization, and student movements seeking social and political reform. Though influenced by the radical ideology of China's Cultural Revolution and the global youth revolt of the 1960s, these movements were not directly affiliated with the underground CCP presence in Hong Kong. While many of the student activists were drawn to the united-front work of the CCP or even recruited into the Party secretly, many other activists were as critical of Communist authoritarian rule in China as they were of the colonial status quo.[63] In the 1980s, when the Hong Kong sovereignty question emerged, many activists in these movements converged to form the core of the movement that sought the autonomy and democracy of Hong Kong after 1997.[64]

Hong Kong in the *Longue Durée*

Throughout its long history of more than a millennium, Hong Kong has seen waves of migrants from the mainland settling in the area to avoid turmoil, hardship, or state repression at the center of the Chinese empire. Being far from China's inland political and economic centers and having access to the maritime world of commerce, Hong Kong has been a region where the political and military powers of the Chinese empire could not easily reach. But, as demonstrated by the fisher rebellion in 1197, then the Cantonese gentry's support of the Taiwan-based resistance against the Qing state in the late seventeenth century, and the bloody Hakka rent resistance against the Cantonese landed gentry elite in the nineteenth century, Hong Kong has not only been a space for evading the Chinese state, but also a seedbed of resistance, challenging Chinese imperial rule and its local representatives.

This pattern of evasion and resistance continued into the British era, when industrialists and workers from mainland China resettled in Hong Kong, first to avoid the civil wars in the mainland, then to escape from Communist rule. These new urban industrial communities became torn between the Chinese party-state and the British Empire. Minimally incorporated into the British colonial regime, some industrialists developed their affinity to the Communist regime and became alienated from British rule. Others maintained their connections with the KMT regime in Taiwan and continued their anti-Communist inclinations. In postwar Hong Kong, the working-class communities were first drawn to the CCP-affiliated grassroots organizations and then repelled by the radicalism manifested in the 1967 anti-British uprising.

In the early history of Hong Kong, the periphery status of the communities there vis-à-vis the imperial center was a result of geography. Where transportation and communication technology advanced, the state space expanded, and the political center became capable of tightening control over distant places. However, throughout the colonial history of Hong Kong, its remoteness from the centers of the British Empire and the Chinese state and the resulting autonomy became codified and institutionalized into the political status quo and its formal relations with political centers. One example of such codification and institutionalization was the constitutionally warranted autonomy of the British colonial government from London.[65] The other instance was the Sino-British Joint Declaration in 1984, which authorized the transfer of Hong Kong's sovereignty from London to Beijing in 1997 under "One Country,

Two Systems," which was further codified in the Basic Law. These documents warrant Hong Kong's autonomy and political distance from Beijing for 50 years until 2047. Hong Kong lives on as a liminal space and a political periphery, outliving the physical geographical limit of the political centers' state spaces.

The expansion of the new middle class in the 1970s paved the way for the democratic movement of Hong Kong in the 1980s. This opposition movement navigated between the ailing British Empire and the rising Chinese state, aspiring to carve out and maintain an autonomous social and political space of Hong Kong after the sovereignty handover of 1997. When these opposition movements continued to morph after the handover, they inherited the spirit and legacies of the many resistance and evasion efforts of earlier communities throughout Hong Kong's long history. At the same time, they were also empowered by Hong Kong's newly gained centrality as China's offshore financial market and the gateway of international capital's entrance into China at the turn of the twenty-first century. The contradictory combination of the long-term political marginality and the recent financial centrality of Hong Kong created a precarious space that enabled the waves of rebellion from the Umbrella Movement in 2014 to the 2019 uprising.

Part I
Capital

3 THE MAKING OF CHINA'S OFFSHORE FINANCIAL CENTER

The sovereignty handover of Hong Kong in 1997 coincided with the onset of the Asian financial crisis that pulled Hong Kong's economy into a long downturn. The economic stagnation from 1997 to 2003 culminated in the SARS epidemic in 2003. In the aftermath of SARS, Hong Kong's financial markets and the economy at large rebounded in the context of China's accession to the WTO and consolidation of Hong Kong's role as China's offshore financial center. This consolidation came with a set of Beijing policies, including the Closer Economic Partnership Arrangement (CEPA) between Hong Kong and mainland China, signed in 2003. CEPA further lowered tariffs and other restrictions on Hong Kong goods and capital entering mainland China and vice versa.

Chinese officials and state media did not shy away from using Hong Kong's post-2003 economic rebound to emphasize that Hong Kong's economy was one-sidedly dependent on China's mercy to thrive. This perspective seemed logical in the context of China's economic peak and its strong economic rebound in the aftermath of the 2008 global financial crisis. Many also point to Hong Kong's shrinking share of China's GDP as an indication of Hong Kong's declining significance to the Chinese economy after 1997.[1]

The common wisdom about Hong Kong's falling economic value to China, however, and about its increasing economic dependence on China, is misplaced. As a low-income country, when China's GDP grew rapidly, all small developed economies' GDP as a share of China's GDP declined, as shown by the comparison in Figure 3.1.

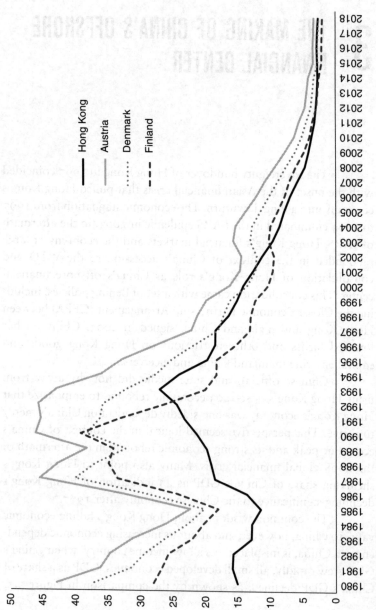

Figure 3.1 Hong Kong share of China's GDP in comparative perspective
Source: World Development Indicator

This is merely an indication of China's rapid growth as a developing country. It says nothing about the change in Hong Kong's economic significance to China.

This chapter will look at how Hong Kong's role as China's offshore market originated in British times and served China's economic development well in the Mao era and the early stage of market reform in the 1980s. Such a role continued to be indispensable to the China boom after the sovereignty handover. I will then look at the global forces and Beijing's policies that enabled the continuation and expansion of such a role for Hong Kong. Being a free financial market at the doorstep of China, where the financial system still resists full liberalization to this day, Hong Kong is a unique window or springboard for Chinese enterprises to raise capital and undertake essential financial operations in the global economy. The last two sections look at how Chinese money has become the dominant economic force in Hong Kong after 1997.

The Hong Kong Gateway from Mao's Autarky to the China Boom

From the heyday of Mao's economic autarky to the China boom after Deng initiated market reform, Hong Kong has always been an important trade and investment gateway for China. After the CCP secured control of most of China in 1949, the British prepared for an evacuation scenario when the People's Liberation Army (PLA) reached just north of British Hong Kong. Then the CCP decided to keep the British in Hong Kong, adopting a Hong Kong policy of "fully utilize and plan for the long run" (*changqi dasuan chongfen liyong*). This policy served Mao China well and continued until the late 1970s, when Beijing started to signal its intention of seeking Hong Kong's transfer to Chinese sovereignty in 1997.[2]

From the 1950s through the 1970s, Chinese state enterprises in Hong Kong, most notably the Bank of China and China Resources, have been an important channel through which the PRC could absorb foreign exchange via their trading activities and remittance services. The Chinese trading companies in Hong Kong allowed China to employ its limited foreign-exchange holdings to import foreign capital goods.[3] The role of Hong Kong in China's development became more important after the early 1960s, when Beijing broke with Moscow and Soviet assistance to China ended.

After Nixon's visit to China in 1972 and the resumption of trade between China, the US, and its allies in the Cold War, Hong Kong's entrepôt trade, which was illicit under the UN embargo, thrived in the open again. Though most of China was still under economic autarky in the 1970s, the provincial government of Guangdong, adjacent to Hong Kong, already experienced soaring trade through Hong Kong. Chinese entrepreneurs and US companies in Hong Kong started to participate in the annual China Import and Export Fair (also known as the Canton Fair) in Guangzhou. Hong Kong's elite Chinese families, like the families of Tung Chao-yung and Tang Hsiang-chien, who had deep US connections, worked with the American Chamber of Commerce in Hong Kong to lobby the US to grant China most-favored-nation status.[4] This would allow Chinese products to be exported to the US market with low tariffs. It finally became a reality in 1979, right after the US and the PRC established diplomatic relations.

While Hong Kong served as the only window to the outside world for autarkic Mao's China, its role as the gateway to and from China became even more important through the different stages of China's market reform. The first stage of reform was characterized by the decollectivization of agriculture and the revival of a market-oriented peasant economy and rural industries in the form of township and village enterprises (TVEs). In this stage, economic dynamism came mainly from the domestic market. The Shenzhen special economic zones, just north of Hong Kong, came into being as export processing zones. Manufacturing capital from Hong Kong started moving there, and Hong Kong investment into other sectors, like hotels and retail, began to enter China, mostly in Guangdong province. However, foreign direct investment (FDI) and the export sector did not yet constitute a large share of the Chinese economy in the 1980s, as most surplus labor in the countryside was retained in the rural TVEs and the booming agricultural sector.

By the 1990s, in the aftermath of the Tiananmen crackdown and the collapse of the Soviet Union, Beijing turned the economy toward export-oriented growth and fostered radical privatization of the urban state sector. The one-off devaluation of the renminbi (RMB, the Chinese currency) against the dollar of more than

30 percent in 1994, followed by a peg to the dollar, boosted China's export manufacturing. Beijing's measures to hold back the development of TVEs and agriculture after 1994 released the massive rural labor force to the coastal export-oriented manufacturing establishment. The Clinton administration's policy of guaranteeing Chinese goods low-tariff access to the US market, regardless of human rights concerns, and the landmark US free trade agreement with China in 1999 cleared the path for China's accession to the WTO in 2001. China became the workshop of the world after 2001.[5]

Short of capital, know-how, and connection to foreign consumer markets, coastal governments competed with one another for FDIs to fuel local export manufacturing growth. As such, China became the prime destination for East Asian labor-intensive, export-oriented manufacturing capital seeking low-cost labor. Between 1990 and 2005, investment from Hong Kong, Taiwan, South Korea, Japan, and Singapore together made up 71 percent of the stock of FDI flowing into China, with capital from Hong Kong constituting over half.[6]

Hong Kong also played a crucial role in the reform of state enterprises in the 1990s. As we shall see later, many large state-owned enterprises (SOEs) became state-supported transnational corporations by going public in the overseas capital market. Hong Kong's Stock Exchange, with its advanced financial architecture and access to global financial capital, had been the primary venue for Chinese enterprises' overseas capitalization. Hong Kong's real-estate developers were key players in the making of the private real-estate market in the 1990s, which was created through the privatization of socialized housing formerly provided by SOEs.[7]

At first glance, the increasing dominance of debt-financed and state-directed fixed-asset investment in the Chinese economy since the 1990s, largely in the form of infrastructure construction, seems not to involve Hong Kong. But it does. First, most construction projects undertaken by local governments and state enterprises relied on state bank financing. A large portion of liquidity in China's banking system originated from a "sterilization" process in which exporters and foreign investors surrendered their foreign-exchange holdings to state banks in exchange for an equivalent amount of RMB created by the People's Bank of China, China's central bank. A large part of liquidity in China's banking system, therefore, originated from the rising foreign-exchange reserves, which stemmed from FDI inflow and export, for which Hong Kong was an important nexus.

Second, state companies were the key actors that received low-cost loans from state banks to undertake most infrastructure and capital-intensive projects. When the investment sector started to suffer from overcapacity, they aggressively sought overseas investment opportunities. Hong Kong became a default gateway through which Chinese enterprises went overseas. This has been a new development since the late 1990s. China's urge to export its capital redoubled after the mammoth monetary stimulus in 2009–2010 in response to the global financial crisis of 2008. Under the stimulus, the CCP ordered state banks to open the floodgate of lending to state enterprises or state-connected enterprises to expand capacity. This resulted in a rapid buildup of excess capacity and falling profit in the economy, particularly in the construction sector.

Consequently, Chinese corporations became more eager to seek investment and business opportunities overseas, with Hong Kong as their first stop after 2010. The next chapter will look at this in more detail. In sum, Hong Kong played a special and indispensable role at every stage of the China boom. Hong Kong has been an offshore nexus that facilitated China's export and import of goods and capital, gluing China to the world economy when the Chinese economy was not yet fully open.

For a long time, many China observers, liberal economists, and policymakers in China supposed that China's move toward a completely open economy, driven by private enterprise, was inevitable. China's accession to the WTO in 2001 has been conditional upon China's pledge to eventually lift all capital control measures; open up its financial sector to foreign banks; and create a level playing field for private, state-owned, domestic, and foreign enterprises. By the time China completes its transition to a fully open market, Hong Kong's role as an entrepôt of goods and capital for a semi-open China will be over. But as it turns out, the CCP is not interested in lifting capital controls or policy preferences for SOEs.[8] The CCP sees its control of credit through state banks and its command of the economy via monopolistic SOEs as important foundations of its rule. The state did not wither but rather expanded its role in the economy during the two decades after China's accession to the

WTO. With China's financial system remaining semi-closed to the world and the continued dominance of the state sector under the model of state capitalism, China's connection to the global economy continues to hinge on Hong Kong, which maintains a semi-porous and heavily regulated economic border with China but a free economic border with the world.[9] Hong Kong is a nexus that connects China's state capitalist economy with the global free trading system. We should not take for granted the conditions that enable Hong Kong to continue playing this role after 1997.

International Foundations of Hong Kong's Financial Centrality after 1997

Hong Kong's continuous function as China's offshore financial center after the handover not only depends on the institutional legacy of British rule and China's policy on Hong Kong, but also is grounded in the international community's treatment of Hong Kong after 1997. British Hong Kong had connected China to foreign capital and the global market. At the same time, China maintained the complete or partial closure of its economy in order to benefit from its integration with the global economy through Hong Kong while shielding itself from the risks associated with economic openness from the 1950s through the 1990s. While Hong Kong could easily perform this role as China's offshore trading and financial center when it was politically separate from China under British rule, this role was not guaranteed under Chinese sovereignty after 1997. The CCP's idea to institute a "One Country, Two Systems" arrangement after Hong Kong's sovereignty handover was first and foremost an attempt to ameliorate the confidence crisis among the business elite and the middle class in the territory. It was also an attempt on Beijing's part to perpetuate Hong Kong's role as China's offshore market beyond the handover.[10]

International recognition of Hong Kong's autonomy vis-à-vis Beijing after 1997 is of utmost importance, as Beijing's plan to perpetuate Hong Kong's role as China's offshore financial center would not have worked had governments and companies worldwide not treated it as such. In 1992, US Congress passed the United States–Hong Kong Policy Act to regulate US relations with Hong Kong after

1997. The Act stipulated that the US would regularly monitor whether Hong Kong's autonomy from mainland China, its rule of law, and its pre-existing freedom were maintained after 1997, as promised in the Sino-British Joint Declaration. Upon verification of such autonomy, the US would "continue to treat Hong Kong as a separate territory in economic and trade matters, such as import quotas and certificates of origin." The Act's stated purpose was to support the UK and the people of Hong Kong in ensuring Hong Kong's autonomy following the handover. The Act served as a template for other countries' policies and treatment of Hong Kong as a separate customs territory. These steps were widely recognized as necessary to upholding Hong Kong's freedom in the wake of the 1989 Tiananmen crackdown.[11]

Besides this stated political objective to safeguard Hong Kong's freedom, the Act benefits Beijing, too. The Act's pledge of treating Hong Kong separately from mainland China in trade, investment, and immigration warrants the continuation of Hong Kong's role as a useful offshore platform for the Chinese economy beyond 1997. For example, the Act stipulates that "the United States should continue to grant the products of Hong Kong nondiscriminatory trade treatment (commonly referred to as 'most-favored-nation status') by virtue of Hong Kong's membership in the General Agreement on Tariffs and Trade."[12] This policy was import-ant before China's accession to the WTO in 2001, and continued to be essential to China's development even after China joined. With the US's certification of Hong Kong and China as two separate customs territories, an arrangement that was followed by other economic entities in the world, China and Hong Kong held two separate memberships in the WTO under different terms. Hong Kong maintained a more open trade and investment linkage with the world economy than China.

Hong Kong had been a separate member of the GATT, the WTO's predecessor, since 1986. It participated in the Uruguay round of GATT negotiations that led to the formation of the WTO in 1995. Hong Kong is therefore a founding member of the organization. On the eve of Hong Kong's sovereignty handover, the British Hong Kong government sent a memo to the WTO headquarters, stressing Hong Kong's autonomy from Beijing under the Sino-British Joint declaration.[13] In the agreement on China's accession to WTO in 2001, paragraphs from this 1997 memo were incorporated to confirm that Hong Kong's separate membership in the organization would coexist with China's:

> Hong Kong, then a British Crown Colony, became contracting party of GATT on 23 April 1986. On 1 July 1997 the People's Republic of China resumed the exercise of sovereignty over Hong Kong. From that date, Hong Kong became a Special Administrative Region of China. As such it would, inter alia, retain the status of a separate customs territory, and would continue to decide its economic and trade policies on its own ... Hong Kong will continue to be a WTO Member using the name of "Hong Kong, China".[14]

While Hong Kong's economic border with the global market has been fully open, China has kept a semi-open, heavily regulated economic border even after joining the WTO. At the same time, the economic border between Hong Kong and mainland China has been liberalized, though still regulated under the 2003 CEPA.

The dual Hong Kong–China WTO membership arrangement allowed China to keep its partial economic closure. Despite this closure, China could obtain full and free access to the global market and global capital via Hong Kong in whatever areas it chose. For China, it is the best of both worlds. For instance, China continued to forbid foreign banks from fully owning their operations in China and upheld tight capital control long after it acceded to the WTO. This enabled the CCP's iron grip on China's financial sector. But Chinese individuals and enterprises could still have full access to foreign banking and could move their wealth in and out of China freely via Hong Kong. Another example is that China maintained high tariffs for imported farm products such as tropical fruits and frozen meats. However, it could selectively import farm products at low tariffs to Hong Kong, which it did in large quantities and then re-exported the majority of them to mainland China.[15]

Another advantage that Beijing enjoys from Hong Kong's internationally recognized autonomy is that investment registered as originating from Hong Kong enjoys far greater freedom worldwide, especially in Western countries, when compared to investments originating from mainland China. Many countries, including the US, the UK, and Australia, put Hong Kong investment under lighter national security scrutiny than mainland China's investment, particularly investment coming from SOEs. This is one reason why mainland Chinese corporations have been eager to either register as a Hong Kong company (e.g., Lenovo) or send their investment to the world via their Hong Kong subsidiaries. Much capital that China exports to Hong Kong is for re-export to somewhere else, rebranded as Hong Kong capital.[16]

This internationally recognized autonomy of Hong Kong involves international treatment of Hong Kong and mainland Chinese courts as two different systems, too, under the condition that the former continues to practice common law and stays free from the CCP's control. Judgments in the court system in Hong Kong have been recognized and are enforceable in many other court systems in the world and vice versa, either through reciprocity agreements or through common law. This reciprocity between Hong Kong courts and many courts in the world continued after 1997, although courts' judgments in China and those in other countries are not mutually enforceable. In 2011, the Hong Kong government became the first in Asia to revamp its arbitration institutions to abide by the 2006 version of the Model Law on International Commercial Arbitration of the United Nations Commission on International Trade Law. Hong Kong has also been a separate member of the New York Convention on the Recognition and Enforcement of Foreign Arbitral Awards. Commercial arbitration in any member state is enforceable in all member states. Hong Kong's long-standing involvement in these international legal and arbitration systems, together with the "arrangement between Hong Kong and the Mainland for reciprocal enforcement of arbitral awards" signed in 1999, turned Hong Kong into an international arbitration center. China's arbitration and legal systems, on the other hand, do not fully follow international standards and do not have full reciprocal enforceability with most major economies. Outward-oriented Chinese companies and foreign companies having businesses in China overcome the legal limitations of the Chinese market by relying on the legal and arbitration apparatus of Hong Kong.[17]

Another key institution that warrants Hong Kong's role as China's offshore market is Hong Kong's separate currency and financial system. The complete openness of Hong Kong's financial system to the world economy, the free convertibility of the

Hong Kong dollar, and a separate and presumably independent financial regulation system and monetary authorities enable Hong Kong to continue performing its role as a financial intermediary between China and the world. We will see later that Hong Kong's financial sector is exceptionally important to the Chinese state sector.

Hong Kong's economic centrality beyond the sovereignty handover serves China's national development well. Figures 3.2 and 3.3 show that, to this day, the majority of FDI going into China originates from Hong Kong. The majority of China's outgoing FDI has Hong Kong as the top destination too. Many investments from Hong Kong to China do not originate from Hong Kong – they come from elsewhere but assume a Hong Kong identity. Likewise, many investments from China to Hong Kong do not stay in Hong Kong, but move on to other places in the world as Hong Kong investments. Hong Kong continues to be the main gateway through which global capital moves into China and Chinese capital moves out to the world.

Since China joined the WTO in 2001, Beijing has cultivated selected state enterprises to become national champions with a global reach through favorable policies and subsidies. This revived expansion of the state sector came at the expense of private-sector growth. The expansion of the state sector redoubled in the aftermath

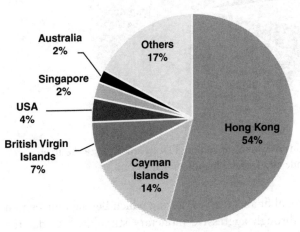

Figure 3.2a Destinations of China's outgoing FDI by stock (2017)
Source: Hong Kong Trade and Development Council

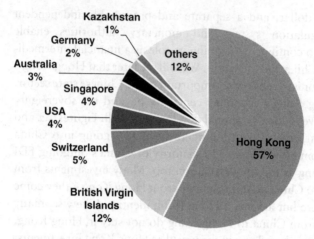

Figure 3.2b Destinations of China's outgoing FDI by flow (2017)
Source: Hong Kong Trade and Development Council

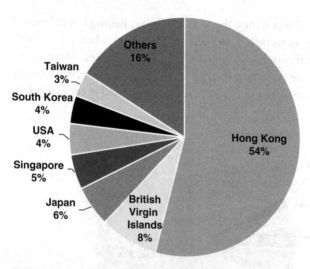

Figures 3.3a Origins of China's incoming FDI by stock (2018) Source:
Hong Kong Trade and Development Council

of the 2008 global financial crisis, during which Beijing rejuvenated
the economy through aggressive monetary stimulus.[18] Under the
stimulus, state banks opened the floodgates of low-cost loans to
state enterprises and to local governments to speed up their

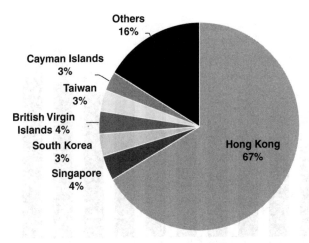

Figure 3.3b Origins of China's incoming FDI by flow (2018)
Source: Hong Kong Trade and Development Council

investment projects. This generated an impressive rebound in the economy, but it also created excess capacity and depreciation pressure on the RMB, unleashing a wave of capital export and capital flight when viable investment projects ran out within China for the already debt-laden companies. This new wave of capital outflow intensified over the 2010s when China's economic growth continued to slow and private property continued to be insufficiently protected.[19] China's offshore market in Hong Kong became the primary channel through which China's surplus capital ventured overseas in search of investment opportunities and safe havens.

Hong Kong is also the main venue where Chinese enterprises obtain loans and raise capital in foreign currencies, mainly US dollars. After 1997, most foreign loans owned by Chinese enterprises originated from the financial market in Hong Kong.[20] Most overseas initial public offerings (IPOs) of Chinese enterprises happened in Hong Kong as well. As shown in Figure 3.4, Hong Kong has been the prime location for overseas capitalization of Chinese enterprises.

Hong Kong has been an irreplaceable conduit for the wealthy Chinese elite to channel their family and individual wealth overseas. It is an open secret that many Chinese officials freely move their money and even their relatives to Western countries under the cover of being "Hong Kong investment" and "Hong Kong residents." Some of the

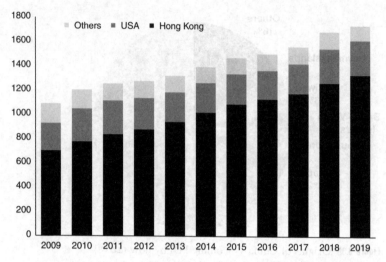

Figure 3.4 Number of Chinese companies' stocks trading in overseas financial markets
Source: Ryan Capital

most high-profile family members of the Chinese leaders, such as Gu Kailai, the wife of Bo Xilai (Politburo member before his downfall in 2012) and Li Xiaolin, daughter of Li Peng (premier of China from 1988 to 1998), had established Hong Kong residency before they obtained residency in other countries.[21] Reportedly, children of key Politburo Standing Committee members, including Xi Jinping, Li Zhanshu, and Wang Yang, all held billions of dollars' worth of property in Hong Kong.[22] The art market and vintage red wine market in Hong Kong have been important venues for the mainland Chinese elite to store and move their wealth too.[23] This accumulated wealth of the Chinese elite in Hong Kong, unlike their property in mainland China, could be converted into other currencies and freely move to other countries at any time they see fit.

Over the years, there has been speculation that the free-trade zones that the Chinese government set up in Shenzhen and Shanghai, such as Shenzhen's Qianhai free-trade zone (FTZ) and the Shanghai FTZ, both established in 2013, would surpass Hong Kong as China's offshore financial market. However, both of these FTZs failed to achieve a fraction of the economic significance of Hong Kong. Foreign companies are reluctant to move their Hong Kong operations to those FTZs, which lack judicial independence, freedom of information, a separate central bank and monetary system, and, most importantly, international recognition of separate customs territory status.[24] This attests to the reality that Hong Kong's function to the Chinese economy as an offshore financial center does not result from the Chinese government's policy alone. That function rests in a larger part upon Hong Kong's historical institutional legacy (such as the common-law tradition of the courts) and international recognition of Hong Kong's economy as separate from that of mainland China.

The Rise of Mainland Chinese Capital

The presence of Chinese state companies in Hong Kong predated China's market reforms. As we saw in the first section, state companies like Bank of China and Chinese Resources had been operating under the auspices of the British colonial government to handle financial and trade activities between the PRC and Hong Kong, which was the only channel for China's economic interaction with the outside world at the height of the Cold War. After the beginning of China's market reform in the 1980s, these enterprises became ever more profit-oriented. The imminent sovereignty handover of Hong Kong to China further enhanced the prowess of these enterprises. Simultaneously, more state enterprises set up subsidiaries as "window companies" in Hong Kong.[25] More Chinese enterprises incorporated in Hong Kong, such as Lenovo.

Some of the biggest Chinese state enterprises incorporated in Hong Kong or elsewhere outside China became public on the Hong Kong Stock Exchange and are collectively known as "red chips" in the financial markets. On top of the red chips long established in the local economy, an increasing number of Chinese companies, mostly state-owned, incorporated within China flocked to the Hong Kong Stock Exchange since the exchange started accepting listing of PRC-based companies in 1993 as "H share" companies. Though these companies did not necessarily have many businesses in Hong Kong, they used Hong Kong to raise capital internationally. Hong Kong's unique attraction for these companies was the combination of its proximity to China and its judicial autonomy from China. In the 2000s, leading Chinese private enterprises incorporated outside China and controlled by mainland Chinese individuals also started to be listed on the Hong Kong Stock Exchange. They overshadowed the state-owned H shares and red chips, with Alibaba and Tencent being recent, well-known examples. Table 3.1 shows that these companies have been increasing in number and are among the most prominent companies trading in Hong Kong's financial market over the years. They cover a wide range of business fields, from finance to energy to utilities.

The growing dominance of red chips, H shares, and Chinese private enterprises in Hong Kong's capital market is also reflected in their rising share in total market capitalization, as shown in Table 3.2. They constituted more than 73 percent of the market on the Hong Kong Stock Exchange as of 2019.

The rise of China Mobile (formerly China Telecom) on the Hong Kong Stock Exchange illustrates how these mainland-based companies came to be incorporated or listed in Hong Kong in collaboration with Western financial giants. The creation of China Mobile, which is among the few "national champion" companies in China and is on the Fortunes Global 500 list, is emblematic of China's reform of SOEs in the 1990s. Before then, China's telecommunication services were provided through fragmented facilities operated by provincial governments. In the early 1990s, Goldman Sachs "aggressively lobbied Beijing" to create a national telecommunication company and ultimately succeeded.[26] Under the auspices of international bankers, accountants, and corporate lawyers, China Mobile was created as a new company representing the consolidation of previously provincially owned telecommunication assets. After years of American bankers' efforts to build its international image, China Mobile completed its initial public offering in Hong Kong and New York in 1997 and, despite the Asian financial crisis, raised USD 4.5 billion.

Utilities, energy, and finance have always been the dominant sectors among red chips and H shares in the Hong Kong capital market. Chinese financial companies have been growing particularly rapidly. Table 3.1 shows that financial companies were not among the top H shares and red chips listed on the Hong Kong Stock Exchange in the year 2000. However, by 2014, over half of the top H shares' and red chips' total market capitalization was from banks or insurance companies. In 2019, Chinese financial firms continued to be important, though they were overshadowed by Alibaba and Tencent, two Internet giants in China and the world.

Table 3.1 *H shares, red chips, and mainland Chinese private companies among the top 50 companies on the Hong Kong Stock Exchange by market capitalization*

Year	Company	Classification	Market capitalization (HK$ million)	% of equity total
2000	PetroChina Co. Ltd	H share	22,857.14	0.48
	China Mobile Ltd	Red chip	792,586.3	16.53
	China Unicom (Hong Kong) Ltd	Red chip	150,008.3	3.13
	China Merchants Holdings (International) Co. Ltd	Red chip	11,582.63	0.24
	Shanghai Industrial Holdings Ltd	Red chip	12,749.56	0.27
	China Everbright Ltd	Red chip	12,419.3	0.26
	Legend Holdings	Private	36,625.01	0.76
			Total	**21.67**
2014	China Construction Bank Corp.	H share	1,531,458.33	6.15
	Industrial and Commercial Bank of China Ltd	H share	491,254.29	1.97
	Bank of China Ltd	H share	365,429.35	1.47
	Ping An Insurance (Group) Co. of China Ltd	H share	294,551.67	1.18
	Bank of Communications Co. Ltd	H share	253,485.89	1.02
	China Life Insurance Co. Ltd	H share	226,583.78	0.91
	PetroChina Co. Ltd	H shares	181,450.54	0.73
	China Petroleum & Chemical Corporation	H share	159,458.99	0.64
	Agricultural Bank of China Ltd	H share	120,496.19	0.48
	China Pacific Insurance (Group) Co. Ltd	H share	109,346.82	0.44
	China Mobile Ltd	Red chip	1,845,762.61	7.41
	CNOOC Ltd	Red chip	466,119.44	1.87
	CITIC Ltd	Red chip	329,221.94	1.32

Table 3.1 *(cont.)*

Year	Company	Classification	Market capitalization (HK$ million)	% of equity total
	BOC Hong Kong (Holdings) Ltd	Red chip	274,363.65	1.10
	China Unicom (Hong Kong) Ltd	Red chip	248,904.58	1.00
	China Overseas Land & Investment Ltd	Red chip	188,410.14	0.76
	China Resources Land Ltd	Red chip	119,248.42	0.48
	Tencent	Private	1,053,930.94	4.23
	Hanergy Thin Film Power Group Ltd	Private	116,949.88	0.47
	Lenovo Group Ltd	Private	113,522.22	0.46
	Hengan International Group Co. Ltd	Private	99,236.38	0.40
			Total	**34.95**
2019	China Construction Bank Corp.	H share	1,618,008.56	4.25
	Ping An Insurance (Group) Co. of China, Ltd	H share	685,921.83	1.80
	Industrial and Commercial Bank of China Ltd	H share	520,764.27	1.37
	Bank of China Ltd	H share	278,462.18	0.73
	Bank of Communications Co. Ltd	H share	193,965.72	0.51
	China Merchants Bank Co. Ltd	H share	183,865.59	0.48
	China Life Insurance Co. Ltd	H share	161,101.44	0.42
	China Mobile Ltd	Red chip	1,341,144.13	3.52
	CNOOC Ltd	Red chip	578,631.03	1.52
	China Overseas Land & Investment Ltd	Red chip	332,520.72	0.87
	CITIC Ltd	Red chip	303,120.54	0.80
	BOC Hong Kong (Holdings) Ltd	Red chip	285,993.71	0.75
	China Resources Land Ltd	Red chip	276,680.46	0.73

Table 3.1 *(cont.)*

Year	Company	Classification	Market capitalization (HK$ million)	% of equity total
	China Unicom (Hong Kong) Ltd	Red chip	224,590.23	0.59
	China Resources Beer (Holdings) Co. Ltd	Red chip	139,824.02	0.37
	Alibaba Group Holding Ltd	Private	4,446,881.70	11.68
	Tencent Holdings Ltd	Private	3,587,872.92	9.43
	Meituan Dianping	Private	591,768.25	1.55
	China Evergrande Group	Private	284,657.13	0.75
	Country Garden Holdings Co. Ltd	Private	272,621.38	0.72
	Xiaomi Corporation	Private	258,962.59	0.68
	Longfor Group Holdings Ltd	Private	218,178.77	0.57
	Sunac China Holdings Ltd	Private	206,828.89	0.54
	ANTA Sports Products Ltd	Private	188,456.62	0.50
	Shenzhou International Group Holdings Ltd	Private	171,217.03	0.45
	Haidilao International Holding Ltd	Private	165,890.00	0.44
	Hansoh Pharmaceutical Group Co. Ltd	Private	149,925.03	0.39
	Sunny Optical Technology (Group) Co. Ltd	Private	147,965.02	0.39
	Geely Automobile Holdings Ltd	Private	139,705.04	0.37
			Total	47.17

Source: HKEX

The Nexus of RMB Internationalization

The increasing dominance of Chinese capital in Hong Kong's financial market went in tandem with Beijing's

Table 3.2 *Market capitalization of mainland Chinese companies on the Hong Kong Stock Exchange (HK$ million and %)*

	2014	2015	2018	2019
H shares	5,723,993.53	5,157,109.86	5,937,289.44	6,423,518.74
Red chips	5,214,967.56	5,137,712.98	5,374,871.03	5,443,942.64
Private enterprise	4,078,538.74	4,931,492.39	8,838,322.09	16,062,221.74
Total	15,017,499.84	15,226,315.23	20,150,482.55	27,929,683.12
% of market total	60.33	62.34	67.79	73.39

Source: HKEX

designation of Hong Kong as the global wholesale center for RMB business in its campaign to internationalize RMB. With the increase in the international use of RMB, more foreign businesses would buy and hold RMB through the financial institutions of Hong Kong. While all major banks in Hong Kong had been vying for the RMB business, Chinese financial institutions in Hong Kong enjoyed a significant competitive advantage because of their mainland connections. Above all, the Bank of China Hong Kong, a red chip on the Hong Kong Stock Exchange, was designated by China's central bank as the official clearing and settlement bank of RMB in 2003.

Since the global financial crisis triggered by the US financial meltdown in 2008, the Chinese government has been worried about its accumulation of USD-dominated assets, mostly in the form of US Treasuries, in its foreign-exchange reserve. At the height of the crisis, there was speculation that the USD's value would collapse, threatening the value of China's foreign-exchange reserve. To reduce its dependence on USD in its trade settlement and to curtail the need to accumulate USD assets, Beijing started a campaign to internationalize the use of RMB. Beijing sought to increase the amount of trade settled in RMB, gradually displacing the USD's dominant role in China's trade. This would reduce China's large accumulation of USD and risky US Treasury bonds in its foreign-exchange reserve.

An increase in RMB's global use would also increase the holding of RMB in foreign countries, hence enhancing China's overseas influence.[27]

One big hurdle for actualizing this RMB internationalization plan is that it would require Beijing to eventually make RMB freely convertible, as the international market's appetite for an inconvertible currency would be minimal. To make RMB freely convertible, Beijing would have to liberalize its capital account fully. But this means that the CCP would need to let go of its control of the banking sector and its monopoly on credit creation – something the CCP is very reluctant to do. It sees its control of credit as a key source of power over the economy and society. Hong Kong's offshore financial market offers Beijing a pathway to internationalize RMB without fully liberalizing its capital account. The regulated permeability between the Chinese and Hong Kong financial systems allows Beijing to pursue RMB internationalization by injecting a large pool of freely convertible offshore RMB to Hong Kong while maintaining the onshore RMB's inconvertibility in mainland China.

The centrality of Hong Kong in RMB's internationalization process is well illustrated in China's successful bid to get RMB included in the IMF currency basket that constitutes the special drawing rights (SDRs) in late 2015. The SDR is essentially an accounting unit created by the IMF for use as a substitute for hard currencies like the USD held by central banks as foreign-exchange reserves. The value of the SDR is determined by the values of its constituent currencies and the weight of each constituent currency as determined by the IMF. The IMF creates SDR units out of thin air regularly and allocates them to its members' central banks according to their economic standing. A central bank can use the allocated SDR units to purchase its constituent hard currencies or use its hard-currency reserves to purchase SDRs from other central banks. The inclusion of a currency in the SDR basket is perceived to be a recognition of the currency's status and stability by the IMF.

The IMF invented the SDR in 1969 as a remedy to the insufficient global supply of the USD and gold as major reserve assets around the world amidst rapid global economic expansion. But not long after its invention, Nixon abolished the gold standard of the USD. The US authorities then turned on the printing press and inundate the world with new USD supply. The urgent need for the SDR as a substitute for scarce hard currencies in central banks' foreign-exchange reserve disappeared.[28] The long-forgotten SDR attracted much attention again in 2009. The global financial break-down originating in the US unleashed a global fear about the USD's imminent collapse among countries that hold a large number of USD assets in their foreign-exchange reserves, China in particular. In March that year, Zhou Xiaochuan, the head of China's central bank, issued a statement calling for an increase in the use of SDRs and replacing the USD with the SDR as the leading world reserve "currency." Zhou also advocated for an expansion of the SDR currency basket so that its stability would be less dependent on any particular country's financial health. In November 2011, the then Chinese president Hu Jintao amplified such advocacy by incorporat-ing it as the centerpiece of his proposal to reform the global financial system, which he laid out in his speech at the G20 summit.[29]

Beijing's proposal of replacing the global dollar standard with an SDR standard was in tandem with Beijing's effort to push for RMB inclusion in the SDR basket. The inclusion of a currency in the SDR basket is comparable to the inclusion of a certain stock in a major stock index. It induces significant world demand for the included currency. Chinese leaders must have assumed that an RMB inclusion would be tantamount to an official endorsement by the IMF that the RMB is as reliable and liquid as the existing currencies in the basket – the USD, the euro, the pound, and the yen – and safe to use as reserve currency. Such endorsement would naturally increase the world demand for RMB. The symbolic pride of having RMB recognized as a peer of the USD and the euro would also benefit the CCP's legitimacy in its people's eyes.

From the IMF officials' vantage point, such inclusion could encourage Beijing to liberalize its financial system and capital account further. But in 2010, in its five-yearly review of the SDR basket composition, the IMF rejected RMB inclusion, as it concluded that RMB had not met the "freely usable" criteria of SDR constituent currency. According to the IMF definition, a freely usable currency is "widely used to make payments for international transactions," and is "widely traded in the principal exchange markets."[30]

The IMF designation of RMB as not freely usable in 2010 was hardly surprising. China's financial system has not been open to the global financial circuit. Beijing maintained tight foreign-exchange control as a safeguard against the volatile financial flow and erosion of the Communist Party's command of the economy through its control of credits and deposits. After 2010, Beijing redoubled its effort to make RMB fulfill the IMF technical requirements for its inclusion in the SDR. The tricky part is how the Communist Party could meet the requirements without forfeiting its control of China's financial sector. Hong Kong was, once again, the key to solving this problem.

By early 2015, the IMF started to signal that it was on the way to certifying that RMB had fulfilled its SDR inclusion requirements. The fund decided in November that year to include RMB in its SDR currency basket. The data most widely cited as proof of RMB's "free usability" was that the use of RMB in international payments had shot up from below the top fifteen currencies in 2011 to the fifth most-used currency as of September 2015, trailing just behind the USD, the euro, the pound, and the yen. This appears to be an impressive achievement. Nevertheless, a more careful look into the data shows that the fifth rank represents only 2.45 percent of all international payments in all currencies, still far below the 43.3 percent for the USD and 28.6 percent for the euro. This composition and ranking have stayed more or less unchanged ever since then, as shown in Figure 3.5.

Remarkably, among the 2.45 percent of international payments carried out in RMB, more than 70 percent are transactions conducted in Hong Kong, as shown in Figure 3.6. In other words, the internationalization of RMB that helps the currency fulfill the IMF technical requirements is mostly due to the expanded circulation of offshore RMB in Hong Kong. It involved an increase of RMB deposits in Hong Kong banks (mostly by Hong Kong's retail currency investors betting on RMB appreciation), sales of RMB-denominated "dim sum bonds" in Hong Kong, and the "through-train" Hong Kong–Shanghai stock arrangement.[31] Beijing has carefully managed the increasing use of RMB in Hong Kong under a quota regime. As such, RMB's "free usability" in the world is, in large part, attributable to its "free usability" in Hong Kong. China did not further open its capital account to the world. What made China fulfill the IMF technical requirement was, in fact, China's controlled opening to Hong Kong.

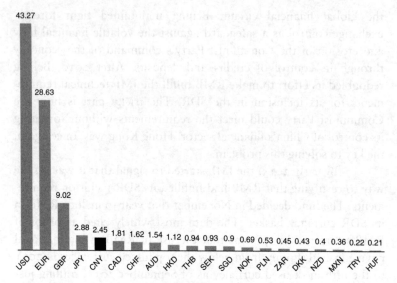

Figure 3.5a Ranked major currency shares as international payment currencies in value (%), September 2015
Source: SWIFT

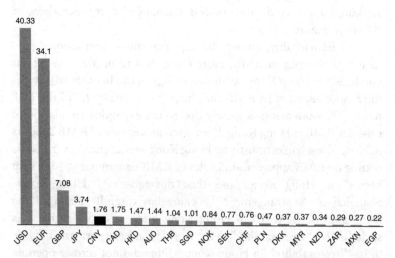

Figure 3.5b Ranked major currency shares as international payment currencies in value (%), June 2020
Source: SWIFT

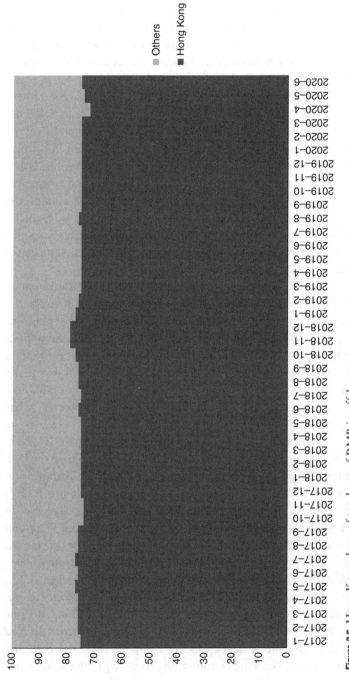

Figure 3.6 Hong Kong share of total use of RMB in offshore payment
Source: SWIFT

In such a manner, the offshore RMB market in Hong Kong played a central role in RMB internationalization. It allowed Beijing to boost RMB's international status without compromising the CCP's control of China's financial system. Policy advisers and financial think tanks in China have been keenly advocating for the consolidation of Hong Kong's role as the offshore financial center to aid the ascendance of RMB as a global currency in the years to come. They agreed that the only viable way for RMB to assume the role of a major global currency without China's capital account fully liberalizing is to develop Hong Kong as a wholesale RMB center. Other financial markets around the world (such as London and Singapore) could become RMB retail centers. To achieve this, developing the Hong Kong's Stock Exchange's connection to the mainland financial markets, building an RMB bond market in Hong Kong, and expanding RMB-denominated financial products run by Chinese state banks in Hong Kong become ever more important.[32]

The IMF and the international financial community assume that Beijing's controlled opening of the Hong Kong–mainland financial border is a transitory phase, where RMB is on its way to becoming a genuinely freely convertible currency. Under this assumption, Hong Kong's elevated role as an offshore financial center facilitating RMB internationalization would be transitional. It will eventually lose its uniqueness after onshore RMB becomes freely usable like other currencies in the SDR basket. This is not, however, what Beijing prefers. Beijing has never been earnest about liberalizing its financial system and capital account. Internationalizing the RMB via Hong Kong's offshore market is more a long-term plan than the IMF wishfully expects.[33] Beijing's appetite for financial liberalization diminished further in the summer of 2015, right before RMB's inclusion in the SDR basket. That summer, a stock market rout in China and a sudden depreciation of RMB set off capital flight and a vicious cycle of market turbulence and depreciation. Beijing moved in swiftly to stem capital outflow via draconian administrative measures and further tightened its control of the financial market.

After 2015, the RMB internationalization project was put on hold. Advocates for financial liberalization in China became silent. With the liberalization of China's financial sector delayed indefinitely and the need for Chinese companies to raise debt and capital in foreign currencies continuing to grow, Hong Kong's free financial channel to the world became even more important for Chinese enterprises and elites. China's capital outflow via Hong Kong accelerated despite Beijing's tightening capital controls and Hong Kong's function as China's offshore financial center was further consolidated.[34]

4 THE MAINLANDIZATION OF BUSINESS MONOPOLIES

In the early days of the HKSAR, Beijing relied on a united front with the local Hong Kong business elite to govern. This united front emerged in the 1980s and the 1990s when traditional Chinese business allies of the British shifted their allegiance to Beijing in anticipation of the handover, expecting Beijing's protection of their interests and a share of the China boom.[1] This Chinese business elite continued to maintain dense investment and collaboration networks with foreign capital from the US and other Western countries. The mainlandization of Hong Kong's economy created new competition between mainland Chinese capital, local Chinese capital, and foreign capital, which resulted in a shifting of the political balance among different factions in the governing coalition and had significant implications for the Hong Kong policy of the US and other major powers.

The CCP-Local Business Elite Ruling Coalition

Chapter 2 discussed how the British colonial state relied on an alliance with the British and local Chinese business elite to govern Hong Kong. The Chinese business elite in the coalition was the nexus between the colonial government and local Chinese society. Heads of prominent business families received appointments into the Executive and Legislative Councils of the government. The colonial government also recruited them into many consultative bodies, granting them access to information and policy-making processes that could benefit their businesses. This synergy of the ruling elite remained intact for most of the twentieth century.

For a long time, the British banks (led by HSBC) and merchant houses (like Jardines) occupied the economy's commanding height. Their political representation dominated the colonial government. Interlocking directorship of leading British companies in Hong Kong shows that the British business elite constituted a highly cohesive network, with HSBC at the center. In Hong Kong, the British capitalist class had been a highly organized, conscious class force exerting a significant influence on the colonial government.[2]

In the countdown to 1997, many British corporations, seeing the uncertain future of Hong Kong, started to diversify their business overseas and to sell off their assets in Hong Kong. Simultaneously, the local Chinese business elite expanded aggressively to take control of key business sectors. By the time sovereignty changed hands, the local Chinese elite had successfully displaced their British counterparts to control the local economy. For example, Li Ka-shing acquired Hutchison Whampoa, an old British asset holding companies that controlled important infrastructure, telecommunications, and real-estate property in 1979. In 1985, he acquired Hong Kong Electrics, which provided electricity to Hong Kong Island, home to the administrative and financial centers of Hong Kong.

When the transition to Chinese sovereignty began in the 1980s, the British started to expand direct elections in Hong Kong. At the same time, Beijing worked very hard to prevent the British from going too far in democratizing the colony before they left (see Chapter 7 below). The LegCo, which used to be fully appointed by the colonial government, alloted twelve out of the fifty-seven seats to be elected by functional constituencies (FCs) in 1985. Voters in each of the FCs were mostly corporations or members of registered professional bodies. This FC system was a way to consolidate the alliance between the government and the business and professional elite in the last years of colonial rule.[3] In 1991, the number of LegCo representatives increased to sixty, with twenty-one FC seats and eighteen directly elected seats.

After the sovereignty handover, in the 1998 election of the first LegCo, twenty seats came from direct election and thirty from

FCs. Of the thirty FC seats, nearly all were occupied by ethnically Chinese elites from the financial, commercial, industrial, and professional sectors, and, with few exceptions, were Beijing allies (the exceptions being those from the labor, education, and social-welfare constituencies).

To ensure its effective control of the HKSAR through its business and professional allies, Beijing held on to the FC system as the foundation of the LegCo after the sovereignty handover. The number of seats of the LegCo was frozen at sixty until 2008. Seats open for direct election increased from twenty in 1998 to twenty-four in the year 2000, and to thirty in 2004, remaining at thirty in 2008, whereas FCs dominated the rest (see the composition of the 2008 LegCo in Table 4.1). The monopoly business elite, as the allies of the CCP, always made up a safe majority in the FC seats, and the democrats always captured the majority of directly elected seats. In 2012, LegCo seats increased to seventy, with half of them elected by FCs and the other half by direct election.[4] This structure created a symbiosis of an electoral authoritarian state and key sectoral interests.[5]

CCP-led grassroots organizations, such as the Federation of Trade Unions, and political parties, led by the Democratic Alliance for the Betterment (DAB) of Hong Kong, participated keenly in direct elections. Given sponsorship by Beijing's business allies, their unlimited financial resources allowed them to gain roughly 40 percent of the vote for the directly elected seats in each LegCo election.[6] FC seats and directly elected seats captured by CCP-affiliated candidates always constitute a majority in the LegCo. CCP allies also did very well in the smaller, neighborhood-level district council elections, in which a candidate could easily win with as few as a thousand votes.[7] In such small-scale elections, well-resourced CCP-affiliated candidates were adept at establishing patron–client relations with voters through their generous social services and other favors, such as discounted seafood banquets and free medical check-ups for the elderly.[8]

The Basic Law designated that all motions initiated by any councilors in the LegCo needed to win the majority among all directly elected councilors and among all FC councilors separately to become law. In contrast, motions initiated by the government only require a simple majority of the whole LegCo to pass. This rule

Table 4.1 *Composition of the Legislative Council as of 2008*

Functional constituency (30)		Geographical constituency (30)	
Accountancy*	Information technology*	Elected candidates from democratic camp	19
Agriculture/fisheries†	Insurance†		
Architectural/ surveying /planning*	Labor (3 seats)† Legal*		
Catering†	Sports/performing arts/	Elected candidates	11
Commercial (I)†	culture/publication†	from Beijing- affiliated	
Commercial (II)†	Real estate/ construction†	groups	
District council*	Social welfare*		
Engineering*	Textiles and garments†		
Finance†	Transport†		
Financial services†	Wholesale/retail†		
Health services*	Medical*		
Heung Yee Kuk*	Tourism†		
Import and export†			
Education*			
Industrial (I)†			
Industrial (II)†			

† With corporate bodies or their owners/chairmen as electors.
* With individuals (usually registered professionals) as electors.
Source: Hong Kong Electoral Affairs Commission

ensured that the FC councilors could veto any pro-democracy or pro-welfare motion initiated by the democrats. Examples of the democrats' legislative initiatives that could have succeeded in a simple majority vote but were vetoed by FC councilors abound. They included motions to reverse the privatization of public housing amenities, to increase welfare benefits to the unemployed, to introduce antimonopoly measures that check big corporations' market share, and so on. The rule also warrants that the government–business coalition's motions would always pass easily in a simple majority vote of the whole LegCo.

The nomination and election of the chief executive are equally dominated by the CCP–business coalition, as the Election Committee responsible for nominating and electing the chief executive was constituted under principles similar to the FCs in the LegCo. Before 2012, three-fourths of the 800 members of the Election Committee were elected by corporate bodies from thirty-eight sectors, with each sector contributing dozens of members to the committee. The designation of these sectors resembles the sectors that constituted the FCs in the LegCo. The remaining members of the Election Committee came from select members from the district councils, the LegCo, and Hong Kong representatives of the National People's Congress and People's Political Consultative Conference with Beijing's blessing. When the Election Committee expanded to 1,200 members in 2012, business and professional corporate bodies continued to dominate, as shown in Table 4.2.

The business and professional elites' reliability as Beijing's allies in governing Hong Kong increased in tandem with their growing exposure to the Chinese market. The prolonged economic downturn in the aftermath of the Asian financial crisis of 1997–1998 deepened the dependence of Hong Kong's business elites on Beijing. After implementing the CEPA in 2003, the relocation of Hong Kong business and professional services to mainland China accelerated.

As we saw earlier, the British business elite that dominated Hong Kong before 1997 exhibited a highly cohesive network under HSBC's leadership. The Chinese business elite in the ruling coalition after 1997, however, was fragmented. Interlocking directorships among leading Chinese corporations shows that the Chinese elite has been divided into competing factions without a clear hegemonic force. Their internal competition and lack of leadership made the Chinese elite a less viable political force compared with their British predecessors. The competition among these factions often spilled over into the government decision-making process, contributing to the government's indecision and ineffectiveness.[9]

The Displacement of Local Capital by Mainland Capital

While the internal fragmentation of the Chinese business monopolies undermined their collective political influence, the

Table 4.2 *Composition of the Election Committee as of 2012*

	Subsector	No. of members
I	Catering	17
I	Commercial (first)	18
I	Commercial (second)	18
I	Employers' Federation of HK	16
I	Finance	18
I	Financial services	18
I	HK Chinese Enterprises Association	16
I	Hotel	17
I	Import and export	18
I	Industrial (first)	18
I	Industrial (second)	18
I	Insurance	18
I	Real estate and construction	18
I	Textiles and garments	18
I	Tourism	18
I	Transport	18
I	Wholesale and retail	18
I	**First sector total**	300
II	Accountancy	30
II	Architectural, surveying and planning	30
II	Chinese medicine	30
II	Education	30
II	Engineering	30
II	Health services	30
II	Higher education	30
II	Information technology	30
II	Legal	30
II	Medical	30
II	**Second sector total**	300
III	Agriculture and fisheries	60
III	Labor	60
III	Religious	60
III	Social welfare	60
III	Sports, performing arts, culture and publication	60
III	**Third sector total**	300
IV	National People's Congress	36
IV	Legislative Council	70

Table 4.2 *(cont.)*

Subsector	No. of members
IV Chinese People's Political Consultative Conference	51
IV Heung Yee Kuk	26
IV HK and Kowloon district councils	57
IV New Territories district councils	60
IV **Fourth sector total**	300
Grand total	1,200

Source: Electoral Affairs Commission, HKSAR Government

Hong Kong business elite faced increasing economic and political competition from the rising mainland elite in Hong Kong. The mainlandization of Hong Kong's financial market and the expanding RMB business in Hong Kong boosted the prowess of mainland Chinese corporations and elites in the territory. Besides dominating Hong Kong's capital market, as we saw in the previous chapter, Chinese companies began aggressively acquiring businesses in different sectors in Hong Kong. One example is the world of securities firms. Before 2015, most securities firms in Hong Kong were owned and run by local Hong Kong Chinese. Mainland Chinese securities firms began to make inroads into the Hong Kong market in 2005 and accelerated rapidly in 2015. By 2019, the sector of securities brokerage had become controlled by mainland Chinese capital.[10]

Chinese companies' purchases of Hong Kong securities firms surged in the context of Beijing's policy to open channels for Hong Kong investors to participate in the mainland Chinese stock market and vice versa, through the stock market "through-train" system connecting the Hong Kong and Shanghai markets. This policy was part of Beijing's larger strategy to increase Chinese access to international capital while not liberalizing China's capital account. With the advantage of low-cost loans from state banks, a large mainland customer base, and connections to brokers and other players in the mainland's financial markets, mainland securities firms were well placed to outcompete local Hong Kong firms, which only had a local customer base and access to local financial markets. One consequence of this mainland takeover of the sector was that local financiers and financial analysts were increasingly displaced by those with a mainland background, as mainland Chinese firms preferred to hire the latter.[11] In the year 2000, mainland Chinese only occupied about 15 percent of all investment banker jobs in Hong Kong, while the majority were occupied by Hong Kongers. By 2020, the jobs going to mainland Chinese had climbed to 60 percent, while those occupied by Hong Kong locals slumped to 30 percent (the remaining 10 percent were occupied by foreigners).[12]

Thanks to the plentiful initial public offerings (IPOs) of Chinese companies in Hong Kong, Hong Kong has been among the world's largest IPO markets over the last decade. Underwriting Chinese companies' IPOs has been one of the biggest and most profitable businesses in the Hong Kong financial market. The underwriter of an IPO not only earned consultancy fees from the company in question, but also earned the right to subscribe to the company's substantial shares at discounted prices before the IPO. Share prices usually increase steeply right after the IPO, enabling the underwriters to rake in large profits. Before 2010, most IPOs in Hong Kong were underwritten by foreign firms, including Wall Street investment banks like Goldman Sachs and European banks like Credit Suisse and Deutsche Bank. Chinese securities firms have since become the dominant force in Hong Kong's IPO business in tandem with the Chinese capital's inroads into the Hong Kong securities sector.[13]

Today, the biggest players in the Hong Kong IPO market are no longer Wall Street firms. The leading players now are mainland Chinese banks like the China International Capital Corporation (which sponsored Alibaba's gigantic secondary listing in 2019), ICBC International Capital, and Everbright, which expanded into the Hong Kong market by acquiring Sun Hung Kai Financial Limited, one of the oldest and largest securities firms in Hong Kong in 2015. As shown in Figure 4.1, by 2019, Chinese companies had dominated the Hong Kong IPO market. Most of the IPOs in Hong Kong were underwritten by Chinese securities firms, as shown in Figure 4.2. Many of the local Hong Kong securities firms involved in the Chinese companies' IPO business were newer firms founded in Hong Kong in recent years with mainland Chinese background.

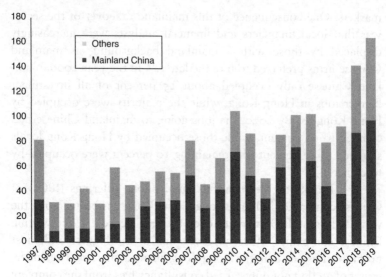

Figure 4.1 Origins of newly listed companies on the Hong Kong Stock
Exchange, 1997–2019
Source: HKEX

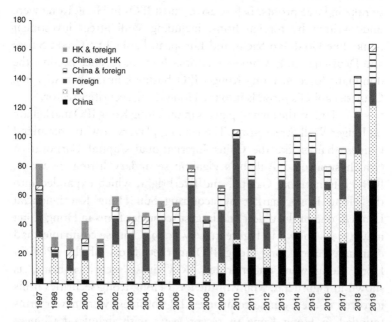

Figure 4.2 Origins of sponsors of all IPOs on the Hong Kong Stock Exchange,
1997–2019
Source: HKEX

Another manifestation of mainland Chinese capital's inroads into the Hong Kong economy is mainland Chinese developers' aggressive bidding for land publicly auctioned by the Hong Kong government. For a long time, Hong Kong's homegrown real-estate developers were the most successful and active bidders in government auctions. The Hong Kong government always limited land supply to support land prices, as land sales have been its most important source of revenue since the inception of colonial Hong Kong. Given this centrality of the real-estate sector in the Hong Kong economy and the limited supply of land, only a few real-estate developers managed to accumulate sizable land reserves over the years, and these land reserves laid the foundation of their economic monopoly in Hong Kong.

Hong Kong did not see a single bid for government land from mainland Chinese companies before 2011. That year saw the beginning of the surge in Chinese companies' participation in government land auctions. Awash with low-cost loans originating from the Chinese state's monetary stimulus after the 2008 global financial crisis, Chinese developers began to flood the Hong Kong land market to drive up auction prices and outbid local Hong Kong developers. Their appetite for Hong Kong land further increased amidst China's economic slowdown (when the government's 2008 mega monetary stimulus fizzled after 2011), and further still following the financial turbulence and RMB depreciation during the summer of 2015. Their land purchases were a form of capital flight: many Chinese companies rushed to move their RMB assets out of China, and holding assets in Hong Kong was the most convenient path.

From 2011 to 2017, Chinese companies' share of successful bids for residential land auctioned by the Hong Kong government rose from 1 percent (measured in the total value of land sold) in 2011 to 100 percent at the peak of the first half of 2017.[14] Chinese land developers pushed up the bidding price to more than 30 or even 40 percent of the asking price. Such a purchase price would mean a meager profit from the final residential development project. Local land developers, who would not take risks to acquire land at prices that would not warrant substantial profit from the final project, could not compete with these Chinese companies, which prioritized locking in land resources over profitability. Local developers were thus squeezed out of the land auction market.[15] Notable examples of mainland Chinese land bidding include the HNA's successful bid for a series of residential plots at astronomical sale prices in 2017.[16]

Besides bidding for residential land, mainland companies also moved aggressively to acquire commercial property. China's Evergrande Real Estate Group's purchase of Mass Mutual Tower (renamed China Evergrande Center) in 2015 and China Everbright's acquisition of Dah Sing Financial Center (renamed Everbright Center) in 2016 were two of the highest-profile cases. Some of the most prominent buildings in Hong Kong's central business district are now all owned by Chinese companies.[17] Mainlanders' displacement of local tycoons in the property market invites comparison to local tycoons' replacement of British companies in the 1980s and 1990s.

After 2015, Beijing heightened its efforts to stem capital flight. This curtailed Chinese companies' bidding for Hong Kong land. After the peak of 2017, Hong Kong companies started to once again outbid mainland companies in land auctions.[18] Despite this ebbing of mainlanders' land acquisitions, Chinese developers had already locked on to some of the most valuable land in Hong Kong and built up a significant land reserve. The balance of power between Hong Kong and mainland developers had shifted to a degree of no return.

Hong Kong's construction sector also witnessed the displacement of local companies by mainland ones. Giant mainland Chinese companies, such as China Overseas Land and Investment Limited, have become increasingly dominant players in Hong Kong's construction business, which used to be monopolized by Hong Kong and Western contractors. Government infrastructure projects increasingly went to mainland contractors. Between 2008 and 2018, 35 percent of projects commissioned by the Highway Department went to mainland companies. For all ongoing projects as of 2018, 62.1 percent went to mainland companies (80 percent if we include a consortium involving mainland companies). For all completed and ongoing projects commissioned by the Civil Engineering and Development Department until 2018, close to 70 percent went to mainland companies.[19]

Some of the most outspoken and politically active Hong Kong business representatives, such as James Tien Pei-chun and Michael Tien Puk-sun, openly fretted about the displacement of local Hong Kong companies by powerful mainland companies. The Tien brothers are the sons of Francis Tien Yuan-hao, a leading Shanghai industrialist who settled in Hong Kong after 1949. James Tien founded the Liberty Party in 1993 and has been its long-term leader. The party was to represent the interests of the Hong Kong Chinese business elite. It has been a core member of Beijing's ruling coalition in Hong Kong. James Tien lamented that the widespread sale of Hong Kong business to mainland companies would lead to the complete control of Hong Kong's daily life by mainland Chinese capital. According to Tien, such control would eventually threaten the viability of the "One Country, Two Systems" arrangement.[20] His brother Michael Tien, another Beijing ally in Hong Kong, echoed his views by asserting that a total replacement of Hong Kong business by Chinese companies would cause serious harm to Hong Kong's business environment.[21] Hong Kong's traditional business elite are all too aware of the political implications of Chinese capital's rising economic weight at the expense of local capital. It is central to the question of who rules Hong Kong.

The Political Ascendancy of the Mainland Business Elite

Corresponding to mainland companies' strong presence in Hong Kong is the increasing social and political influence of the mainland elite. The mainland business and professional elite are tied to mainland and foreign companies. Vying for mainland Chinese business, many foreign financial firms in Hong Kong were eager to recruit Western-educated financiers with mainland Chinese background to take advantage of their connections in China. The highest-profile case of such a hire would be JP Morgan's 2001 choice of Fang Fang. Fang Fang was born and educated in mainland China and received MBA education in the US. He became the chief executive of JP Morgan China in 2007 and was appointed as a member of the Chinese People's Political Consultative Conference National Committee in 2008. This hire put JP Morgan under US scrutiny and eventually led to a US federal investigation. The investigation was part of a probe into Wall Street firms' Chinese princelings hiring program, which was suspected of violating the Foreign Corrupt Practices Act. In connection to this US investigation, Hong Kong's anticorruption agency arrested Fang in 2014.[22] But none of the investigations deterred the growth of mainland Chinese elite in Hong Kong's financial industry at large. The total number of mainland Chinese investment bankers has long surpassed that of local Hong Kong ones, and is on the way to surpassing all other foreign investment bankers operating in Hong Kong.[23]

Before his downfall, Fang Fang actively organized the expanding mainland Chinese elite in Hong Kong. In 2011, Fang Fang established the Hua Jing Society of Hong Kong with other prominent Chinese elites. The society's stated goal was to organize mainland Chinese professionals and cultivate Hong Kong–mainland China exchanges. This society has been active in different social, educational, and philanthropic activities, many involving notable Hong Kong and Chinese officials. Some leading members of the society were key supporters of the Leung Chun-ying election campaign for chief executive of Hong Kong in 2012.

After Leung Chun-ying became the chief executive, he appointed many leaders from within the Hua Jing Society into government bodies. For example, Judy Chen Qing, now the society's permanent honorary chair, was recruited into the HKSAR government Central Policy Unit, the Major Sports Events Committee, and the Civic Education Committee. Fang Fang has also been a member of the HKSAR Commission of Strategic Development. This commission was chaired by the chief executive and included all major government officials. Leung Chun-ying and Carrie Lam are the current sponsors of the Hua Jing Society. The roster of leaders in the Hua Jing Society is a who's who list of mainland elite occupying key positions in different social and economic sectors of Hong Kong, particularly in the financial sector, as shown in Table 4.3.

The Leung Chun-ying administration also set up a Financial Services Development Council in 2013. The council's stated mission was to "promote our financial services industry and Hong Kong as an international financial center on the Mainland and overseas."[24] Among its board of directors are some of the most prominent mainland and Hong Kong financial elite, including Chen Shuang, vice chairman of the Hua Jing Society at the time.

Table 4.3 *Background of leaders of the Hua Jing Society (as of August 2020)*

Position	Name	Background
Sponsor	Leung Chun-ying	Former chief executive of Hong Kong
	Carrie Lam	Current chief executive of Hong Kong
Honorary consultants	Han Shuxia	Former director of the Youth Works Department at the Liaison Office of the Central People's Government at HKSAR
	Chen Lin	Director of the Youth Works Department at the Liaison Office of the Central People's Government at HKSAR
Founding chair	Fang Fang	Former head of investment banking in China at JP Morgan Chase; member of the Standing Committee of the All-China Youth Federation and the National Committee Chinese People's Political Consultative Conference
Lifetime chair emeritus	Judy Chen Qing	Former head of Asia–Pacific Wealth Management at Merrill Lynch; chairman of UNICEF HK; member of the national committee of All-China Youth Federation; daughter of Chen Zuo'er, deputy director of the Hong Kong and Macau Affairs Office of the State Council; wife of Li Ka-shing's nephew
Chairs emeritus	Zhang Yi	Partner at King & Wood Mallesons Law Firm; committee member of the Shanghai Political Consultative Conference and standing committee of All-China Youth Federation
	Rao Guizhu	General manager of Cinda International Holdings Ltd, subsidiary of a state-owned asset management company; committee member of All-China Federation of Women

Table 4.3 *(cont.)*

Position	Name	Background
Vice chairs emeritus	Qin Jing	Chief investment officer at SINO-CEEF; former executive director and general manager at Deutsche Bank's mainland China investment banking branch
	Huang Haibo	Deputy director and head of the Chief Editor's Office of the Chinese Channel at Phoenix Satellite TV
	Huang Zheng	Musician from the mainland who joined the Hong Kong Philharmonic
	Hung Man	Chair and CEO of Crown International Corporation in Hong Kong
	Ni Mu	Director of Shenzhen Zhongke Nano Technology Co. Ltd
	Dong Zhe	Managing director, Promisky Holdings Group Ltd; wife of Frank Chan Shung-fai, a Hong Kong businessman and member of Hong Kong Election Committee; granddaughter of PLA general Dong Qiwu
Chair	Chen Shuang	Deputy director of the legal affairs office of the Bank of Communications headquarters; executive director and CEO of China Everbright Group; member of Tung Chee-Hwa's Our Hong Kong Foundation
Vice chairs	Zhang Yue	Executive director and general manager of Asia Area Investment Banking in Deutsche Bank; formerly at Citi Group
	Meng Mingyi	Investment banking analyst at Nomura; daughter of Meng Xiaosu, the president of the China National

Table 4.3 *(cont.)*

Position	Name	Background
		Real Estate Development Group Corporation and former secretary of Wan Li, who was the chairman of the NPCSC
	Ren Shanshan	Deputy managing director, China Construction Bank International Asset Management Ltd
	Tian Bin	No detailed information available
	Chen Wei	Director of music theater and opera
	Zhan Sheng	Worked at Xinhua News Agency and Ta Kung Pao; Standing Committee member of the All-China Youth Federation; grandson of the iconic CCP-affiliated cartoonist Zhang Leping
	Diao Tong	No detailed information available
	Liu Bin	Chairman of the board of directors at New Success International Group Ltd; worked in the People's Bank of China and China Construction Bank
	Joseph Zeng Xiaosong	Partner and Hong Kong office head of Greenwoods Asset Management; formerly vice president with JP Morgan's FIG Group investment banking department
	Zhao Jiayin	CEO of Guotai Global Investments; National Committee member of the All-China Youth Federation
	Wu Kexuan	Formerly investment banking analyst at Goldman Sachs and UBS before joining Phoenix TV
	Zhou Yuanzhi	President of the New Capital Fund Management (Shenzhen) Co. Ltd
	Guo Qifei	Vice president of HNA Holding Groups Co. Ltd; non-managing director of Aid Partners Technology Holdings Ltd

Table 4.3 *(cont.)*

Position	Name	Background
	Edward Liu Yang	Senior registered foreign lawyer at Reed Smith Richards Butler (shipping litigation and arbitration)
	Zhao Yang	Vice president of Geely Auto group
Secretary general	Su Xiaopeng	Chief strategy officer at China Everbright Ltd
Treasurer	Pu Zefei	Founding partner at River Delta Asset Management (Shanghai) Co. Ltd; member of the board of directors of Hong Kong Jiangsu Youth Association

Source: Hua Jing Society

The Hua Jing Society has been involved in promoting key central government policies related to Hong Kong. For example, after Leung Chun-ying announced that his government would turn Hong Kong into a nodal point for China's Belt and Road Initiative, promoting the initiative became one of the main themes of many activities organized by the society. Before and after the LegCo election of 2016, when the central government took on the fight against political activists promoting "Hong Kong independence," the Hua Jing Society organized protests and a signature campaign to demand disqualification of "pro-independence" legislators. It mobilized its members to participate in several anti-independence rallies with other pro-establishment groups. The society has also been active in social networking events with government officials and pro-establishment politicians in Hong Kong and mainland China.

The activities of formal organizations like the Hua Jing Society are the tip of the iceberg of the mainlander elites' expanding political activism and influence in Hong Kong. The episode described earlier in the introduction about a dinner party in which a small group of wealthy mainlanders with Hong Kong residency lobbied Chief Executive Carrie Lam on key policy issues shows that the elite have routine informal access to the HKSAR government's power-holders. This kind of access had previously been exclusive to local Hong Kong tycoons.

The election of the chief executive in 2012 shows the split of the Hong Kong elite into two factions and manifests the alienation of the local business elite. That election pitted two establishment candidates, Henry Tang Ying-yen and Leung Chun-ying, against each other. Henry Tang is the son of Tang Hsiang-chien Tang, a Hong Kong industrialist originating from Shanghai. The Tang family had been a key ally of Beijing from late colonial times to the HKSAR days. Leung Chun-ying is a professional land surveyor and long-time ally of Beijing. There are persistent rumors that he has long been a CCP member despite his consistent denial.[25]

During the election, local tycoons in the Election Committee mostly supported Tang. Local business supporters have been the backbone of Beijing's ruling coalition in Hong Kong – they were the bases of the Tung Chee-hwa and Donald Tsang Yam-kuen governments. In Tung and Tsang's elections, the local business elite in the Election Committee, representatives of mainland Chinese companies, and other members of CCP organizations voted in unison to support the only establishment candidate. Many expected that the 2012 election would be business as usual, and Henry Tang, as the only establishment candidate, would be effortlessly "elected." However, when Leung Chun-ying announced his candidacy, the election suddenly became competitive. This caught many in the establishment camp by surprise.

While there were two establishment candidates in the election, Beijing did not express any preference until the last minute. Many local tycoons, including Li Ka-shing, supported Tang throughout, even after it became clear at the very end that Beijing supported Leung Chun-ying. Leung received support from the representatives of Chinese state companies in Hong Kong: all the votes from the Hong Kong Chinese Enterprises Association, which represented Chinese state-owned enterprises in the Election Committee, supported Leung from the beginning.[26] The election became a competition between local tycoons and the mainland business elite. In the end, Beijing sided with Leung, and Leung won the election with the votes from members of the Election Committee that Beijing directly controlled, like those from the traditional CCP

Table 4.4 *Vote share of the winning chief executive in the Election Committee in each chief executive election*

1996: 80%
2002: no competition
2007: 84%
2012: 66%
2017: 67%

Source: Election Affairs Commission, HKSAR Government

organizations and parties such as the Federation of Trade Unions and the DAB. Hong Kong members of the National People's Congress also voted for Leung. However, Leung won with the smallest margin of victory since the handover, as shown in Table 4.4.

After becoming the chief executive, Leung Chun-ying did not particularly favor local tycoons, but nonetheless opened more doors for mainland Chinese companies. This contrasted to his predecessor, Donald Tsang, who had much cozier relations with the local business elite.[27] Leung Chun-ying established the previously mentioned Financial Services Development Council. Besides the young mainland Chinese elite from the Hua Jing Society, the council board of directors also included prominent Chinese princelings, such as the son of former premier Zhu Rongji, and heads of leading Chinese state companies, like Everbright and CITIC, as shown in Table 4.5. The recruitment of mainland business elites into important government consultation bodies was a departure from the tradition of including only representatives of British banks (such as HSBC) and homegrown local Chinese elites in such bodies.

Leung Chun-ying government's open embrace of the mainland business elite continued into the Carrie Lam government. Lam became the chief executive in the 2017 election, with only slightly better margins than Leung against another heavyweight establishment candidate, John Tsang Chun-wah. Tsang had been the Finance Secretary in both the Donald Tsang and the Leung Chun-ying governments. In that election, many local business elites initially expressed their support for Tsang.[28]

Table 4.5 *Financial Services Development Council members as of its founding, January 2013*

Title	Name	Background
Chairman of the board	Laura Cha Shih May-lung	Chairman of HKEX; nonexecutive deputy chairman of HSBC Co. Ltd; long-time leadership role in Hong Kong's Securities and Futures Commission; vice chairman of the China Securities Regulatory Commission (CSRC) from 2001 to 2004; a member of HKSAR's Executive Council since 2004; adviser to Carrie Lam's run for chief executive of HKSAR in 2017
Board member	Zhu Yunlai	Son of former Chinese premier Zhu Rongji; worked at Arthur Anderson at Chicago and Credit Suisse First Boston; worked at the Hong Kong branch of China International Capital Corporation Ltd as its CEO
Board member	Chen Shuang	Worked at Bank of Communications from 1992 to 2001 and joined China Everbright Group in 2001; became executive director and CEO of Everbright Limited in 2007
Board member	Michael Fung E	Worked at JP Morgan Chase from 2001 to 2015; was chairman of JP Morgan Private Bank in Asia; president and partner of SouthBay Investment Advisors Ltd
Board member	Benjamin Hung	Long-term senior executive at Standard Chartered Bank Limited; was vice chairman of Hong Kong Association of Banks
Board member	Edward Kwan	Former chief executive officer of HSBC Broking Services (Asia) Limited
Board member	Fred Lam Tin-fuk	Executive director of Hong Kong Trade Development Council (HKTDC); was appointed CEO of Airport Authority Hong Kong

Table 4.5 *(cont.)*

Title	Name	Background
Board member	Jeanne Lee	Chairman of the Hong Kong Securities Professionals Association
Board member	Vincent Lee	Chairman of Tung Tai Group of Companies; independent nonexecutive director at HKEX
Board member	Laurence Li Lu-jen	Was the head of the Corporate Finance Division of the Securities and Futures Commission of Hong Kong
Board member	Anton Liu Ting'an	Deputy chairman and president of China Life Insurance (Overseas) Company Ltd
Board member	Mark McCombe	Worked as chairman of Asia Pacific at BlackRock and senior managing director and chief client officer of BlackRock; before BlackRock, was the CEO of HSBC Hong Kong
Board member	Alasdair Morrison	Was senior adviser of the Asia Pacific Region, Citigroup; was managing director of British conglomerate Jardine Matheson
Board member	Joseph Ngai	Senior partner and managing partner (greater China) of McKinsey & Company, Inc. Hong Kong; adviser for Tung Chee-hwa's Our Hong Kong Foundation
Board member	Qin Xiao	Was chairman of Boyuan Foundation; son of CCP revolutionary elder Qin Lisheng; served as secretary for senior CCP official Song Renqiong; held senior management positions in CITIC and China Merchants Group; served as chairman of the APEC Business Advisory Council
Board member	Mark G. Shipman	Partner and global head of the Funds & Investment Management Sector at Clifford Chance, a pre-eminent international law firm

Table 4.5 *(cont.)*

Title	Name	Background
Board member	William Strong	Was co-chief executive officer of the Asia Pacific Region, Morgan Stanley
Board member	Tse Yung-hoi	Chairman of BOCI-Prudential Asset Management Ltd
Board member	Frank Wong Kwong-Shing	Was chairman and nonexecutive director of Mapletree Greater China Commercial Trust Management Ltd; independent nonexecutive director of China Mobile Ltd; served in the senior management of DBS Bank, Citigroup, JP Morgan and NatWest; was chairman of Hong Kong Futures Exchange
Board member	Florence Yip	Partner and national tax leader of financial services at PwC Hong Kong
Board member	Douglas W. Arner	Law professor at the University of Hong Kong; senior fellow of Melbourne Law School; nonexecutive director of Aptorum Group
Ex officio member	Ka-keung Ceajer Chan	Served as Secretary of Financial Services and the Treasury; was chairman of Kowloon–Canton Railway Corporation (KCRC)

Source: HKSAR government

Mainland companies have reportedly become more involved in local electoral politics in Hong Kong since Leung Chun-ying became the chief executive in 2012. In the 2016 LegCo election, the Central Government Liaison Office, which had been co-ordinating establishment election campaigns since the handover, abandoned a few traditional Beijing allies with local rural elite and local business elite ties. These traditional elite candidates were made to forfeit their electoral ambition to give way to a few new rising stars directly cultivated by the Liaison Office. At least one came from a Chinese state company background, with her father serving as a senior executive in a mainland state enterprise. Throughout the election, mainland companies in Hong Kong mobilized their large army of employees to campaign and vote for establishment candidates.[29]

In retrospect, the Donald Tsang era marked the heyday of the local business elite's political influence and economic monopoly. On the other hand, the Leung Chun-ying era witnessed the aggressive expansion and rising political influence of mainland Chinese capital at the expense of Hong Kong local businesses. Feeling marginalized within the establishment, local tycoons became more vocal in expressing their disagreement with the government's various policies. The Liberal Party, a political party representing the local business elite, split with the government in their LegCo voting in some cases and wavered in their support of the government in others. Their weakening support contributed to the failure of a few government initiatives, such as the government's aborted attempt to tighten regulations over the Internet in 2015 after prominent members of the Liberal Party, including its former chairman, James Tien, openly expressed their opposition to the government bill.[30] In the midst of the 2014 Umbrella Occupation, James Tien even called for the resignation of Leung Chun-ying as a solution to the crisis.[31]

The local business elite's alienation from the authorities culminated in the extradition legislation crisis, as we saw in the introduction. Many local tycoons saw the legislation as jeopardizing their property and safety. Many of them publicly showed their opposition to or reservations about the legislation. Having been dependent on the alliance with the British and then Beijing to protect their economic interests for so long, only time will tell whether these local elites can become a viable independent political force.

In the aftermath of the 2019 unrest, some prominent mainland Chinese elites with Western education and Hong Kong residency formed the Bauhinia Party, a new establishment party, in 2020. Among the founders of the party were Chairman Li Shan, Wong Chau-chi, and Chen Jianwen.[32] Li is a delegate to the National Committee of the Chinese People's Political Consultative Conference and a member of Credit Suisse's board of directors. Li was the student of Zhu Rongji in the 1980s, who later became the Chinese premier in the 1990s. When he worked at Goldman Sachs, he accompanied the then chief operating officer, Henry Paulson, to meet with Zhu Rongji, in 1997. Moreover, he left Goldman to join the China Development Bank after a personal invitation from Zhu.[33] Wong Chau-chi, an alumnus of Harvard University who was born and raised on the mainland, is the chairman and chief executive of the Hong Kong-listed multimedia firm CMMB Vision; a director of the private equity fund Chi Capital; and formerly with Goldman Sachs, Citibank, and BNP Paribas. Chen is chairman of Bonjour Holdings Limited, a cosmetic company listed in Hong Kong. He is also currently a director of Haifu International Finance Holding and has diverse investments on the mainland, including commercial real estate, national resources, and manufacturing.

In an interview conducted in an official magazine run by the Liaison Office, Li outlined the party's platform, in which the overarching goal was to secure another fifty years of the "One Country, Two Systems" arrangement after 2047. The platform also included:

> Supporting effective governance of the HKSAR government ... providing the government with high-quality governing talents and supporting party members to join the government ... supporting their candidates to run for chief executive ... supporting party members to become the core members of major social, philanthropic, and nongovernmental organizations.[34]

The establishment of their party instantly invoked the caution of the traditional local business elite. For example, James Tien judged that the party could not do well in the election, for it lacked connection to local society. Therefore, "chances of the new party becoming an influential force within the [establishment] bloc were slim."[35] In any event, the party's formation indicated a new stage of political participation of the mainland business and professional elite, which had hitherto exerted their political influence behind closed doors. Though many see them as natural allies of the CCP, whether the Liaison Office was involved in the formation of the Bauhinia Party and how much Beijing would trust these Western-educated mainland Chinese elites are not yet known. Whether they are able to become a viable political force in Hong Kong still remains to be seen, but the trend of more active political participation of Hong Kong residents with mainland background is certain.

Hong Kong in the US–China Rivalry

While mainland capital's rising economic power and political influence vis-à-vis local capital jeopardized Beijing's united front with the latter in ruling the city, it also menaced US economic interests in Hong Kong. Since the early 2000s, Beijing has become a challenger to US geopolitical hegemony, often exploiting Hong Kong's special status in the world trading system. This development pushed Washington to rethink its Hong Kong policy. We saw in the last chapter how well the US–Hong Kong Policy Act has served mainland China's and Hong Kong's economic interests. The US and other Western countries have also benefited from this status quo. It allowed their companies to do business with Chinese companies and the wealthy elite while China's financial system was still closed. For example, Western investment bankers, who are barred from doing business with Chinese clients in mainland China, can do so freely in Hong Kong. Western companies also rely on the separate legal and arbitration system in Hong Kong to settle disputes with their Chinese partners, as they do not trust the court system in mainland China.

However, Beijing's increasing use of Hong Kong as a backdoor to bypass Western sanctions on China and its allies has become a geopolitical problem from the US perspective. It is well known that China has been taking advantage of the special status and identity of Hong Kong since right after the sovereignty handover to make sensitive international deals to avoid the attention of Western countries. For example, in 1998, the Hong Kong-based entertainment company Chong Lot Travel Agency struck a deal with the Ukrainian government to acquire two retired Soviet-era aircraft carriers, *Varyag* and *Minsk*. The Travel Agency was founded by businessman Xu Zengping, who was a PLA veteran. On the surface, it appeared to be a deal about turning old aircraft carriers into floating theme parks for entertainment. In reality, this operation was part of the PLA's efforts to acquire and refit Soviet aircraft carriers. While *Minsk* did become a floating theme park in Shenzhen, Chong Lot sold *Varyag* to the PLA, which turned it into the first aircraft carrier of China, the *Liaoning*. The *Liaoning* was commissioned in 2012, and it became a symbol of China's ambition and capability of projecting its power into the Pacific Ocean at the expense of US influence.[36]

As another example, in 2013, the Nicaraguan government granted a fifty-year concession agreement to a Hong Kong-registered company, the Hong Kong Nicaragua Development Investment, to construct the Nicaragua Canal. The canal was supposed to divert Atlantic–Pacific traffic away from the Panama Canal, which has long been a US-controlled trading and geopolitical chokepoint. Chinese billionaire Wang Jing established the Hong Kong company that was involved right before the Nicaragua deal. Many believed that the company had the backing of the Chinese government and served Beijing's geopolitical ambition to expand its influence in South America. Though this project eventually faltered in 2015 due to insurmountable political resistance in Nicaragua and the Hong Kong Chinese company's financial difficulties, it still put Washington on alert.[37]

China also used Hong Kong to bypass the international sanction and export-control regime. Since the Cold War, the US and its allies have placed strict controls on the export of civilian–military dual-use technologies to a range of countries, including China. Items controlled under this regime are wide-ranging, including equipment for thermal sensors, video game consoles, high-speed computers, artificial intelligence-related hardware, and many more. Such an export-control regime further tightened for China after the 1989 Tiananmen massacre. Any entities in China would need a special license from the US government to import such items. If such a license was granted, the exported items would be subject to tight scrutiny concerning their destination and final use.

Nonetheless, the US–Hong Kong Policy Act of 1992 stipulated that Hong Kong would stay out of the export control after the 1997 handover. It stated that the "United States should continue to support access by Hong Kong to sensitive technologies controlled under the agreement of the Coordinating Committee for Multilateral Export Controls (commonly referred to as 'COCOM') for so long as the United States is satisfied that such technologies are protected from improper use or export."[38] By enabling Hong Kong to import such technologies freely as a separate customs territory, the Hong Kong Policy Act offered China a convenient backdoor to get access to these technologies.

Chinese technology companies benefited from this backdoor through setting up subsidiary offices and laboratories in Hong Kong, where they could develop their products with equipment that they could not have been able to obtain in mainland China. It has also been reported that Chinese entities often bypassed US sanctions by smuggling sensitive technologies into mainland China through Hong Kong. One recent example is the smuggling of military-grade US drones to China.[39] It is difficult to estimate the scale of such smuggling activities that have not been uncovered. Chinese companies also used this Hong Kong backdoor to help China's geopolitical allies and US foes to break international sanctions. For example, China set up Hong Kong companies to import controlled items and transship them to North Korea and Iran.[40] When the US export control authorities identified those companies in Hong Kong and put them on a blacklist for failing to verify the final destinations of the exported items, those companies would close down and reopen with a different name.[41]

After Xi Jinping launched the Belt and Road initiative to boost Chinese investment and trade links to other developing countries, Washington perceived such a project as a deliberate attempt to displace US influence in Eurasia. Washington also worried that China would use this project to benefit countries under US sanctions, like Syria and Iran. Two prominent cases of US persecution of Chinese nationals revealed the centrality of Hong Kong in China's expansion into Belt and Road countries. The first case is the US arrest of Patrick Ho Chi-ping in 2017. Ho was the Secretary for Home Affairs in the HKSAR government during the Tung Chee-hwa administration. He was also a member of the National Committee of the Chinese People's Political Consultative Conference. He grew up in Hong Kong, studied in the US, and practiced as an ophthalmologist in Hong Kong for nearly two decades before joining the Tung Chee-hwa government. After he finished his term, he headed the CEFC think tank, established by the Shanghai energy company CEFC China Energy. CEFC China Energy, as a private Chinese company, acquired oil fields and energy companies in Belt and Road countries and transferred their acquisitions to Chinese state-owned companies. CEFC, the think tank, was registered as a Hong Kong entity. It also maintained an office in the Washington, DC area. CEFC organized forums and conferences on topics ranging from US–China relations to sustainable agriculture. It held an Economic and Social Council (ECOSOC) special consultative status in the UN.[42]

Ho used the CEFC's Hong Kong identity and its ECOSOC special consultative status to access UN resources and people. He offered monetary gifts to African politicians via a bank in Hong Kong to facilitate CEFC China Energy's bids for African oil fields. As many of the deals between Ho and the African politicians were conducted on US soil, the US authorities arrested Ho. They convicted him on corruption charges in 2017. The court found Ho guilty and sentenced him to a fine of $400,000 and three years in prison in New York City.[43] This case exposed how China has been using the international financial network of Hong Kong and the convenience of a Hong Kong identity to conduct shady international deals to expand its global influence.

Another prominent case is the arrest of Sabrina Meng Wanzhou, the CFO and daughter of the founder of Huawei. As Huawei is a tech giant in China with intricate ties with the Chinese military, the US government views it with great suspicion. The US sees it as a core actor in China's project to dislodge US dominance in an international telecommunication network. Following a request from the US, the Canadian authorities arrested Meng in 2018 in Vancouver and started legal proceedings for her extradition to the US. She was indicted for conspiring to help Iran break international sanctions via Huawei's two satellite companies in Hong Kong, Skycom and Canicula Holdings Ltd. According to the indictment, the two Hong Kong companies imported computer equipment from the US's export control list and transshipped it to Iran in violation of international sanctions.[44]

Among similar cases, these two alerted the US and other Western countries that Beijing had been exploiting Western recognition of Hong Kong's special status to acquire sensitive technology, assist the US's foes, and expand its influence overseas.[45] On this reckoning, the US and its allies have started rethinking their Hong Kong policy. This rethinking appeared to start as early as 2013, when Edward Snowden, the former US National Security Agency employee and whistleblower who exposed the US global surveillance program, escaped from Hawaii to Moscow via Hong Kong. When Snowden was hiding in Hong Kong, the US government requested the Hong Kong government to extradite him to the US, as the US maintained an extradition treaty with Hong Kong independent of China. The HKSAR government refused

US requests and let Snowden slip away. The US government protested, but assumed that HKSAR's negligence of the US request was due to an order from Beijing.[46]

After 2015, Western governments started extending some of their sanctions over China to Hong Kong. In 2018, the White House imposed a new aluminum tariff on China. It explicitly stated that Hong Kong was not exempted from the tariff. As Hong Kong has zero aluminum production, the inclusion of Hong Kong in the tariff was an attempt to plug the Hong Kong transshipment loophole through which China could get around the tariffs. As another example, the Netherlands banned the export of surveillance equipment to China in 2018 to deter China from developing a massive, Orwellian "Skynet" system for monitoring citizens. The sanction included Hong Kong on the ban list to ensure that Chinese companies could not use Hong Kong to bypass the ban.[47]

At the same time, Hong Kong's investment in Western countries started to attract more scrutiny. In 2017, US security agencies decided that the Hong Kong owner of the Long Beach container terminal in California violated national security regulations and had to sell the terminal. The terminal owner was Orient Overseas, a Hong Kong company founded and run by the Tung Chee-hwa family and acquired by China's state-owned shipping giant COSCO. Though Orient Overseas remained a Hong Kong-registered company, US national security officials viewed its ownership of a US container terminal as an unacceptable national security risk. After lengthy negotiations with US regulators, Orient Overseas sold the terminal to Macquarie Infrastructure Partners, a US asset management company, in 2019.[48]

The heightened scrutiny of Hong Kong's investments extends beyond the US. In 2018, the Australian government blocked the bid for the APA Group, the country's biggest gas pipeline company, by CK Infrastructure Holdings, which is a Hong Kong company controlled by the Li Ka-shing family. The Australian government's Foreign Investment Review Board and the Critical Infrastructure Centre decided that the sale of a key infrastructure company to a Hong Kong company was against its national interest, as it was no longer feasible to distinguish a Hong Kong company from a mainland Chinese one.[49]

After the US and its allies began to rethink their policy on Hong Kong, they no longer turned a blind eye to Beijing's accelerating encroachment on Hong Kong. They became more vocal in expressing their concern about Hong Kong's deteriorating autonomy. In the previous chapter, we saw the mainlandization of the Hong Kong economy, particularly in its financial market, at foreign companies' expense. This trend is well illustrated in Figure 4.3. For a long time, US and Japanese corporations were the largest foreign capital operating and maintaining Hong Kong offices. But in recent years, mainland Chinese companies have overtaken both the US and Japan as the biggest presence of outside business in Hong Kong.

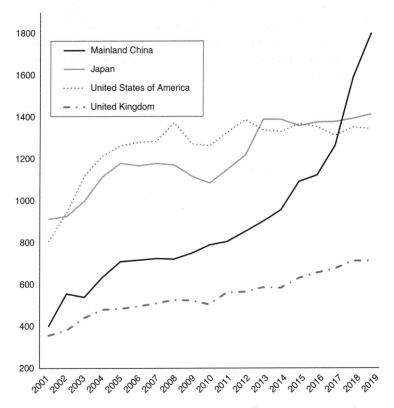

Figure 4.3 Number of nonlocal companies with offices in Hong Kong, by origin
Source: Hong Kong Census and Statistics Department

The displacement of foreign business interests in Hong Kong's financial market and beyond makes the US and other countries worry less about the collateral damage to their business interests if they choose to become more assertive against China over Hong Kong.

As a result of these new geopolitical and economic calculations, the White House and Congress did not hesitate to support the resistance movement in Hong Kong in 2019. The US–China relationship has been deteriorating ever since President Barack Obama's second term. Hong Kong inevitably became a focal point of escalating US–China rivalry, given that Hong Kong's unique utility to China hinges largely on the US certification of Hong Kong's autonomy. Beijing's imposition of the National Security Law on Hong Kong in 2020 provoked the US declaration to stop recognizing Hong Kong as a separate entity from China. Hong Kong was drawn into the eye of the storm of the US–China rivalry. We will turn back to this development and its repercussions in the concluding chapter.

Part II
Empire

5 "ONE COUNTRY, TWO SYSTEMS" BEFORE HONG KONG

Beijing views Hong Kong's return to China after 150 years of colonial rule as a manifestation of China's national rejuvenation from the "century of humiliation" starting from the imperialist dismemberment of the Qing empire in the nineteenth century. Its plan to absorb Hong Kong into the People's Republic under the "One Country, Two Systems" arrangements is not as novel as it appears. It is a repetition of Beijing's strategy to absorb Tibet in the 1950s. In the late 1970s and early 1980s, when Deng Xiaoping first floated the idea of using "One Country, Two Systems" to tackle the Hong Kong question, Deng himself, as well as several Chinese leaders, repeatedly compared their vision of post-1997 Hong Kong to 1950s Tibet, when the Dalai Lama government continued to run Tibet under Beijing sovereignty. In 1981, as Deng explained to the visiting UK foreign minister,

> [To understand the idea of "one country, two systems" that I proposed for Hong Kong,] we can study the experience of our solution to the Tibet question. In solving the Tibet question, we reached an agreement with the Dalai Lama that we would not reform Tibet for a prolonged period.[1]

Deng's frequent reference to Tibet in the 1950s as a blueprint for Hong Kong is not so surprising. Deng was the head of the CCP Southwestern Bureau in 1949–52, in charge of the negotiations with the Dalai Lama government regarding Tibet joining the PRC. In the early 1980s, Deng's government also reopened communication with the Dalai Lama government in exile, seeking his return to Tibet.[2] As such, we cannot fully understand Beijing's conception of, and strategy to tackle, the Hong Kong question without first revisiting the tumultuous history of China's failed experiment with "One Country, Two Systems" in 1950s Tibet.

Remarkably, the language used in the 1984 Sino-British Joint Declaration on Hong Kong and the Basic Law showed many parallels with the Seventeen-Point Agreement that Beijing and the Dalai Lama government signed in 1951 to allow Tibet self-governance. Legal scholar Paul Harris compares the documents and notes,

> In 1951 China and representatives of the Dalai Lama signed the "17 point agreement for the Peaceful Liberation of Tibet". The drafting phraseology of this document shows that some one was looking at it when drafting Hong Kong's Basic Law. It provides that "the Tibetan people have the right of exercising national regional autonomy under the unified leadership of the Central People's Government" (Article 3); that "the Central People's Government will not alter the existing political system in Tibet" (Article 4), and "will not alter the established status, functions and powers of the Dalai Lama" (Article 4).[3]

The "One Country, Two Systems" arrangement failed in Tibet in 1959 with the Lhasa uprising, the PLA crackdown, the flight of Dalai Lama to India, and the complete takeover of Tibet by the central government. Despite this failure, Beijing's official account to this day does not shy away from claiming that the local autonomy of 1950s Tibet was the first experiment with "One Country, Two Systems" in the PRC, and that Beijing's solution to the Hong Kong question is based on this experiment.[4] Li Hou, the secretary-general of the Basic Law Drafting Committee, later acknowledged that the CCP policy document on Tibet in the late 1940s was used as a template for a key CCP document on Hong Kong policy in 1982.[5] Some dissident authors have warned that Tibet's rough transition to "One Country, One System" in 1959 is what Beijing has intended for Hong Kong from the beginning.[6] Some contend that the "Tibetization" of Hong Kong has already begun. They see Beijing applying the same strategy to Hong Kong that it employed to establish control over the Tibetan population after 1959 through diluting the local population with mainland settlers.[7]

Beijing's contentious experiment of absorbing Tibet and Hong Kong into the People's Republic of China represented the larger challenge of constructing a nation-state in a culturally heterogeneous territory that the CCP inherited from the Qing multiethnic empire. The ethnic and cultural complexity of the empire and the homogenizing urge of creating a culturally uniform modern nation-state makes for constant tension that underlies the conflict between Beijing and its newly incorporated peripheries, including Hong Kong after 1997.[8]

As many PRC textbooks and official articles attest, Beijing policies toward minority regions, particularly those with pre-existing states before being incorporated into the PRC, like Tibet and Xinjiang, have been very much influenced by the legacies of how ethnic minority areas were managed in the Ming and Qing empires. The experiences of the CCP passing through ethnic minority areas in its revolutionary years matter, too. These texts often include discussion of the Hong Kong and Taiwan questions, showing that Beijing does view these two under the same framework of ethnic frontier management.[9]

The Frontier Questions from the Qing Empire to the Chinese Nation

The Qing empire of 1644–1911 was a multiethnic empire ruled by the ethnic minority Manchus. Its territory's transformation into the People's Republic of China over the twentieth century is a trajectory that deviates from most other cases of modern nation-state formation. Many other multiethnic world-empires, such as the Ottoman Empire, disintegrated into multiple relatively homogeneous nation-states in their incorporation into the Westphalia international system of sovereign states. In contrast, Chinese nation builders incorporated or claimed nearly all of the Qing territory, including territories lost to Western powers like Hong Kong, as a singular nation-state despite the cultural and ethnic heterogeneity in this vast geographical space.[10]

The transition from the Qing empire to the Chinese nation is far from complete or resolved.[11] The allegiance of the original Qing empire's geographical periphery to the newly imagined Chinese nation is often problematic. Nation builders from the 1911 Revolution to the founding of the People's Republic of China in 1949 experimented with different strategies to define and institute Chinese nationhood that could warrant such allegiance on the nation's frontiers and in the claimed but not yet incorporated territories. Many of these strategies and institutions contain conceptions and practices originating from the Qing empire's governance of its frontiers and the Soviet policy on nationalities.[12] They continue to shape power, identities, and resistance in these regions today.[13] Though the Communist party-state always claims it is building a modern nation-state, the incorporation and governing of the vast and diverse geographical space inherited from the Qing empire necessitate that it adopt ruling strategies overlapping with those of Qing times. This makes the PRC an empire pretending to be a nation-state.[14]

In Qing times, the unity of the empire, the size of which doubled over the eighteenth century by incorporating Taiwan and large areas in Central Asia, was grounded on its universalistic convictions of Confucianist moral values. The rulers' multiculturalist disposition toward local customs and sociopolitical orders in the non-Han regions, exchanging respect for local particularities and local self-governance for the local ruling elite's allegiance to the imperial center, helped facilitate that unity. But at the same time, the tolerance of local cultures was not meant to be perpetual. The local native elite was supposed to eventually accept universal Confucianism. They would be outnumbered by Han migrants who were deliberately encouraged to move in to dilute the local population. Over time, indirect rule through native chieftains (*tusi*) would be replaced by the area's formal incorporation into the centralized imperial state's bureaucratic and educational structure. This process is known as "transforming chieftainships into direct administration" (*gaitu guiliu*).[15] To be sure, the transformation from indirect to direct control and assimilation across the empire's frontier was far from even. It progressed more thoroughly in certain areas, such as the ethnic frontier in Yunnan and Guizhou, but was never completed in many Tibetan regions in the southwest before the empire's fall.[16]

After the Qing collapse in 1911, the nationalist elite established the Republic of China, which grounded its territorial claims on the Qing empire's geographical coverage at its largest extent in the late eighteenth century. The KMT that controlled the Republic of China government after 1927 never managed to establish direct control of many of the peripheral regions, including Xinjiang, Tibet, Taiwan, and Hong Kong, which were under the domination or rule of the British, the Japanese, or the Soviets throughout most of the Republican period of 1911–1949. In this period, the Soviet-backed CCP, as a contender for national power with the KMT, proposed to build a new China, based on a system of the federation of republics resembling the Soviet Union.

The CCP, following Lenin's and the Third International's policy of granting right to self-determination to minority nationalities, recognized the People's Republic of Mongolia, which broke away from Republican China with Soviet support and declared its founding in 1924. The KMT government, however, never recognized its independence and continued to claim its territory as part of the Republic of China.[17] The 1931 constitution of the Chinese Soviet Republic that the CCP established in its revolutionary base in the Jiangxi province postulated that "[t]he Soviet Government of China recognizes the right of self-determination of the national minorities in China, their right to complete separation from China, and the formation of an independent state of each national minority."[18]

The CCP's support of minorities' right to national self-determination during its revolutionary years was more than empty words. In 1936, when the Red Army was in the middle of its Long March, breaking away from KMT encirclement to establish a new Red base in the northwestern frontier closer to the Soviet Union, it fostered a united front with the Tibetans in Sichuan. The CCP used the Red Army to assist them in establishing a Bopa People's Republic (*bopa* means "Tibetan" in the local Tibetan language). The Declaration of the First National People's Congress of the Bopa People's Republic announced that "the only way to perpetually free us from these sufferings is to count on the power of all Tibetan people to become independent ... Our banner is 'Tibetan independence,' our immediate goal is to 'revive Tibet and exterminate Chiang [Kai-shek]'!"[19] This Bopa People's Republic was supposed to be a Soviet Republic and was going to be a constitutive part of a future Chinese Federation of Soviets. However, this fell apart after the CCP entered a new United Front with the KMT when the war with Japan fully broke out in 1937.

While the CCP was seeking support from minorities on China's inland frontiers by promising them self-determination and nationhood, it also actively sought overseas support on China's maritime frontiers, including the Taiwanese under Japanese colonial rule and ethnic Chinese in Hong Kong. Ethnic Chinese in Taiwan and Hong Kong played a significant role in supporting the Republican Revolution of 1911 and were deeply involved in the KMT–CCP struggle from the 1920s. The national identities among these transnational groups were contested, constantly in flux amidst the competing nation-building projects of the CCP and the KMT.[20] The CCP even once recognized Taiwan's right to self-determination, as Mao told US journalist Edgar Snow in 1936: "if the Koreans wish to break away from the chains of Japanese imperialism we will extend them our enthusiastic help in their struggle for independence. The same thing applies for Taiwan [Formosa]."[21] The CCP's attempt to include these overseas Chinese communities into the imagined Chinese nation by promising them autonomy and freedom continued well after establishing the PRC, which has been implicated in Beijing's policy over Hong Kong and Taiwan, as we shall see later.

By the time the CCP won national power over the KMT, it had given up the idea of federalism and turned to espousing a centralized system under which frontier regions inhabited by ethnic minorities, as recognized in the CCP's laborious ethnic classification process in the 1950s, were designated "national autonomous regions." Such regions enjoyed nominal autonomy but were governed directly by Beijing through the CCP's chain of command and mostly Han cadres.[22] The abandonment of the federal system and the embrace of a unitary system happened quite drastically in late 1949. The Common Program, written under the auspices of the CCP as an initial draft of the future Constitution of the PRC, carried an explicit designation of "rights to self-determination" among nationalities and a "free federal system" in its multiple drafts up to the August 1949 version. The relevant clauses disappeared only in the final version dated September 1949. In a telegram dated October 5, 1949, the CCP Central Committee directed all PLA field officers that "the slogan advocating the right to self-determination among nationalities should no longer be emphasized ... [as] the reactionary KMT rule has been toppled and the situation has fundamentally changed."[23] It became clear that Beijing was not interested in granting serious autonomy on its ethnic frontiers.

Among the several frontier regions with pre-existing states, Xinjiang was where the CCP managed to swiftly install the centralized unitary system. In 1944–1949, part of Xinjiang was governed by the Soviet-sponsored East Turkestan Republic, which modeled itself as a Soviet protégé like the People's Republic of Mongolia. The republic, nonetheless, dissolved after its leadership perished in a mysterious plane crash on their way to Beijing in late August 1949.[24] Ever since Beijing established direct rule in Xinjiang, it resorted to Han settler colonization and heavy-handed military repression to maintain control over the region. In the run-up to the Sino-Soviet split, the Soviet Union was suspected of fanning anti-Beijing sentiments and "local nationalism" among the Uyghurs via the influence of neighboring Kazakhstan.[25]

In contrast, Beijing could not extend swift centralized rule to Tibet, Taiwan, or Hong Kong. Entrenched state institutions and power blocs – the Dalai Lama's government in Tibet until 1959 and in exile from 1959 to present day, the KMT Republic of China government that fled to Taiwan in 1949, and the British colonial government and its Chinese elite allies in Hong Kong – competed with the sovereignty claims of CCP nation builders. Striving to establish effective governance in those regions, Beijing experimented on or offered "One Country, Two Systems" arrangements as the condition for their integration into the People's Republic of China. "One Country, Two Systems" was experimented with in Tibet from 1951 to 1959. Beijing offered it to Taiwan for the first time in the early 1960s, but the KMT government, under US military protection, has never been interested. Then Beijing promoted the "One Country, Two Systems" arrangement to London and the Hong Kong people as a condition for its absorption of Hong Kong into the PRC after 1997.

Chinese leaders emphasized in the 1980s that "One Country, Two Systems" in Tibet would have been successful had the Dalai Lama and Tibet's upper elite not become "treacherous" and revolted. But examining closely how Beijing's relationship with Tibet evolved in the 1950s, we find that the relationship was strained by some general tensions between local autonomy and central control similar to the Hong Kong–Beijing relationship after 1997. At least part of the CCP elite saw the "One Country, Two Systems" arrangement as little more than a tactical move to buy time when they were readying for full elimination of the pre-existing elite and government institutions in the frontier regions. Revisiting the rise and collapse of "One Country, Two Systems" in Tibet in 1951–1959 can help us understand the crisis of governance in post-handover Hong Kong and foresee what is to come for Hong Kong.

From Autonomy to Bloodbath in 1950s Tibet

Before the Qing empire, the social and political order of Tibet had been stable since its consolidation in the seventeenth century. Under this order, Buddhist monks and the aristocracy constituted the ruling class. The Tibetan theocratic state represented them under the supreme authority of the Dalai Lama, who was selected through the identification of his reincarnation, many times from among the commoners. At the bottom of society were the peasants, hereditarily bound to lords and estates.[26] In the Qing empire, the Dalai Lama government was patronized by the Manchu court, which kept the political and religious institutions in Tibet intact and actively intervened in selecting each reincarnated Dalai Lama and served as the source of legitimacy of the theocratic state.[27]

This order loosened in the nineteenth century, when British influence began to reach the Tibetan plateau via India as Qing power receded. The British strived to keep China's influence out of Tibet. The KMT government never exercised effective control there. As such, Tibet became a de facto independent nation. In the 1920s, some Westernized Tibetan elites began to advocate turning Tibet into a modern nation-state by constructing a rational bureaucracy, a professional army, and a universal education system. But they were repressed by the conservative ruling elite that adamantly resisted secularization of the Tibetan state and feared that such modernization efforts would increase their tax burden.[28]

Aspiration for modernization survived despite the theocratic reaction. In the 1930s, a group of Tibetan intellectuals educated in mainland China formed the Tibetan Communist Party (TCP). The party's platform was to establish a socialist and independent Tibet, apparently modeled after the People's Republic of Mongolia, an independent socialist state with Soviet support. The TCP was no more than a small group of underground activists who attempted to realize their platform by influencing potential sympathizers among Tibet's ruling elite. Some of their members were connected to the elite via familial or alumni networks.[29]

In the late 1940s, the CCP, while emerging triumphant in the civil war, started working to incorporate Tibet into the prospective socialist state. The CCP's Tibet strategy, advised as well as executed by Deng Xiaoping, who was head of the CCP's Southwestern Bureau at the time, was to promise the Tibetan ruling elite that reform would be gradual and that the existing Tibetan way of life would be preserved. The Dalai Lama government would continue to run Tibet's internal affairs. Socioeconomic reform of Tibet would not happen unless the Dalai Lama saw fit.[30]

This CCP proposal was supported by the TCP, which saw Tibet's integration into a socialist China as a golden opportunity for Tibet's modernization. Consequently, the TCP dropped the cause for Tibet's independence and merged with the CCP. The Tibetan Communists then reached out to the ruling elite in Lhasa to promote the CCP's proposal of the "One Country, Two Systems" configuration, without naming it that. By late 1950, the People's Liberation Army (PLA) already controlled Tibet's eastern city of Chamdo, and the British had left South Asia. Under these circumstances, the theocratic state saw no other choice than to accept Beijing's offer. This resulted in the signing of the "Seventeen-Point Agreement" between Beijing and Lhasa in 1951.[31]

The Seventeen Point Agreement promised to sustain Tibet's existing political and religious institutions. The eventual reform of Tibet's sociopolitical system was predicated on the agreement and initiative of the Dalai Lama government. The CCP also tried to find a place for Buddhism in the newfound Communist nation. As Mao postulated during his dialogue with the Dalai Lama in 1953 and 1955,

> Tibet's religion . . . is and will be respected and protected. As long as the people still believe in religion, it will be inadvisable and impossible to eradicate or damage religion deliberately . . . Siddhartha, the founder of Buddhism, spoke for the oppressed people of his time . . . Therefore, you Buddhists and we Communists can co-operate. We

share the goal of extricating the mass from suffering, though we still have many differences.[32]

Mao's kind words remind us of Deng Xiaoping's kind words about the "Hong Kong way of life" and its capitalist system's contribution to the Chinese motherland when he tried to win the support of the Hong Kong business elite.

Despite the Seventeen-Point Agreement and Mao's kind words, the Dalai Lama government's and Beijing's disposition toward each other was far from settled. Within the CCP, there was pressure to disregard the agreement and initiate class struggle and land reform to establish the CCP's absolute control of the region. In the early 1950s, this radical voice was balanced by the moderate, pragmatic strategy of relying on the "united front" with Tibet's ruling elite to ensure Tibet's stability. This pragmatic approach, upheld by the cadres from the CCP's Southwestern Bureau, prevailed in large part because of CCP's great logistic difficulty in supplying its cadres and the army in the remote and thin-aired Tibetan Plateau.[33]

CCP radicals' opposition to the pragmatic line was adamant. The radical–moderate split became particularly acute in 1956, when rapid rural collectivization started in China. Influenced by the heated political atmosphere of the times, Chinese cadres in Tibet could not wait to initiate land reform, or "democratic reform" according to official terminology, in Tibet. In July 1956, the CCP Working Committee in Tibet started to talk about the upcoming land revolution.[34] The radicals also made Beijing agree to establish a Tibet Autonomous Region Preparatory Committee (TARPC) in 1956, headed by Zhang Jingwu, which became one of the key forces advocating for implementing immediate socioeconomic reform in Tibet. But Mao and the Central Committee of the CCP also cautioned that "democratic reform" in Tibet will not be implemented any time soon.[35]

Top leaders, including Premier Zhou Enlai, reassured the Dalai Lama that land reform would not start for at least another six years and would never start without the Dalai Lama's consent. Zhou even promised that the reform could be postponed for another fifty years if the Dalai Lama saw fit.[36] However, the TARPC rapidly became a second power center in Lhasa and, although the Dalai Lama himself was also on the TARPC, it seized power from the

Dalai Lama government. This resembles the rise of the Liaison Office in Hong Kong, the de facto local CCP headquarters, as the second power center beside the HKSAR government, which we will turn to in the next chapter.

On the side of the Dalai Lama government, the ruling elite was equally divided. Alongside secular modernizers like the Tibetan cadres of the CCP, who used to be members of the TCP, a segment of the theocratic establishment, including the Dalai Lama himself, opined that reform of Tibet's sociopolitical order was inevitable and beneficial to Tibet. They deliberated that if social reform was inevitable anyway, it was better that it be carried out sooner by themselves than later and imposed by Beijing.[37] The Dalai Lama even considered applying to become a member of the CCP.[38]

In the meantime, the anti-Beijing force grew among the population and the elite in Tibet. After Tibet's incorporation into the PRC, a People's Association emerged as a quasi-political mass party. The leaders of the association were constituted by Tibet's middle class, composed mainly of private administrators and managers of aristocratic and monastery estates, and they were not without sympathizers within the Dalai Lama government. They were not only against the CCP, but also against the Dalai Lama leadership, which was accused of selling out Tibetans' interest to Beijing. They launched signature campaigns and public meetings to demand the departure of the PLA from Tibet.[39]

Up to the mid-1950s, the Dalai Lama and most of the Tibetan ruling elite strived to maintain a cozy relationship with Beijing. But the tensions between the two sides escalated rapidly when anti-Chinese guerrilla warfare broke out in ethnic Tibetan regions in Sichuan, Gansu, and Qinghai provinces of China. Beneath this tension lay Lhasa's and Beijing's diverging conceptions of what "Tibet" meant in the Seventeen-Point Agreement. To Beijing, Tibet was no more than the region effectively controlled by the Dalai Lama government as of 1950 – henceforth, Tibet proper – and ethnic Tibetan regions in Chinese provinces were not spared from agrarian collectivization. But to Lhasa, Tibet was tantamount to the cultural, ethnic, and historical Tibet, including those Tibetan regions in Chinese provinces. Having their land confiscated, manorial lords and monks from the monasteries in the Tibetan areas in the PRC's southwestern provinces took up arms against the Chinese authorities. This conflict empowered the anti-Beijing activists and elite in Lhasa, who saw what happened in these regions as a prelude to what would happen in Tibet proper.[40] The relationship between Lhasa and Beijing deteriorated dramatically as the armed rebellion grew. Overwhelmed by the PLA, the rebels flooded into Tibet proper to recoup. They strengthened the anti-Chinese movement led by the People's Association. Lhasa's offering of shelter to the rebels made Beijing believe that the Dalai Lama government, or at least part of it, was behind the insurgency.

Despite Mao's reassurance in 1957 that socialist transformation in Tibet proper was out of the question in the foreseeable future, the voice for a once-and-for-all showdown with the Dalai Lama government grew within the CCP. The theory that "the essence of the nationalities question is the question of class" gained ground in Beijing after 1958.[41] This theory yearned for complete cultural assimilation and the establishment of direct rule in Tibet. It saw any quest for local autonomy and cultural diversity as nothing but a disguised attempt of the feudal ruling class to maintain or revive their exploitation of the people. Worse still, Beijing increasingly distrusted the Tibetan cadres of the CCP. The Party arrested or rotated many of them out of Tibet during the Anti-Rightist campaign in 1957. The demise of this group of mediators, who used to command Beijing's and the Dalai Lama's trust, broke the most important link of communication between Beijing and Lhasa.[42]

Tension rose further when military conflicts between the PLA and the Tibetan insurgents spread to the vicinity of Lhasa. The showdown between Beijing and Lhasa finally came in March 1959, when a rumored kidnapping of the Dalai Lama by the PLA instigated a full-scale anti-Chinese uprising in Lhasa. The PLA repressed the unrest relentlessly, and the current and fourteenth Dalai Lama, together with key officials in his government, fled to India amid the chaos. Within a few months, the CCP had quelled any remaining resistance in Tibet.[43]

Following the crushed uprising and the flight of the Dalai Lama, Beijing established direct and full control of Tibet via a batch of Han Chinese cadres, who were sent there to replace the Tibetan CCP cadres purged under the charge of "local nationalism." After 1959, Tibet was assimilated into the homogeneous Chinese nation under the monolithic principle of class struggle through land reform, the destruction of religious institutions, and the suppression of religious practices. Beijing also started the policy of encouraging large-scale migration of Han Chinese settlers to Tibet to dilute the local Tibetan population and marginalize the latter in jobs and other opportunities. These policies maintained the appearance of tranquility in the 1960s and the 1970s, but discontent bubbled under the surface. It sowed the seeds for the successive waves of unrest that erupted in the 1980s and continue to this day.[44]

In the next chapter, we will see that the efforts of Beijing to lure the Hong Kong Chinese elite to shift their allegiance to Beijing and to accept Chinese sovereignty in the 1980s and 1990s, as well as Hong Kong's constrained autonomy under a Beijing–Hong Kong Chinese business alliance in the first ten years after the handover, the radicalization and growing anti-Beijing sentiments of the population, and the increasing mutual distrust between Hong Kong's business elite and Beijing, are in many ways a replication of the path from constrained autonomy to assimilationist direct rule in Tibet in the 1950s.

The Taiwan and Hong Kong Questions in the Mao Era

The failure of "One Country, Two Systems" in the bloodbath of Tibet in 1959 did not deter Beijing from using this offer to lure the KMT government in Taiwan to join the PRC. In the 1950s, before the failure in Tibet, Beijing had already worked through middlemen in Hong Kong to convey to the KMT its proposal for resolving the Taiwan question with the unnamed "One Country, Two Systems" model. For example, when a pro-CCP writer in Hong Kong, Cao Juren, who was also a former classmate of Chiang Kai-shek's son, Chiang Ching-kuo, met with Mao in Beijing in 1958, Mao outlined Beijing's proposal for China–Taiwan unification:

> [after Taiwan's reunification with the mainland,] he [Chiang Kai-shek] can keep his army, I will not pressure him to downsize his army and his government. I will let him practice the Three Principles of the People. He can continue to fight communism there [in Taiwan], so far as he does not send fighter planes and spies to subvert the mainland. If he

does not send white spies to the mainland, I will not send red spies to Taiwan ... and the Taiwanese people can maintain their original way of life.[45]

Beijing reiterated this proposal in the 1960s despite the debacle in Tibet in 1959. In 1960, Mao summarized the CCP offer to Taiwan as "One Premise and Four Principles" (*yigang simu*). The premise was that Taiwan would agree to unify with the PRC. The four principles outlined that, after unification, (1) the Chiang Kai-shek government would continue to govern the internal affairs of Taiwan while foreign-policy decision making would be transferred to Beijing, (2) Beijing would financially support Taiwan's defense and economic development, (3) socioeconomic reform would not proceed immediately and would only happen with the consent of Chiang Kai-shek, and (4) the KMT and the CCP would not send spies or sabotage the other's work. Zhou Enlai reiterated this proposal to Chiang via a middleman again in 1963.[46]

Beijing's proposal to Taiwan was nearly identical to the Seventeen-Point Agreement on Tibet. The KMT government never openly entertained this idea. During the turbulent years of the Cultural Revolution in China, Beijing ceased to pursue this proposal. In 1978, after Deng Xiaoping assumed the leadership of the CCP, he made the offer of "One Country, Two Systems" to Taiwan again. The CCP issued "A Letter to Taiwan Compatriots" on January 1, 1979, reiterating that people in Taiwan could maintain their existing way of life after unification with the mainland.

At the same time, London, in light of the upcoming expiration of the lease on the New Territories in 1997, started to take the initiative to explore Beijing's position on Hong Kong.[47] In the spring of 1979, the then governor of Hong Kong, Lord MacLehose, visited Beijing to meet with Deng Xiaoping. He asked about Beijing's intentions for Hong Kong after 1997. Deng expressed that China would take over all Hong Kong but would respect Hong Kong's special status.[48] With the British being anxious to resolve the issue of the future status of Hong Kong after 1997 and Taiwan's disinterest in the "One Country, Two Systems" proposal, Beijing shifted its priority to solving the Hong Kong question and started to express its inclination to apply the "One Country, Two Systems" model to Hong Kong after 1997. It is not an accident that Deng Xiaoping, who was key to formulating and implementing the "One Country, Two Systems" model in Tibet in the late 1940s and the 1950s, was eager to give the experiment a second try in Hong Kong. By casting the "One Country, Two Systems" experiment in 1950s Tibet in a positive light and blaming the Dalai Lama for its failure, Deng led the Chinese government in negotiating with the UK government over Hong Kong's future after 1997.

Even after London had resumed its governance of Hong Kong at the end of World War II, the KMT did not give up the Republic of China's claim of sovereignty over Hong Kong. Nevertheless, the KMT never managed to press this claim on the British when it was overwhelmed by a renewed civil war with the CCP. When CCP's People's Liberation Army swept through China and established the People's Republic of China in 1949, it became possible that the CCP might invade Hong Kong. London even made an evacuation plan in case of such a PLA invasion. But London soon learned that Beijing had no intention of taking Hong Kong from the British.[49]

Over the late 1940s and early 1950s, the UK coped with the demand for decolonization worldwide by making some of its colonies self-governing dominions. The UK introduced elections in those territories and cultivated friendly relationships with local politicians as a path toward eventual independence with favorable terms for the British. Examples closest to Hong Kong would be Malaysia and Singapore, which became self-governing territories and independent states over the 1950s. Around the same time, Hong Kong's colonial administration started to consider expanding elections in Hong Kong. In 1946, Hong Kong governor Mark Young drafted a plan to introduce a municipal council in Hong Kong with two-thirds of the seats directly elected. This was apparently in preparation for decolonization. However, opposition to the plan by the colonial elite in Hong Kong and the fear of Communist infiltration through the election made the British abandon the plan after it was made clear that Beijing had no intention of taking Hong Kong.[50] Through the 1950s, Hong Kong's Urban Council, which specialized in urban sanitary, recreational, and other practical issues, maintained a minority of directly elected seats. The proportion of elected seats kept expanding, but it did not reach half of the seats until 1973.[51]

Though the UK did not suggest its intention to turn Hong Kong into a self-governing territory in preparation for independence, like it did in the Malaya peninsula and elsewhere, Beijing did worry about it. According to declassified British documents, Chinese premier Zhou Enlai expressed his opposition in 1958 to an alleged British "plot or conspiracy to make Hong Kong a self-governing dominion like Singapore." He warned that "China would regard any move toward dominion status as a very unfriendly act. China wished the present colonial status of Hong Kong to continue with no change whatever." In 1960, Chinese officials expressed a clearer threat to London: "We [Beijing] shall not hesitate to take positive action to have Hong Kong, Kowloon and the New Territories liberated" if Britain permitted "self-government" of Hong Kong.[52]

Beijing's growing worry about London turning Hong Kong into a self-governing territory and paving the way for its eventual independence was not only related to British decolonization elsewhere. It was also concurrent with the designation of the rights to self-determination of colonized people at the United Nations under the Declaration on the Granting of Independence to Colonial Countries and Peoples (also known as the Declaration of Decolonization) passed by the United Nations General Assembly in 1960. According to this declaration, colonized peoples were entitled to the right to self-determination over whether they would become an independent state, join with another country, or stay with the colonial motherland, via referendum. The declaration maintained a list of "Non-self-Governing Territories" or colonies entitled to such a right to self-determination. British Hong Kong and Portuguese Macau were on the colonies list. Hong Kong, therefore, enjoyed the right to self-determination under international law.[53]

This was surely a thorn in Beijing's side – so much so that in 1972, after the People's Republic of China joined the UN in the place of the Republic of China in Taiwan, Beijing requested that Hong Kong and Macau be taken off of the UN colonies list. It succeeded. Hong Kong and Macau were taken off and stripped of their right to self-determination under the UN Decolonization Declaration. This is why Chinese official media never recognized Hong Kong before 1997 as a British colony, but a "Chinese territory under British colonial rule."[54]

By 1982, when the Sino-British negotiations over Hong Kong's future status started, Beijing's determination to resume China's sovereignty over all of Hong Kong at all costs had become crystal clear. The pre-emptive move of China to remove Hong Kong from the UN colonies list made it difficult for anyone to argue the case of Hong Kong's decolonization through self-determination or independence on the grounds of international law.[55] Beijing's biggest challenge was the fear of Hong Kong's business elite and the wider population about a Chinese takeover. The stock market and the value of the Hong Kong dollar plunged, showing significant capital flight. Mass exodus of business and professional elites started. It looked possible that by the time Beijing took over, Hong Kong would have become a socially and economically desolate backwater. To prevent this scenario, Beijing started to woo Hong Kong's business and professional elite, its reform-minded activists, and nascent opposition leaders. This is why Beijing began reassuring the Hong Kong public about the "One Country, Two Systems" model, despite its failure in Tibet less than three decades prior.

6 FROM AUTONOMY TO COERCIVE ASSIMILATION

Although "One Country, Two Systems" ended in a debacle in Tibet in 1959 and never gained traction in Taiwan in the 1960s, Beijing tried to reboot the arrangement in 1979 when Deng Xiaoping expressed its desire to negotiate Taiwan's unification with the mainland under the "One Country, Two Systems" formula. The KMT in Taiwan rebuffed this idea immediately. Around the same time, the Hong Kong question started to emerge, as the future status of the New Territories and Hong Kong at large after 1997 remained unclear. Beijing then started negotiating with London about solving the Hong Kong question through "One Country, Two Systems."

Forging a United Front in Support of Sovereignty Handover

The news about the Beijing–London negotiation regarding the future status of Hong Kong and the determination of Beijing to reclaim sovereignty over Hong Kong after 1997 triggered widespread anxiety in the colony. With the vivid memory of the destruction of the Cultural Revolution and of the Communist-led local unrest in 1967, Hong Kong's general public panicked when the Sino-British negotiation unfolded in 1982–1984. The panic was best illustrated by the mass exodus of the rich and professional class through emigration, plunges of the stock market, and even maniacal stocking of nonperishable food by citizens anticipating unrest or even war.[1] To allay the fears about imminent Communist rule,

Beijing indicated that it would allow Hong Kong to exercise self-governance, maintain its liberty, and continue its capitalist system for fifty years after the sovereignty handover.

According to one of the few credible public opinion polls of the time, as shown in Table 6.1, the colony's residents were willing to support any proposal about Hong Kong's future except returning to China. Among the plethora of proposed solutions to the 1997 question at the time, even the most wildly impractical ones – like "letting Beijing be the owner and London be the manager of Hong Kong as a company" and "Hong Kong independence" – obtained more support than returning to China. Maintaining the status quo of British rule was the most popular choice.[2]

Against this backdrop of widespread consternation, different organized political forces in Hong Kong strived to devise practical proposals about Hong Kong's future and to garner social support for their proposals. The entrenched leftist organizations supported Beijing's policy unconditionally, emphasizing that Hong Kong's return to China was part and parcel of a national liberation process to rid China of all humiliations originating from the age of imperialism. Equally unsurprising was that both the British and Chinese business elite, who had been co-opted into the

Table 6.1 *Views about different solutions to the Hong Kong question, 1982* *

Proposal	Support for proposal	Will stay in Hong Kong if proposal is actualized
Maintaining colonial rule	95%	95%
British administration under Chinese sovereignty	64%	72%
Hong Kong independence	37%	68%
Hong Kong becomes a special administrative region of China	42%	50%
Hong Kong returns to China	26%	58%

* Based on 1,000 respondents selected through stratified sampling; respondents can say yes to more than one proposal.
Source: Hong Kong Observer Society 1982, 70–81

colonial power structure and thrived under the government's protection of their business monopolies, supported the continuation of the status quo of colonial rule. They feared that Hong Kong's unification with Communist China would empower the working class in Hong Kong and turn Hong Kong into a socialist economy or a welfare state with heavy taxes. They worried that it would end the low-tax and low-regulation business environment of Hong Kong. This fear was best illustrated when, in 1983, a delegation of representatives from major corporations visited Beijing to express their worry candidly:

> We are of the view that if Beijing firmly intends to regain administrative control over Hong Kong in 1997, public confidence in the territory will immediately nosedive and it will lose its prosperity in a very short time indeed … It would be difficult to maintain Hong Kong's prosperity and stability for long by the self-administration formula. If, for example, people with lower incomes should, after 1997, make unreasonable demands, resulting in a complete breakdown of the present [capitalist] system, what would the Chinese government's attitude be? If the Chinese authorities insist on maintaining [that] the capitalists keep their wealth, how would the Chinese leaders be able to explain this to the one billion people at home?[3]

In contrast to both the steadfast opposition to China's claim over Hong Kong's sovereignty among the colonial elite and the unreserved support of Beijing's position among the leftists, several reform-oriented grassroots and middle-class political organizations expressed their conditional support of Hong Kong's incorporation into the PRC. The most conspicuous and long-lasting of these organizations was Meeting Point, which supported Hong Kong's return to China under local autonomy and democracy.

Meeting Point's founding members were mainly service professionals (such as teachers, social workers, journalists, professors) and veteran student activists sympathetic to Chinese socialism back in the 1970s. Its membership represented the local social and democratic movements that emerged in the 1970s that will be discussed in greater detail in Chapter 7. Meeting Point was vocal throughout the debate over Hong Kong's future in the 1980s and 1990s before it merged with other political activists to form the Hong Kong Democratic Party in 1994, which became the flagship organization of Hong Kong's democracy movement beyond 1997.

It was later revealed that the founding of Meeting Point in 1983 was part of the work of the CCP United Front of Hong Kong. Its founding leader, Lau Nai-keung, became one of the most loyal CCP voices in Hong Kong after 1997. He served as a member of the Chinese People's Political Consultative Conference, and was a keen supporter of Leung Chun-ying's candidacy in the chief executive election in 2012. The headquarters of Meeting Point before 1997 was the property of Paul Yip Kwok-wah, widely believed to be the head of the CCP underground in Hong Kong. Yip charged Meeting Point far less than market rent. Yip also helped Meeting Point members establish contacts with Chinese officials.[4]

Meeting Point supported the claim that Hong Kong's return to China was an important part of China's national liberation project. It saw the sovereignty handover as a golden opportunity for reforming Hong Kong's authoritarian political system and unjust socioeconomic order under British rule.[5] In its proposal on the future of Hong Kong, it declared that

> Hong Kong is part of China and it is unquestionable that China has sovereignty over the territory ... Nationalism is one of the basic principles in considering the problem of Hong Kong's future ... The existing political system must be reformed before China regains sovereignty. One basic principle for reform is providing opportunities for people to participate in politics. Hong Kong's citizens' participation in running local affairs should be expanded ... Social welfare services should be actively developed and existing medical services should be improved. A comprehensive social security program should be established. More reasonable labor laws should be enacted and labor unions should be encouraged to develop.[6]

Attempting to bring democratic and social reforms by supporting a return to China, Meeting Point and other like-minded activists were dubbed the "Democratic Reunionists" (*minzhu huiguipai*) in the 1980s.

In response to these diverging dispositions during and after the Sino-British negotiations, Beijing articulated flexible nationalist discourses to expand support for its claim of sovereignty over Hong Kong. On the one hand, Beijing allied with the Democratic Reunionists to attack the colonial status quo and promised political and social reforms. Beijing never gave up the language of class struggle in its discussion of the Hong Kong question. A 1982 editorial of the *People's Daily* framed the difficulty in securing Hong Kong's (and Taiwan's) return to China as a question of class enemies' obstruction:

> The exploiting class only disappears in the areas governed by the CCP, and they persisted in the Hong Kong and Taiwan regions ... The majority of the bourgeois class there are patriotic and aspired to the unification of the motherland ... But some of them still want to use economic, political, and other filthy means to ... sabotage our socialist system ... In this regard, class struggle continues to exist.[7]

To the delight of the Democratic Reunionists, Beijing also promised that the future autonomous government of Hong Kong would be elected democratically. In 1982, the two universities' left-leaning student unions sent a letter to the then premier of China, Zhao Zhiyang, to express their support for Hong Kong's returning to China. Because the letter expressed their doubts about the future of Hong Kong under Chinese rule, Zhao Ziyang, in his reply, promised that Beijing

> will insist on the principle of democratic self-governance by the Hong Kong people; the central government will not interfere in Hong Kong's internal affairs, and the Hong Kong government, as well as its highest leader, will be elected through universal suffrage.[8]

The Sino-British Joint Declaration in 1984, a document that set the international legal foundation for the sovereignty handover in 1997, included the vague guarantees that the post-1997 chief executive and the legislature of Hong Kong could eventually be generated through elections.[9] Martin Lee Chu-ming, a leader of Hong Kong's democratic movement in the 1980s through the 2000s, recalled that when he learned about this item, he "was thrilled, because it promised that the people of Hong Kong could elect their Chief Executive and legislature and, through them, hold the government accountable to the people. To me, that meant democracy."[10]

Simultaneously, Beijing also started to woo the pro-British business elite to its side by guaranteeing protection of the capitalist order and their privileges after handover. To balance the militant language of class struggle, Beijing coined the notion of "lousy patriotism" (*mamahuhude aiguo zhuyi*), meaning that the only criteria for being eligible to become leaders in the future Hong Kong government would be patriotism in its loosest sense. Anybody showing support for Hong Kong's return to China was a patriot, regardless of their political disposition in the past. Deng Xiaoping remarked that "no matter whether they believed in capitalism, feudalism, or even slavery," they could be regarded as patriotic in so far as they supported China's sovereignty over Hong Kong.[11] It is in this spirit that Beijing agreed to guarantee in the Sino-British Joint Declaration that "the current [capitalist] social and economic systems in Hong Kong will remain unchanged, and so will the life-style ... Private property, ownership of enterprises, legitimate right of inheritance and foreign investment will be protected by law" for fifty years.[12] This flexible, pragmatic conception of patriotism was part and parcel of the "liberal nationalism" that prevailed in China's official discourse in 1979–1989. Under this liberal nationalist discourse, the Chinese nation under the CCP was a community of citizens joining their efforts to pursue progress, opening, and China's revival in the international community.[13]

After completing the Sino-British negotiations in 1984, a Drafting Committee and a Consultative Committee were created to facilitate the creation of the Basic Law, the mini-constitution of the future HKSAR from 1997 to 2047. The Consultative Committee was to advise the Drafting Committee of public opinion. It included 180 representatives, all appointed by Beijing, with a wide range of social backgrounds and political orientations, including representatives from the student movements and many Democratic Reunionists. The Drafting Committee, which was the only authorized body to create the Basic Law, comprised fifty-nine members and was heavily dominated by Chinese officials and the Hong Kong business elite, with only two representatives, Martin Lee and Szeto Wah, from the democratic movement.[14]

The Democratic Reunionists, who retained their Chinese nationalist belief that Hong Kong's return to China was a culmination of China's national liberation and a chance to reform the colony into a social-democratic city-state, saw the drafting process of the Basic Law as a battleground to realize their aspirations for social and political reform. They intended to bring in clauses that would expedite the realization of universal suffrage (such as the proposal that the first post-1997 government would be democratically elected) and labor rights (such as the introduction of collective bargaining rights for labor) in the draft. At the same time, the conservative Chinese business elite, who sought to become the new allies of Beijing once they realized that the departure of the British was inevitable, sought to delay universal suffrage and to make the Basic Law a vehicle to warrant the continuation of the favorable business environment and government protection of their privileges after the handover.[15]

As such, Beijing's United Front in support of China's sovereignty over Hong Kong after 1997 has been divided between a reformist bloc, which represented the interests of the lower and the new middle classes, and a conservative bloc representing the Chinese business elite. Fearing the exodus of investment from Hong Kong and eager to lure Hong Kong investment to mainland China to aid China's market reform, Beijing increasingly sided with the business elite at the expense of the reformists. Beijing also shared the business elite's opposition to the rapid and full democratization of Hong Kong immediately after the handover. Beijing worried that it would lose control of the city and that the British would continue to exert their influence via supporting their candidates in the election. Beijing supported the conservatives' proposal to limit the direct-election component in the post-1997 government and delay universal suffrage indefinitely. Beijing also sided with the business elite to veto many social welfare enhancement proposals, though the Democratic Reunionists and the traditional CCP-affiliated labor unions supported them. In response, the Democratic Reunionists came to rely on grassroots mobilization to magnify their voices for reform.[16]

Though the Democratic Reunionists were marginalized in the CCP United Front, they never totally broke with Beijing and still maintained the faint hope that they could win over Beijing with popular support. This United Front was supposed to be the embryo of the governing coalition after the sovereignty handover. Its fragile unity held on until 1989 when the Beijing Democratic Movement and its aftermath radically altered the political landscape of Hong Kong.

Racialist Nationalism and National Security

From the beginning of the Tiananmen democratic movement in April 1989, the Democratic Reunionists were quick to mobilize Hong Kong citizens to support the protesting students. They anticipated that a victory for the students and their sympathizers in the CCP would shift the terms of debate over Hong Kong's future political and social order in their favor.[17] To their disappointment, the democratic movement ended in a bloody crackdown and the purge of the student sympathizers from within the CCP.

After the crackdown on June 4 and the fully fledged turn toward conservative Chinese politics, the CCP's United Front in Hong Kong fell apart. Before June 4, the Democratic Reunionists organized large-scale rallies supporting the students and raised an astronomical amount of donations to be directed to the Tiananmen movement. After June 4, they organized a rescue mission to smuggle persecuted dissidents out of China. They were not hesitant to call the CCP government a "butcher regime." Beijing accused them of being subversive traitors collaborating with foreign powers to topple the Chinese government. Their representatives in the Basic Law Drafting Committee, Martin Lee and Szeto Wah, resigned to take a stand against the regime. Beijing did not approve their resignation and instead ousted them from the committee.[18]

In Hong Kong, the business elite, who could not wait to endorse the Tiananmen crackdown and formed the first foreign delegation to greet Chinese leaders in the summer of 1989, rose to become the "genuine patriots" in Beijing's eyes. After Beijing ousted the democrats from the Basic Law Drafting Committee, the committee swiftly passed the most conservative proposals for all controversial issues after 1997, from political systems to social welfare reform. China's National People's Congress approved the final draft of the Basic Law in April 1990.

The Drafting Committee hastily added Article 23 to the final version of the Basic Law. Under Article 23, the future HKSAR government bore responsibility for devising legislation to outlaw any organizations, activities, and speeches that would threaten the Chinese government. The Basic Law maintained the promise of ultimate universal suffrage in the chief executive's election and in the whole body of the LegCo, though it did not mention any timetable. It also did not specify what universal suffrage meant. Article 45 of the Basic Law stipulated,

> The method for selecting the Chief Executive shall be specified in the light of the actual situation in the Hong Kong Special Administrative Region and in accordance with the principle of gradual and orderly progress. The ultimate aim is the selection of the Chief Executive by universal suffrage upon nomination by a broadly representative nominating committee in accordance with democratic procedures.[19]

Whereas Article 68 stipulates,

> The method for forming the Legislative Council shall be specified in the light of the actual situation in the Hong Kong Special Administrative Region and in accordance with the principle of gradual and orderly progress. The ultimate aim is the election of all the members of the Legislative Council by universal suffrage.[20]

The annex of the Basic Law specified that after 1997, half of the LegCo seats would continue to be elected through functional constituencies. The chief executive would be nominated and elected through an Election Committee constituted along the same principles as the FCs. It mentioned that the election method could be amended with a two-thirds majority vote in the LegCo as early as ten years after the sovereignty handover. This delayed universal suffrage without a timetable fell far short of the democrats' demand for a universal right of suffrage after the sovereignty handover. The final version of the Basic Law also dictated that the document's final interpretation rested not in the Supreme Court in Hong Kong but the National People's Congress of China. In retrospect, it was a significant backdoor that allowed Beijing to alter the Basic Law at will after 1997.[21]

With the Democratic Reunionists pushed into the enemy category, Beijing's nationalist appeal to Hong Kong hardened. The flexibility of "lousy patriotism" gave way to a hard division between genuine "patriots" and "traitors" determined by whether one was a friend or an enemy of the regime. Beijing was anxious to freeze the colonial, authoritarian system and leveled harsh criticism at the democrats by attributing their quest for genuine autonomy and democracy after 1997 to an international conspiracy to "turn Hong Kong into a base to subvert China's central government."

At the same time, the official nationalist discourse in China mutated from the liberal nationalism of the 1980s into a more primordial, racialist conception that defines the Chinese nation as a mystical Han-centric Chinese community bounded by racial blood ties. Part of this Han racialist nationalism in the 1990s and beyond was a revival of the cult of the Yellow Emperor, portrayed as a common ancestor of all Chinese in official propaganda.[22] Phrases like "blood is thicker than water" (*xuenong yushui*) became a routine characterization of the relationship between China and Hong Kong. The Chinese government organized tours for the newly patriotic business elite from Hong Kong to attend the state's annual sacrificial ceremony in the official Yellow Emperor Mausoleum. The mausoleum was conveniently located in the CCP's old revolutionary base in Yan'an, Shaanxi, and underwent a large-scale expansion and restoration in 1993.

In the 1990s, the CCP no longer attacked the antinomies of Beijing's Hong Kong policies in the language of class struggle, as it had done in the old times. Instead, Beijing officials, the media, and Beijing allies in Hong Kong began to denigrate the democrats in racialist, patrilineal diatribes using terms like "forgetting about your ancestors" (*shudian wangzu*) and "traitors to the Han race" (*hanjian*). Martin Lee, the leader of the Democratic Party, and Anson Chan Fang On-sang, who transformed from a high-ranking civil servant under British rule to the first chief secretary of the HKSAR government and then to an elected opposition legislator in 2004–2008, were the two who received the most frequent attacks.[23]

Beijing's racialist nationalist discourse over Hong Kong was best illustrated in the Monument for Commemorating the Return of Hong Kong to China, erected in the Yellow Emperor Mausoleum in 1997. The statement inscribed on the monument, dated on the day of the 1997 handover, strikingly resembles the structure of a traditional Han Chinese genealogical inscription in an ancestral shrine. This kind of inscription usually starts with praise of the founding generation, followed by tributes to the major merits of earlier generations, and ends with a blessing for future generations:

> We, descendants of the Yellow and Yan Emperor, summoned funds and erected this memorial to mark the historical moment and to console our ancestors ... Now the traveling sons are back home to search for their roots, and all descendants can now joyfully gather in the same family hall ... China is reunified into one, and all under the same bloodline will prosper as one. Forefather Deng Xiaoping coined the uniquely genius theory of One Country, Two Systems, and Hong Kong People govern Hong Kong. President Jiang Zemin further enacted this spirit ... May our ancestors bestow us with their spiritual power from heaven to bless and guard our nation.[24]

After the sovereignty handover, the Hong Kong government maintained its nominal autonomy from Beijing under the Basic Law and the Sino-British Joint Declaration. But Beijing never relaxed its grip over the selection of its chief executive and his or her ministers, or over any major decisions they made. Beijing was also anxious to delay any democratization reform that the Basic Law warranted. The chief executive and the LegCo's election methods were frozen and dominated by business and professional corporate bodies in the Beijing-friendly Election Committee for the chief executive election and the FCs for the LegCo. Directly elected democrats in the Chief Executive Election Committee and the LegCo could never gain a meaningful majority.

In the early days after the handover, Beijing's Hong Kong policy manifested two contradictory tendencies. The first was to continue to leaving Hong Kong affairs to the Hong Kong government and restrain Beijing's overt intervention, as promised in the Basic Law. The second, however, was to emphasize the imperative of Hong Kong residents' absolute loyalty to Beijing and the ultimate power of the central government over Hong Kong affairs. The tension between these two tendencies resembles the tension between the radicals and the pragmatists regarding Tibet's governance within the CCP in the 1950s.

Beijing's attempt to encroach on Hong Kong's existing freedom and autonomy started right after the handover. The Liaison Office of the Central People's Government in the Hong Kong Special Administrative Region, or simply the Liaison Office, was established in 1997 as the highest representative body of China's central government in Hong Kong. Bestowed with the official responsibility of being a liaison between the HKSAR government and the central government, it became increasingly outspoken about Hong Kong affairs. Its officials actively pursued contacts in different sectors in Hong Kong politics and society. It also became more overtly involved in co-ordinating the pro-establishment candidates' election campaigns in each election.[25] In 2002–2003, Beijing suggested that the Hong Kong government should not wait to initiate the highly controversial antisubversion legislation stipulated in Article 23 of the Basic Law. The legislation that the HKSAR government began writing in the fall of 2002 was a draconian version that would outlaw even the ownership of publications categorized by Beijing as a threat to China's national security.

The legislation garnered opposition not only from the democrats and social-movement groups (discussed in greater detail in Chapter 7), but also many business elites, who expressed reservations about the legislation, at least about the draconian version being pushed by the government. David Li Kwok-po, the head of the Bank of East Asia and an heir of a long-established banking family in Hong Kong whose dominance pre-dated World War II, spoke openly in December that the banking sector worried that the legislation would strangle the freedom of information on which the financial sector relies. His reservations carried significant weight, as Li was the representative of the LegCo's banking sector.[26] The US also officially expressed its "serious reservations" about the law, which would "blur the dividing lines between the Chinese and Hong Kong legal systems."[27]

The legislative process was interrupted by the SARS epidemic that brought the city to a standstill in spring 2003. Once the epidemic abated in May 2003, the legislative process roared ahead at full speed. The prolonged economic downturn after the Asian financial crisis of 1997, the government mismanagement of the epidemic, and the government's obsession with implementing a law that many saw as a grave violation of "One Country, Two Systems" by outlawing speech that Beijing deemed to be subversive led to an explosion of grievances. Opposition to the law culminated in the half-million demonstration on July 1, 2003.

Despite widespread protests by citizens, the government refused to make any compromises. It moved ahead and tried passing the legislation on July 16, according to the original schedule. The opposition called for a large-scale rally outside the LegCo and did not rule out more disruptive action to halt the legislative process. As the possibility of a violent confrontation rose, the Liberal Party, led by James Tien and representing pro-Beijing Hong Kong business interests in the establishment, announced that the government would not have their votes in the LegCo. Tien resigned from the Executive Council to express his disagreement with the government. With the ruling coalition splintered on the legislation, the government had no choice but to withdraw the bill.

After the defeat in legislating Article 23, Chief Executive Tung Chee-hwa resigned in spring 2005, citing health issues as the reason for his resignation. But it was widely believed that his resignation had everything to do with the defeat of the legislation. He was replaced by Donald Tsang, a senior civil servant under British rule and the Chief Secretary for Administration in the Tung Chee-hwa government, for the remainder of the term. Tsang was elected in the Election Committee's by-election in 2005 and was re-elected in 2007, being chief executive until 2012.

The Tsang government tried to broaden its support base by recruiting some professionals and political entrepreneurs with democratic backgrounds. In 2010, he even worked with the Democratic Party to reach a compromise to reform the LegCo by increasing direct-election elements in its makeup (see Chapter 7). But just as the Donald Tsang government seemed to be offering an olive branch to the moderate faction of the opposition, Beijing's radical voice, which advocated more direct intervention by Beijing in Hong Kong affairs, never ceased to grow. Such direct intervention did expand in a few key areas under the Tsang government's cover of moderation.

Empowered by the successful opposition to Article 23 in 2003–2004, the democrats started to demand universal suffrage of the chief executive in 2007 and of the whole LegCo in 2008.

According to their reading, the Basic Law did not specify the election method for the 2007 chief executive election and the 2008 LegCo election, and hence 2007 and 2008 were the earliest years in which the Basic Law warranted universal suffrage. This was not only the position of the democrats. It was also the position of establishment parties, including the Liberal Party and the CCP-led Democratic Alliance for the Betterment and Progress of Hong Kong (DAB) in their founding in the 1990s.

In defiance of the pressure from the democrats, Beijing hardened its line and launched an all-out propaganda offensive to reinterpret the "One Country, Two Systems" concept. It asserted that its "One Country" element was the "precondition and foundation" for the "two systems," not vice versa.[28] Furthermore, although universal suffrage was endorsed in the Basic Law as the ultimate goal of Hong Kong's political development, Beijing attacked the democrats' aspirations for "turning Hong Kong into an independent or semi-independent political entity."[29] This propaganda campaign paved the way for the decision of the National People's Congress Standing Committee (NPCSC) in April 2004 to interpret the Basic Law.[30] According to this interpretation, the election methods for the chief executive and the LegCo in 2007–2008 would remain unchanged – there would be no universal suffrage in Hong Kong in the immediate future.

After it was certain that there would be no universal suffrage in 2007–2008, the democrats shifted their goal to seeking universal suffrage in the chief executive and LegCo elections in 2012. Beijing once again shut the door swiftly. The NPCSC decided in December 2007 that there would be no universal suffrage in 2012. However, election methods for both the chief executive and the LegCo could see incremental modifications in 2012.[31] This also kept the democrats' dreams alive by stating that universal suffrage in the chief executive election could be possible in 2017, followed by universal suffrage in the LegCo election afterward.[32]

In retrospect, Beijing's keeping the promise of universal suffrage alive while delaying its realization was a tactical move to buy time by pacifying the democrats – or at least their moderate wing. In the meantime, Beijing was relentlessly tightening its control over all aspects of Hong Kong politics and society after 2003, readying itself for a showdown with the opposition forces when the question of universal suffrage could no longer be delayed.

Seeing Hong Kong Like an Empire

After the 2003 defeat over the Article 23 legislation, Beijing started to prepare a counteroffensive to tighten its direct control of Hong Kong, beyond just beating back the democrats' demands for universal suffrage. When Beijing was devising a new strategy over Hong Kong, it sent officials and scholars to research the Hong Kong question and build connections to different sectors in Hong Kong's politics and society. This wave of studies concluded that the root cause of the rising discontent and increasingly confrontational opposition since 2003 was the lack of identification with the Chinese nation among the youth and nostalgia for colonial rule. According to these studies, this identity question resulted from the Hong Kong people's colonial mind-set instilled by 150 years of British rule. The proposed solution, unsurprisingly, was to redouble the efforts of patriotic education and other related ideological campaigns. The studies also proposed that Beijing become more active in participating in the politics and society of Hong Kong. In other words, Beijing should be more proactive in pursuing direct political and ideological work in Hong Kong rather than relying on its local elite allies.

This diagnosis and proposed solution are best summarized in the works of Jiang Shigong, an influential legal scholar from Beijing. In 2004–2007, he was on dispatch to work in the Research Department of Hong Kong's Liaison Office to study and write about the Hong Kong question. During his tenure, he reportedly reached out to scholars, business leaders, politicians, and other notable community leaders. He also wrote about Hong Kong in Beijing's *Dushu* magazine. After his work in Hong Kong, he went back to Peking University to serve as the vice dean of the School of Law. His publications on Hong Kong later became the guidelines of Beijing's policy toward Hong Kong. He was reportedly a key author of Beijing's White Paper on Hong Kong in 2014 which promoted a stricter interpretation of "One Country, Two Systems," emphasizing the "One Country" component. The White Paper called for all-round governance of Hong Kong by Beijing and paved the way for the NPCSC decision on August 31, 2014, triggering the Occupy movement (discussed in Chapter 8.)

Jiang belongs to the New Left intellectuals in China. In recent years, many New Left intellectuals in China have critiqued American imperialism and neoliberalism of the 1990s. They advocated for a union of apparently conflicting intellectual lineages, including Marxism, Maoism, right-wing statism as epitomized by Leo Strauss and Nazi legal theorist Carl Schmitt, and Confucianism. Liberal intellectuals in China critiqued this group as being complicit or openly collaborative with the increasingly repressive party-state establishment.[33] As part of this New Left group, Jiang Shigong fretted that Deng Xiaoping's denunciation of the Cultural Revolution had thrown the baby out with the bathwater, as this denunciation erroneously discredited the Chinese experiment with "Great Democracy" during the Cultural Revolution. He lamented that China had lost its indigenous discourse on democracy and become speechless in the face of the Western promotion of bourgeois democracy.[34] At the same time, he was one of the key writers to introduce Carl Schmitt's legal philosophy to China. As the "crown jurist" of the Nazi regime who refused to de-Nazify after World War II, Schmitt saw that the sovereign's priority is to differentiate enemies from friends and guarantee absolute decisiveness on the part of the sovereign to exterminate its enemies. This priority is far more important in politics than the priorities of the state's legal and legislative legitimacy. To Schmitt, liberal democracy represents a "Semitic" influence that weakens the sovereign's power and hence threatens the survival of the state and the nation.[35]

Jiang's articles published in *Dushu* during his tenure in Hong Kong's Liaison Office view Beijing's solution to the Hong Kong question – to establish complete control of the former British colony – as a significant step toward China's revival as a Confucianist empire. He later revised the articles and put them together into a monograph,[36] in which he asserts that though the "One Country, Two Systems" formula served as a genius arrangement that secured Hong Kong's reunion with China in 1997, this legal arrangement is incapable of tackling the most important question regarding China's sovereignty over Hong Kong – that is, the question of Hong Kong people's identity. Replacing their original Hong Kong identity, developed under British rule, with a Chinese identity was seen as being the key to establishing Beijing's full control of Hong Kong. Jiang suggests that the solution has to be sought through political rather than legal means. Beijing has to think beyond the "One Country, Two Systems" framework in its endeavor to transform all Hong Kong residents into true Chinese patriots. Short of that, China's sovereignty over Hong Kong can only be formal and never substantive.

To Jiang, most Hong Kong people embrace the socialist motherland and have done so since the 1950s, including the Hong Kong Chinese who collaborated with the British. They are, supposedly, inherently patriotic because of their familial ties to mainland China dating back generations.[37] The most important task, therefore, is to help Hong Kong Chinese rediscover their latent patriotic heart. Jiang stipulates that the British were shrewd at "winning the hearts and minds" of Hong Kong people during the period of colonial rule, and Beijing should learn from the British experience. It is noteworthy that Jiang translated "winning hearts and minds" into "washing the brains and winning the minds" (xi'nao yingxin), deviating from the original English saying.[38] Jiang's thesis is tantamount to saying that all Hong Kong Chinese are "patriots-in-themselves" waiting to be transformed by the vanguard patriots in Beijing into "patriots-for-themselves." It suggests that Beijing's ideological work in Hong Kong is essential and must obliterate any local identities.

Jiang acknowledges that the "One Country, Two Systems" arrangement in Hong Kong originated from the Seventeen-Point Agreement between Beijing and the Dalai Lama government in Tibet in 1951. He asserts that it is significant not only because it warranted Hong Kong's reunion with China but also because it presaged the revival of China as an empire (Jiang 2008: 123–58). To Jiang, the Chinese empire, which reached its heyday in Qing times, was grounded on the radiation of Confucianist civilization and successive incorporation and transformation of its periphery zones into its core territory. For newly incorporated regions with distinct customs and leadership, the Qing emperor would allow the local elite to exercise local autonomy and maintain local customs, but not for long. Over time, the region would be integrated into the empire's core territory, being culturally assimilated and having their local autonomies and identities eradicated. After establishing direct rule in those regions, the empire would move on to incorporate new territories. The PRC's incorporation of Hong Kong and Taiwan, as well as the prospective assimilation of Hong Kong, illustrates the revival of a similar successive imperial expansion of China in the twenty-first century.

What Jiang implies is clear. Hong Kong's "One Country, Two Systems" is just a transitional arrangement to aid in the smooth transition of Hong Kong's sovereignty from London to Beijing. Once the transition finishes, Beijing's task is to establish substantive sovereignty over Hong Kong through direct control over all aspects of Hong Kong life. In later interviews, Jiang explicitly remarked that the interpretation and practice of "One Country, Two Systems" need to transgress the "era of Deng Xiaoping."[39] Hong Kong's local autonomy needs to be downplayed. What awaits Hong Kong is what Tibet has experienced since 1959: forced assimilation and direct Beijing rule.

Throughout the book, Jiang does not shy away from using the word "empire" with a positive connotation. He repeatedly stipulates that the revived Chinese empire should learn from "skill and art of empire" (*diguode jiyi*) of the British. In other venues, he emphasizes that China's contribution to global governance was to amalgamate China's imperial traditions with "skills and achievements ... employed by Western civilizations to construct world empire" in order to create a "world empire 2.0" (*shijie diguo di'erban*).[40] Jiang's embrace of Maoism, fascism, and imperialism in his discussion of Hong Kong is not exceptional. It is emblematic of the CCP's increasing assertiveness toward Hong Kong. While the PRC has been always an empire pretending to be a nation-state, Jiang's open endorsement of Western and Chinese imperial legacies represents a grand coming out of the new Chinese empire.

Jiang's work is not purely intellectual discussion. It carried significant weight in influencing Beijing's policy toward Hong Kong. From the beginning, Jiang's role at the Liaison Office was to collect information on Hong Kong and devise policy recommendations for Beijing in the aftermath of the 2003 anti-Article 23 protests. Many of his suggestions became actual policies. For example, Jiang's diagnosis that Hong Kong's recalcitrance was rooted in the public's lack of Chinese national consciousness and that this could be remedied through educational and ideological work coincided well with

Beijing's agenda in Hong Kong, as shown by the attempt of the HKSAR government to introduce the compulsory Moral and National Education Curriculum in all schools in 2012. His advocacy for the central government's direct intervention in Hong Kong politics and society also materialized in the expansion of the Liaison Office's power and activities in Hong Kong.

The Making of the CCP's Direct Rule

The Moral and National Education Curriculum guidelines published by the government in 2012 dictated that teachers would need to inculcate and evaluate students' patriotic affection in schools. It also included modules that educated students that the CCP was "progressive, selfless and united."[41] The guidelines spurred a large-scale mobilization that rejected the curriculum as brainwashing. The government revoked the plan to implement the curriculum in September due to public pressure, as we shall see in detail in Chapter 8. But after this setback, the HKSAR government did not cease to intervene in and revise the school curriculum, textbooks, and examination questions to cultivate patriotism among young people.[42]

Jiang's proposal of increasing the central government's direct involvement in Hong Kong politics also coincided with expanding the role of the Liaison Office in Hong Kong. In 2008, one year after Jiang finished his tenure at the Liaison Office Research Department, Cao Erbao, then the head of the Liaison Office's Research Department, published "The Governing Forces in Hong Kong under the Conditions of One Country, Two Systems" in *Study Times* (*xuexi shibao*), an official journal of the CCP Party School.[43] The article articulated a direct governing role of the central government in Hong Kong, which was at odds with the original formulation of "One Country, Two Systems" in the Sino-British Joint Declaration and the Basic Law.

In the original formulation, the HKSAR government, elected locally, is responsible for all aspects of Hong Kong governance besides issues of national defense and foreign affairs. The "One Country" and Chinese sovereignty in Hong Kong are solely expressed in that any elected chief executive and officials of their government need to receive a formal appointment by the central government. After appointment by the central government, the HKSAR government is supposed to have full authority to govern Hong Kong. On the other hand, Cao points out in his article that the HKSAR government is only one of two governing bodies in Hong Kong. One governing body, according to Cao, is not sufficient in manifesting the central government's constitutional power over Hong Kong, hence the need for a second governing team constituted entirely of mainland Chinese Party cadres specializing in Hong Kong affairs to be dispatched to Hong Kong.

To Cao, the formation of this second governing team in Hong Kong is an essential "manifestation of the 'One Country' principle," for it illustrates "the important change in the historical position of the Hong Kong works of the CCP as a national ruling party."[44] Most importantly, it redefines Hong Kong's autonomy as autonomy under China's unitary authority system. This means that the HKSAR government has responsibility over issues explicitly authorized by the central government. The governing responsibility for all other issues naturally belongs to the central government. The article also points out that the Liaison Office is the embodiment of the central government's constitutional power and the CCP as China's national ruling party in Hong Kong. It explicitly spells out the Liaison Office's mission is not just about liaison between the HKSAR and the central government. It is, in fact, a ruling organ of the CCP in Hong Kong.

After the sovereignty handover, speculations about the Liaison Office's interference in Hong Kong media, schools, and elections abounded. Many believed that the chief executive has to govern with the advice and approval of the Liaison Office. Many already saw the office as a second power center or even the HKSAR government's real power center. But even if that were true, the office's real function was never explicit. Cao's article raised eyebrows among the opposition and the international community, as it openly articulated the role of the Liaison Office in Hong Kong in a way that contradicted the official designation of the Liaison Office as merely a communications office facilitating contacts between the HKSAR and the central government.[45] The acknowledgment of a ruling organ of the CCP and the central government in Hong Kong contradicted what most people perceived about the nature of the "high degree of self-government" of Hong Kong according to the Sino-British Joint Declaration and the Basic Law.

The explicit articulation by Chinese officials that the Liaison Office was a secondary, or even the primary, power center in Hong Kong became routine, as if Beijing was anxious to clarify to the people in Hong Kong and the rest of the world who was truly in charge in Hong Kong. In 2019 and 2020, Liaison Office cadres became more vocal in commenting on Hong Kong politics by issuing statements to express opinions about what the HKSAR government should do to deal with the anti-extradition protests. It invoked strong pushback from the opposition, which pointed out that the Liaison Office was a central government department bound by Article 22 of the Basic Law. The article states, "No department of the Central People's Government and no province, autonomous region, or municipality directly under the Central Government may interfere in the affairs which the Hong Kong Special Administrative Region administers on its own in accordance with this Law." As such, its behavior was in violation of the Basic Law. But the Hong Kong and Macau Affairs Office of China's State Council and the Hong Kong government retorted openly that the Liaison Office was not set up according to Article 22 of the Basic Law. It bore the prime responsibility of exercising supervisory power (*jiandu quan*) over Hong Kong affairs. This new reformulation confirmed retro-actively that the Liaison Office has been always the de facto highest authority in Hong Kong.[46]

In light of the history of "One Country, Two Systems" in Tibet that we discussed in the last chapter, such an attempt at building a second power center under the direct command of Beijing to compete with the local government is not surprising. It was what the Tibet Autonomous Region Government Preparatory Committee did to challenge the Dalai Lama government in 1956–1959. That competition was always meant to end with the eradica-tion of the Tibetan government and the establishment of the Tibet Autonomous Region government under direct and complete CCP control.

Before the explicit acknowledgments in Cao's article and the open recognition of its "supervisory role" in Hong Kong, it has been an open secret that the Liaison Office was increasingly involved in participation in the political, social, and cultural lives of Hong Kong.[47] Besides gathering information and making friends from all walks of life in Hong Kong, the Liaison Office was allegedly involved in election meddling by co-ordinating among pro-establishment candidates at all election levels. It was reported that establishment candidates could not run unless they obtained the blessing of the Liaison Office.[48] There have been rumors that the Liaison Office was behind Leung Chun-ying's campaign for chief executive in 2012 against Henry Tang, and that it was behind all the sex and corruption scandals leaked to the media that tarnished Tang's candidacy. A leading financial newspaper owned by Richard Li Tzar-kai, the younger son of Li Ka-shing, was reportedly threatened by the Liaison Office for its negative coverage of Leung Chun-ying.[49] There is never enough hard evidence to prove the case, but it is telling that Leung's first stop in the morning after his election was a visit to the Liaison Office to thank it for its support.

It is reported that Liaison Office cadres have been active in building connections with and influencing media editors, school principals, leaders of professional associations, and others. Many professional and business elites work through the Liaison Office to expand their businesses and careers in mainland China, rendering the office much leverage.[50] It is also reported that the office was involved in mobilizing establishment votes at all levels of elections. Besides co-ordinating and supporting grassroots neighborhood organizations and Chinese companies' employees that confer a large portion of traditional establishment votes, the Liaison Office also helped to organize new mainland immigrants to Hong Kong into native-place organizations according to their home provinces or counties in China. Research finds that under the influence of native-place organizations, these immigrants have become an increasingly important voting bloc for establishment candidates, because they are generally more conservative on most political issues.[51]

Immigration policy was another tool weaponized against Hong Kong's autonomy. Under the immigration regime of Hong Kong after 1997, Hong Kong's Immigration Office retained control of global immigration visas except from mainland China. Immigration from China had been governed by a "family reunion quota" system that was first established in the 1980s and expanded in 1995 to a daily quota of 150. Under this system, Chinese public security authorities would screen and approve mainland Chinese citizens who applied to reunite with their relatives in Hong Kong. Hong Kong authorities do not have any information about the backgrounds of these mainland immigrants until they arrive, let alone being able to verify their qualifications for being admitted to Hong Kong. There have been reports of these visas being sold or used by the CCP to send Party members to Hong Kong.[52]

The Liaison Office and the grassroots native-place associations under its wing command the information of those migrants and often establish contacts with them even before their relocation to Hong Kong. The organizations then incorporate these migrants into the social network they maintain and assist them in job seeking and other social services. Seven years after their arrival in Hong Kong, they become eligible voters if they are at least eighteen years of age. After 1997, the growth of the Hong Kong population has been driven mostly by mainland immigration, as shown in Table 6.2.[53] Mainland immigrants are becoming an increasingly significant block of voters.

Empirical surveys find that this group of voters are more prone to voting for establishment candidates, as seen in Table 6.3.

Table 6.2 *Rising composition of mainland new immigrants in the Hong Kong population*

Year	Population growth	Entry of mainland migrants on one-way permit	New mainland migrants as share of population growth
2006	68,500	54,170	82%
2007	34,100	33,865	99%
2008	25,500	41,610	163%
2009	32,500	48,587	150%
2010	55,700	42,624	76%
2011	60,300	43,379	72%
2012	65,500	54,646	83%
2013	43,900	45,031	103%
2014	44,700	40,496	91%
2015	57,700	38,338	66%
2016	65,200	57,387	88%

Source: post852.com; Hong Kong Census and Statistics Department; Hong Kong Immigration Department

Table 6.3 *Backgrounds, political orientations and voting preferences of mainland new immigrants compared with those born locally*

	Locally born	Born in the mainland and moved to Hong Kong before 1997	Born in the mainland and moved to Hong Kong after 1997
Age (%)			
18–30	18.9	3.2	33.3
31–60	62.8	43.3	44.7
61 and above	18.3	53.5	21.9
Respondents	(1,659)	(630)	(114)
Education (%)			
High school graduate or below	44.9	76.8	69.3
College graduate or above	55.1	23.2	30.7
Respondents	(1,649)	(629)	(114)
Self-declared political orientation (%)			
Democrat/ localist	44.9	30.5	39.8
Neutral	27.2	18.9	14.2
Establishment	12.3	24.7	18.6
No orientation	11.4	19.4	20.4
Other	1.9	1.8	0.0
Don't know	2.3	4.8	7.1
Respondents	(1,637)	(624)	(113)
Voting in directly elected seats in last LegCo election (%)			
Democrat/ localist	56.1	38.3	50.9
Establishment	27.2	44.6	34.9
Other	6.0	4.1	0.9
Didn't vote	10.7	12.9	13.2
Respondents	(1,558)	(587)	(106)

Source: Wong et al. 2020

While Jiang's policy prescriptions for Beijing's solution to the Hong Kong question – ideological transformation and direct involvement of the central government in Hong Kong politics – became actual policies of Beijing, his theoretical and historical justifications for such prescriptions give us a glimpse of Beijing's grand vision for the nature of the Beijing–Hong Kong relationship. It is unequivocally a vision of an empire, a vision according to which the local elite's self-governance is only a transitory state for the imperial center to ready itself for direct rule and complete assimilation of the local population. Such transition from indirect to direct rule happened in many ethnic minority areas in the southwest of the Ming and Qing empires, and it happened to Tibet in 1951–1959. It is not surprising that Beijing has been envisioning the full substantive subordination and assimilation of Hong Kong after 1997 all along, despite its promises about local autonomy to comfort the Hong Kong population and the international community before the sovereignty handover.

In the early summer of 2014, Beijing published the "The Practice of the 'One Country, Two Systems' Policy in the Hong Kong Special Administrative Region" White Paper. Jiang Shigong was one of the leading authors, and the *People's Daily* published a lengthy interview with him upon the White Paper's publication to elaborate on the spirit and details of the document.[54] The White Paper offers an interpretation of "One Country, Two Systems" that is unknown to the people in Hong Kong. According to the White Paper, the "Two Systems" is subordinated to the "One Country" part of the formulation. The rights of self-government of Hong Kong are rights granted by the central government, which can take back the rights at any time. It also emphasizes that the central government enjoys the total authority of governing Hong Kong. In many ways, the White Paper is just a more explicit repetition of Cao Erbao's arguments in his 2008 article and Jiang Shigong's advocacy articulated in his series of articles published between 2004 and 2007. What used to be expressed as "scholars'" opinions has become an official policy document. It is widely seen as a formal declaration of the death of "One Country, Two Systems" as we know it.

The White Paper heralded the August 31, 2014, decision of the NPCSC to initiate yet another "interpretation" of the Basic Law by setting out the detailed guidelines of how universal suffrage of the election of the chief executive would be implemented in 2017. According to the decision, the existing Election Committee for the election of the chief executive would be transformed into a Nomination Committee, and each candidate for the chief executive would need to have the vote of more than 50 percent of all members of the committee before they could stand for the popular vote. Given that the Nomination Committee, like the existing Election Committee, is populated by a supermajority of Beijing allies, the strict guidelines that the NPCSC imposed mean that Beijing would have full power to ensure that only loyalists would have a chance to run for the chief executive. This resembles the election of village leaders in mainland China, where the Party nominates all the candidates for villagers to vote on (we will come back to this in Chapter 8).

To many, the NPCSC August 31 decision spelled the death of any prospect for universal suffrage in Hong Kong, as the international standard for universal suffrage includes citizens' equal rights to be nominated. It became the trigger for the seventy-nine-day Occupy movement that sought genuine universal suffrage. After the dissipation of the Occupy movement, Beijing accelerated the tightening of its grip over Hong Kong, realizing the vision of the White Paper at full speed. The failed 2014 uprising could have been the equivalent of the failed Lhasa uprising of 1959 that opened the gate for rapid transition from "One Country, Two Systems" to "One System" under the iron fist of the Party. Nevertheless, to the surprise of many, Hong Kong's civil society has not died amidst the post-Occupy crackdown. The resistance of civil society came back with an unexpected vengeance in 2019.

Part III
Resistance

7 THE CLASS POLITICS OF DEMOCRATIC MOVEMENTS

It is often assumed that, because Hong Kong is an economically prosperous city, it is also a city with social and political stability and one in which people are practical and prefer self-help over collective action in solving their problems. This assumption abounds in popular and journalistic writings on Hong Kong. There is also an academic version of it: sociologist Lau Sui-kai and political scientist Kuan Hsin-chi published two classics on this topic – *Society and Politics in Hong Kong* and *The Ethos of Hong Kong Chinese* – in the 1980s.[1] Based on surveys conducted in the 1970s and 1980s of a cross-section of the Hong Kong population, they claimed that the Hong Kong Chinese population was politically apathetic. Lau coined the concept of "familial utilitarianism" to describe the "ethos" of the Hong Kong Chinese. According to this conceptualization, most Hong Kong residents were "utilitarianist" as they were prone to maximizing their economic self-interest through pragmatic means. They were "familial" in the sense that they relied mostly on intra-familial resources to attain their economic goals. They were reluctant to resort to collective action like protests. Unlike in utilitarian individualism, thought to be common in liberal Western societies, the basic unit of self-interest and action was not individuals but families. There was a high level of collectivism within the family, though not among families. Lau and Kuan claimed that this ethos explains the long-term social and political stability of Hong Kong in the colonial era.

Lau himself used this concept of utilitarian familialism to justify the conservatives' argument against political reform during Hong Kong's countdown to the sovereignty handover in the 1980s, 1990s, and beyond. Lau himself became a prominent think tank figure in the pro-Beijing camp on the eve of 1997. He became the head of the Central Policy Unit of the Hong Kong government in 2002–2012. He was also appointed a delegate to the Chinese People's Political Consultative Conference in 2003. He is now the vice president of the Chinese Association of Hong Kong & Macau Studies, the most prominent think tank organization on Hong Kong policy in Beijing. Lau did not hesitate to use his theory to support Beijing's agenda of thwarting Hong Kong's democratization. As Hong Kong residents do not care about politics and value stability highly, why open up the regime and risk creating instability? Kuan, on the other hand, parted ways with Lau after the sovereignty handover and became involved in the democratic movement. He joined hands with a group of barristers and professionals opposing the Article 23 legislation in 2003 and became the founding chairman of the Civic Party, the new opposition party founded in 2006 that we will turn to later.

Beginning in the 1990s, a younger generation of scholars have dismantled this theory of utilitarian familism among Hong Kong Chinese. Some argue that contrary to Lau and Kuan's portrayal of a rosy, stable Hong Kong, social conflicts and political movements were abundant throughout the colonial period beyond just the 1966–1967 unrest. In the supposedly stable 1970s, Hong Kong saw a proliferation of different grassroots social movements that merged into the democratic movement in the 1980s.[2] Other survey research found that the "ethos" described by Lau and Kuan was not uniform or static, but varied across social classes and contexts.[3] Even if we suppose that the theory of utilitarian familism is right, it is unclear how and why it would be transmitted to the younger generation of Hong Kongers. In any event, the escalating and ever-radicalizing protest movements in Hong Kong after the sovereignty handover have dispelled the myth about the political apathy and obsession with stability among Hong Kongers. The 2019 protest, to be sure, turned Hong Kong into an epicenter of one of the most militant and persistent protest movements in the world.

The 2019 uprising did not emerge out of thin air. It was rooted in a long evolution of social and political movements in Hong Kong, dating back to colonial times. In this chapter, we will trace the origins of the Hong Kong democratic movement to the protest movements of the 1970s. We will also look at how these movements radicalized after 1997. In the next chapter, we will see how these movements grew with the rise of a localist political consciousness and fostered the 2014 Occupy movement, as well as the 2019 resistance against the extradition bill.

The Genesis of the Hong Kong Democratic Movement

We have seen that upon the founding of the People's Republic of China in 1949, the CCP decided to maintain Hong Kong's colonial status quo. China was eager to keep Hong Kong as its diplomatic and commercial window to the world. The CCP accepted the continuation of British governance of Hong Kong while the British tolerated underground CCP activities in the colony. Meanwhile, the colony saw an influx of Chinese refugees. Some of them were industrialists who fueled Hong Kong's industrial takeoff in the 1950s. A majority of the refugees were former peasants and workers who settled in urban slums, providing the rising industries with low-cost labor. These working-class communities became a breeding ground for CCP-affiliated organizations, including many unions, schools, news agencies, and filmmakers.[4]

In the 1950s and 1960s, CCP-affiliated grassroots organizations grew against the backdrop of rampant corruption in the government, police brutality, class polarization, and institutionalized discrimination against the Chinese population. Leftist unions frequently flexed their muscles with paralyzing strikes. Their film companies made box-office hits that portrayed the working class's misery and helped disseminate propaganda about the new socialist China. Their grassroots community organizations, bolstered by PRC's resources, were often more expedient than the colonial administration in delivering relief in the aftermath of natural disasters like fires, landslides, and typhoons, which constantly threatened working-class neighborhoods that were usually made up of wooden shacks on hilly terrain.[5]

In the spring of 1967, the CCP-affiliated mass organizations, under the influence of the Cultural Revolution, used a minor labor dispute to launch an all-out offensive against the colonial authorities through sustained rallies, demonstrations, and an attempted general strike. It was meant to generate a revolutionary crisis that ignited all social and political contradictions at once, paving the way for a CCP takeover or at least a co-governance of the colony by the British and the leftists (the latter was what the leftist insurgency in Portuguese Macau had achieved in late 1966). The insurgency, however, alienated the majority of the Chinese population, who feared a Communist takeover, and was abandoned by Beijing, which in August indicated that China had no intention of taking Hong Kong at the time. With dwindling popular support, hardcore militants resorted to terrorist tactics like roadside bombs and the assassination of anti-Communist Chinese intellectuals, which further marginalized them.[6]

The insurgency had completely dissipated by early 1968. Though many CCP organizations – including schools, publishers, filmmakers, and labor unions – resumed their operations under the authorities' watchful eyes, the terrorist phase cost them popular support and they became demoralized throughout the 1970s. With a renewed sense of urgency in shoring up the colonial state's legitimacy and the influence of Fabian socialism from Britain, the colonial government managed to break the usual resistance from its business allies to initiate a series of social and administrative reforms in the 1970s.[7] Such reforms included institutionalizing public assistance to the poor, implementing nine years of universal public education, installing an effective and internationally acclaimed anticorruption agency, and creating government-sponsored social services. It also expanded its public housing program, which became the world's largest public housing system, accommodating more than half of Hong Kong's population.[8]

In tandem with these reforms was the rise of the student and social movements. In the early 1970s, the memory of the 1967 insurgency was still vivid among radical youths. These students were influenced by the worldwide student revolts in the late 1960s and were sympathetic to the CCP. With "anticolonialism and anti-capitalism" as the unifying theme, the movement sprang up in 1971 against the American handover of the Diaoyu/Senkaku Islands to

Japan. Since the end of World War II, the islands had been under US occupation but were claimed by China. Soon the movement split into a Maoist faction, which focused on spreading propaganda about the achievements of Communist China and paid little attention to local struggles in Hong Kong, and a "social faction," which was critical of the authoritarian nature of the CCP regime and enthusiastic in supporting local grassroots social movements.[9]

Many of the Maoist students later joined the CCP-affiliated leftist organizations. In contrast, many members of the social faction joined an array of independent social movements and political organizations over the 1970s and afterward. They included teachers' unions, community and housing rights organizations (which were involved in the movement to resettle Tanka boat households into public housing in the late 1970s, as we saw in Chapter 2), and independent labor organizations. After Beijing's intention to resume its sovereignty over Hong Kong became known in 1982, many activists from these organizations converged into a democratic movement, which, on one hand, supported China's plan to take back Hong Kong and, on the other, sought political and social reforms during Hong Kong's decolonization.[10] Many of the early leaders and core activists of the democratic movement were leaders of the social movements in the 1970s, such as Szeto Wah, who was the teachers' union leader, or social workers who started their activism in those movements.

When the colonial government started to open up elections to district boards (later renamed district councils in the year 2000) at the neighborhood level in 1982 and further opened up the Urban Council (disbanded in 1999), a representative organization that specialized in sanitary and urban planning issues, for more directly elected seats, the democrats participated actively and were swept to office. This democratic movement increasingly positioned itself as representing the expanding "new middle class" constituted by professionals and managers in both the private and the public sectors, including teachers, social workers, and others.[11]

The Advance of the Middle-Class Democrats

When Beijing, in the early 1980s, first expressed its determination to reclaim Hong Kong's sovereignty in 1997, only the

CCP-affiliated leftist groups, which had been marginalized in Hong Kong society since the 1967 insurgency, supported the unconditional return of Hong Kong to China. Both the British and Chinese business elite advocated the perpetuation of colonial rule. The mainstream public opinion at the time was against return-ing to China (see the previous chapter). A few political groups within the nascent democratic movement supported Hong Kong's return to China under the condition of democratic self-governance and progressive social reform. The core activists of this group formed Meeting Point in 1983. Others formed the United Democrats of Hong Kong in 1990. The two later merged to become the Hong Kong Democratic Party in 1994, and this has remained the flagship opposition party ever since.

In the last chapter, we saw that these Democratic Reunionists strived for democracy and social reforms in the HKSAR government after the sovereignty handover. However, they were sidelined by the emerging alliance between the CCP and the business elite. In the last years of British rule, the democrats' agenda of democratizing Hong Kong's political system resonated with the departing British agenda of maintaining the colonial gov-ernment's legitimacy through democratization.[12] The democrats advocated that all of the LegCo and the chief executive of Hong Kong after the sovereignty handover should be elected through universal suffrage. They pressured the departing British to speed up the democratization of Hong Kong before 1997 to smooth the tran-sition to their ultimate goal. Though opposed by the business elite, this position was popular among Hong Kong citizens. Afraid of fueling the anti-Beijing sentiment in Hong Kong, the CCP had little choice other than to tacitly approve democratization reforms in the last years of British rule, so long as they did not go too far. After all, the CCP's allies and proxies actively participated in every single direct election opened by the British.

In 1982, eighteen district boards, comprising appointed and directly elected members, were established to govern neighborhood affairs across Hong Kong. In 1985, the LegCo, which had been made up of members appointed by the government, started to introduce functional constituency (FC) members. FC members were elected not by individual voters but by corporate bodies, such as business enter-prises and professional associations, or individuals with professional qualifications designated by the government. In 1991, the British opened eighteen of the sixty seats in the LegCo for popular direct election – democrats captured fourteen of them.[13] In the 1995 LegCo election, when the number of directly elected seats expanded to twenty, democrats captured seventeen. The democrats even won big in the nine FC elections, which the departing British turned into a quasi-direct election by allowing employees (instead of corporate bodies) in the occupational categories to vote. After the sovereignty handover, this arrangement was abolished when Beijing restored exclusively corporate bodies and members of professional organizations as voters in FC elections. On the eve of the sovereignty handover, the democrats were successful at all levels of direct elections. They gained extensive media exposure and substantial financial resources through elected public offices.

The democratic movement relied heavily on middle-class support, as they were the biggest contributors of votes. It follows that the Democratic Party and other mainstream democrats adopted a moderate line on all kinds of social and political issues to maintain middle-class support. For example, they supported a limited expansion of welfare, but were against a fully fledged welfare state. They were adamant about demanding democracy in Hong Kong and in mainland China in principle, but they had a distaste for large-scale popular mobilization and preferred a nonconfrontational approach to dealing with the Hong Kong government and with Beijing.

In the runup to the sovereignty handover, the opposition movement included a more radical wing consisting of student organizations, represented by the Hong Kong Federation of Students (HKFS) as an umbrella organization of all student unions in higher-education institutions, and several fringe groups, such as the group led by Trotskyist Leung Kowk-hung, aka "Long Hair." They detested the moderation of the mainstream democrats and preferred confrontational actions. For example, in every annual commemoration of the June 4 massacre after 1989, the radicals parted ways with the moderates after the Victoria Park candlelight vigil to march onto the New China News Agency headquarters, which was the de facto CCP headquarters in Hong Kong before 1997, and clashed with the Hong Kong police stationed there to keep protesters from the main entrance. But these radicals never held elected public office and had been no more than a vocal minority in the movement.[14]

The democrats and the conservative business elite disagreed over the pace of democratization in the 1990s. The former demanded speedy and full democratization before 1997 so that full democracy would be established by 1997. The latter advocated a slower pace of democratization and warned the British that any democratization reform before the sovereignty handover had to be approved by Beijing. The reform had to be slow and piecemeal. Despite their differences about the pace of democratization, they both claimed to support the idea of having universal suffrage in the election of both the chief executive and all of the LegCo as the ultimate goal of Hong Kong's political reform.[15]

The conflict between the democrats and the conservative business elite escalated in the wake of the failed democratic movement in China in 1989. In the spring of 1989, Hong Kong democrats supported Tiananmen protesters by organizing mass demonstrations and fundraising campaigns. On May 21, more than a million Hong Kongers took to the street to protest the implementation of martial law in Beijing, in support of the students. It was the biggest mobilization and rally in Hong Kong history at the time. Amidst the mobilization, key figures in the democratic movement, student organizations, and other social-movement organizations founded the Hong Kong Alliance in Support of Patriotic Democratic Movements in China (HKASPDMC). It became Hong Kong's umbrella organization supporting China's democratic movement in the decades to come.[16]

Following the June 4 massacre, the general public opinion was that Beijing was not to be trusted and that more guarantee was needed to defend Hong Kong's human rights. The democrats called for the "three strikes" – a labor strike, school strike, and market strike – to paralyze Hong Kong. On June 7, the eve of the "three strikes," a riot broke out in the center of Kowloon at midnight. This movement in support of Beijing students looked set to evolve into local turmoil that could jeopardize the plan for the handover of Hong Kong's sovereignty. For fear of causing unrest and alienating their middle-class base, the democrats hastily called off the strikes and the mass movement's momentum dissipated. Some claimed that the riots on the night of June 7 were instigated by mainland Chinese security officers who had infiltrated the territory. British Hong Kong intelligence officers allegedly argued that these security officers would create further disturbance during any planned rallies to incite fear and panic. The decision to call off the strikes was the consensus of the democrats and of the British government.[17]

  The long-term repercussion of the June 4 crackdown on Hong Kong's democratic movement was profound. We saw in the last chapter that the democrats' cozy-cum-working relationship with the CCP ended. While the democrats saw the Beijing regime as an illegitimate one responsible for a hideous crime, Beijing started to see the democrats as enemies controlled by hostile foreign powers in order to subvert the CCP. HKASPDMC stayed on as a permanent organization in Hong Kong, involving most opposition and social-movement leaders. It organized an annual march and vigil to commemorate the June 4 massacre and demand Beijing's accountability for the bloodshed. They manage to raise a large number of donations during each of these annual activities. The June 4 vigil has been a long-term symbol and one of the most popular activities organized by the opposition, continuing well into the post-handover era (until the HKASPDMC was forced to disband under the National Security Law in 2021), as shown in Figure 7.1.[18]

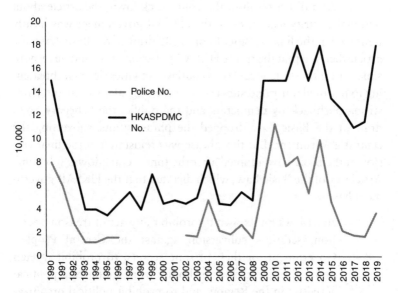

Figure 7.1 No. of attendees of the June 4 candlelight vigil in Victoria Park, Hong Kong, 1990–2019
Source: *Mingpao*, June 4, 2020

Besides the annual commemoration, the HKASPDMC was also involved in China's democratic movement, which went underground after June 4. In the immediate years after 1989, it organized clandestine operations to help wanted student and labor leaders flee China and seek political asylum in Western countries. In later years, it continued to maintain a network in mainland China of lawyers, labor activists, and families of victims of the June 4 massacre.[19]

With the overwhelming support of Hong Kong business elite and Chinese officials, the final version of the Basic Law, passed in 1990, dashed the hopes for immediate universal suffrage after the sovereignty handover. Though it did reinstate the promise of the chief executive's eventual election and all LegCo seats through universal suffrage in Articles 45 (on election of the chief executive) and 68 (on the LegCo election), it delayed implementation indefinitely. It only specified that this change could not occur earlier than 2007 for the election of the chief executive and 2008 for the LegCo in Annexes I and II. It did not specify how the candidates for universal suffrage were to be nominated.

As a direct result of the 1989 crackdown, the article about national security legislation in the HKSAR government was hastily tightened in the final version. In the 1988 draft of the Basic Law, the article dictated that the future HKSAR government would be responsible for establishing local law to outlaw activities deemed threatening to national unity and subversive of the central government. After strong pushback by democrats and the public, the February 1989 draft of the Basic Law dropped the phrase about subverting the central government. But this phrase was reinstated in the final version of the Basic Law adopted after the June 4 crackdown. It became Article 23 of the Basic Law, which dictated that the HKSAR government has to

> enact laws on its own to prohibit any act of treason, secession, sedition, subversion against the Central People's Government, or theft of state secrets, to prohibit foreign political organizations or bodies from conducting political activities in the Region, and to prohibit political organizations or bodies of the Region from establishing ties with foreign political organizations or bodies.[20]

Article 45, which embodies the promise of eventual universal suffrage, and Article 23, which threatens pre-existing liberties that Hong Kongers enjoyed under British rule, became the focal points of contentious political mobilizations by the democrats after 1997. The main theme of the democratic movement in Hong Kong under China was to strive for actualization of genuine democracy as early as possible and defend Hong Kong's existing freedoms against any national security legislation.

New Social Movements and Radicalization

Public outrage at the local ruling circle mounted as the government struggled to revive Hong Kong's economy following the Asian financial crisis of 1997–1998. Its failure to contain the SARS epidemic in spring 2003 only made matters worse. In early summer of 2003, at the peak of discontent, the government responded to pressure from Beijing and redoubled the push for the antisubversion legislation mandated by the Basic Law's Article 23. The actual law that the government proposed was as draconian as could be. It outlawed organizations and the publication, circulation, and ownership of "seditious" materials, with a vague definition of what constituted sedition.[21] It was feared that it would ultimately be Beijing that determined what and who was seditious and who was not. In such a case, Hong Kong autonomy would be severely compromised, as the court in Hong Kong would inevitably need to consider Beijing's political will and preference in ruling on matters of national security. This legislative attempt inspired many otherwise inactive scholars, journalists, librarians, and even members of the Catholic Church and many Protestant congregations to join the democrats in opposing the legislation, as they saw it as a grave threat to pre-existing freedoms of speech and association that Hong Kong had enjoyed since late colonial times.[22]

The accumulation of the public's discontent manifested in a massive demonstration on July 1, 2003, on the sixth anniversary of the sovereignty handover when more than half a million protesters took to the street, united in opposition to the Article 23 legislation. The demonstration, with enthusiastic participation of youngsters coming of age after 1997, expressed a wide range of spontaneous appeals, including universal suffrage in 2007–2008 and an attack on the business monopoly elite, who were seen as culprits in Hong Kong's widespread inequality.[23]

In response to this citizen uproar, Beijing acquiesced to an indefinite suspension of the Article 23 legislation. In 2005, Beijing's handpicked chief executive, Tung Chee-hwa, resigned and was replaced by Donald Tsang, who had been a senior bureaucrat in the late colonial administration. Beijing's choice to replace the head of an old business family with a civil servant in the role of chief executive was a move to exonerate the HKSAR government from any charges of collusion with big business.

These concessions were not enough to temper the discontent of the protesters. After winning the battle against Article 23, the democrats turned to universal suffrage in the election for chief executive in 2007 and for all LegCo seats in 2008, the earliest possible date for universal suffrage, according to many people's – including many pro-establishment politicians' – reading of the Basic Law. On the first anniversary of the July 1 demonstration in 2004, a large crowd showed up under the slogan "Political power returned to the people" and "Universal suffrage in 2007/08."[24]

As we saw in the last chapter, Beijing pushed back strongly against the demand for universal suffrage in 2007–2008. The National People's Congress Standing Committee (NPCSC) interpreted the Basic Law and dictated that universal suffrage was out of the question for 2007–2008. It later decided that the earliest dates for Hong Kong to have universal suffrage in the election of the chief executive and of the LegCo would be in 2017 and 2020 respectively. Besides this strong pushback, Beijing also brought forward the CEPA with Hong Kong to 2003. As seen in Chapter 3, the CEPA ensured that China could enjoy free access to goods and capital from around the world through Hong Kong without fully opening its economy even after joining the WTO. CEPA unleashed a strong economic recovery for Hong Kong. It consolidated Hong Kong's role as China's offshore financial market and accelerated Hong Kong's economic and social integration with China, opening the floodgate of mainland-to-Hong Kong capital, visitors, and labor migrants.

Following the resignation of Tung Chee-hwa and the strong economic rebound under the CEPA, political confrontation cooled down. But under the surface, social cleavages that had led to the 2003 mobilization continued to deepen. Government's collusion

with big business intensified under Donald Tsang. The CEPA accelerated social polarization. Deeper integration between Hong Kong
and mainland China sped up business relocations to China, jeopardizing both working- and middle-class jobs in Hong Kong. The
expanding mainland Chinese migrants across education levels further intensified competition in the labor market for manual and
professional workers alike, leading to wage stagnation. The huge
inflow of Chinese capital into Hong Kong's economy drove up
housing prices and rent, as well as the cost of living across the
board.[25] This made Hong Kong's housing market the world's least
affordable for ten straight years as measured by median home price
as a multiple of median income (see Figure 7.2).

Therefore the post-2003 economic boom mostly benefited
the business elite and the older, propertied middle class, while the
living standards of the younger, salaried, and unpropertied lower
and middle classes deteriorated. Rapid growth of income inequality

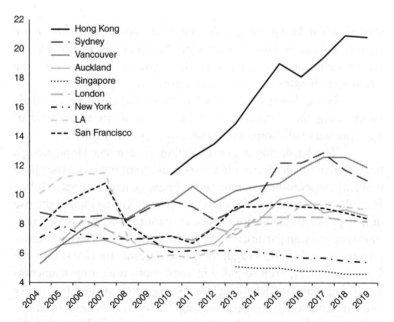

Figure 7.2 Median home price as multiple of median income in Hong Kong in
comparison with some of the most expensive housing markets in the world
Source: Demographia International Housing Affordability Survey

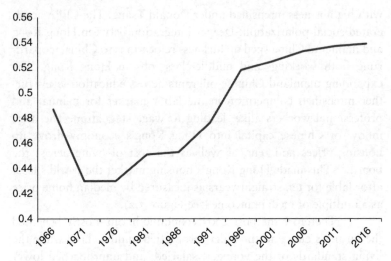

Figure 7.3 Gini coefficient of Hong Kong by household
Source: World Income Inequality Database v.2 by World Bank for 1966–1976; Hong Kong Census and Statistics Department for 1981–2016

started when Hong Kong's development moved from the more equitable phase of industrialization in the 1960s and 1970s to financialization in the 1980s and onward. It continued to grow after the sovereignty handover, as shown in Figure 7.3.[26]

Hong Kong's Gini coefficient of 0.539 in 2016 made Hong Kong the ninth most inegalitarian economy in a world of 157 countries with comparable data, as shown in Table 7.1.

The hardening stance of Beijing in denying Hong Kong's transition to full democracy in 2007–2008, combined with the raised political consciousness among the younger generation that resulted from the successful anti-Article 23 mobilizations, facilitated the rise of new political organizations that were more radical than the traditional opposition parties, like the Democratic Party. The new organizations included the League of Social Democrats (LSD) and the Civic Party (CP), both founded in 2006. Both took a more uncompromising stance on defending Hong Kong's pre-existing civil society and on demanding universal suffrage. The original leaders of the LSD included a firebrand anticommunist radio talk show host, Raymond Wong Yuk-man; the leader of a fringe Trotskyist group, "Long Hair" Leung Kwok-hung; and disillusioned left-leaning

Table 7.1 *Ten economies with the highest inequality in the world,* c. *2016*

Rank	Country	Gini by household	Data date
1	Lesotho	0.632	1995
2	South Africa	0.625	2013
3	Micronesia, Federated States of	0.611	2013
4	Haiti	0.608	2012
5	Botswana	0.605	2009
6	Namibia	0.597	2010
7	Zambia	0.575	2013
8	Comoros	0.559	2004
9	Hong Kong	0.539	2016
10	Guatemala	0.530	2014

Source: www.cia.gov/library/publications/the-world-factbook/rankorder/2172rank.html

Democratic Party politicians like Albert Chan Wai-yip and Andrew To Kwan-hang. It attracted many grassroots activists working on diverse issues ranging from LGBT rights to Internet free speech. The Civic Party was initiated by barristers, scholars, and other professionals who were active in mobilizing for the 2003 anti-Article 23 legislation protest and the 2004 movement seeking 2007–2008 universal suffrage.[27]

The two new parties performed impressively in the 2008 LegCo election. A number of the candidates representing the two parties were nonaffiliated veteran legislators who had already been elected to the LegCo in 2004 (like Leung Kwok-hung of the LSD and Margaret Ng Ngoi-yee of the CP). Altogether the two parties' candidates mustered 23.7 percent of the vote and seven of the thirty directly elected seats, outnumbering the 20.5 percent vote and matching the seven directly elected seats commanded by the Democratic Party (see Table 7.2). The rise of the LSD and the Civic Party spelled the end of the hegemony of the Democratic Party in the opposition movement.

In the meantime, a spate of community movements organized by diverse students and young intellectuals grew to resist the government and large corporations' efforts to destroy historic buildings, traditional neighborhoods, and natural habitats to make way for

Table 7.2 *Distribution of elected candidates in the 2008 LegCo election by political affiliation*

Party	Geographical constituencies		Functional constituencies	LegCo total
	Vote %	Seats	Seats	Seats
Democratic camp				
Democratic Party	20.5	7	1	8
Civic Party	13.6	4	1	5
League of Social Democrats	10.1	3	0	3
Others	13.2	5	2	7
Total	57.4	19	4	23
Establishment camp				
DAB	22.8	7	3	10
Liberal Party	4.3	0	7	7
Others	11.0	4	16	20
Total	38.1	11	26	37
Invalid votes, etc.	4.5			
Total	100	30	30	60

Source: Hung 2010: 71

profitable redevelopment projects.[28] This type of community mobilization calling for the preservation of colonial-era historical buildings mushroomed after 2003, as many of the core activists were drawn to social movements by the 2003 July 1 demonstration. These movements were not restricted to protecting historic urban neighborhoods – they also worked with rural inhabitants to seek preservation of their communities and natural habitats against development projects.[29]

Concomitant with this continuous mobilization of Hong Kong society, formal freedom of speech was more or less maintained throughout the postcolonial period, thanks to the successful resistance to the Article 23 legislation. However, many surveys suggest that self-censorship among journalists and editors was on the rise, and the media became ever more reluctant to criticize Hong Kong's and China's governments. This has something to do with the mainstream media's reliance on investment from local business magnates, who served as

Beijing's proxies in ruling Hong Kong. Mainstream media, both electronic and printed, also relied on commercials from the city's business monopolies, who allegedly boycotted certain media outlets that Beijing deemed to be anti-CCP.[30]

Despite the creeping indirect control of mainstream media by Beijing, the popularization of high-speed Internet facilitated the explosive growth of independent and alternative media platforms launched by social activists with more radical views. These media platforms never pulled any punches in scrutinizing and criticizing the government and the moderate democrats. They also fueled the growth of the new radical wing of the democratic movement and the different community mobilizations against redevelopment projects. Some of these outlets built a large following and even matched some of the most popular mainstream media in their popularity.[31]

The radicalization of the democratic movement and the rise of community movements against redevelopment projects culminated in late 2009 and 2010. The latter movements developed into a large-scale campaign against the construction of the Hong Kong– Guangzhou section of the national high-speed rail system that would uproot various rural and urban communities within Hong Kong. Its unit cost is exceeding all other segments in the national high-speed rail system in mainland China, and the project was to be paid for by Hong Kong government revenue.

By early 2009, the small-scale protests of Choi Yuen villagers, whose village would be demolished to make room for the construction of the high-speed rail, escalated into recurrent demonstrations of thousands of people. The village of Choi Yuen was formed by immigrant tenant farmers who settled near Kam Tin in the New Territories and made a living by vegetable cultivation or husbandry (discussed in Chapter 2). They were excluded by the traditional HYK power structure of rural Hong Kong, as they do not have original-inhabitant status. But their protest drew support from residents in urban neighborhoods who would also be disrupted by the construction, as well as from citizens who were outraged by the astronomical cost of the hastily planned project and its extensive destruction of community life and of the natural environment. Some professional groups and pro-democratic politicians criticized the project because it would only benefit vested interests in the real-estate sector while overloading the local transportation system.

Most LegCo members in FCs, which represented professional and vested-interests group and usually allied with Beijing, supported the government's plan. The democratic legislators, who constituted the majority in the directly elected seats, mostly opposed the project to different extents. With half of the LegCo seats occupied by FC legislators, it was mathematically impossible for the LegCo to deny the government plan. The protesters gradually merged their opposition to the project into a quest for the LegCo's full democratization by abolishing all FC seats.

The legislative sessions designated for debating and voting on the government budget for the project in January 2010 drew almost 10,000 protesters to encircle and blockade the LegCo building, nearly succeeding in detaining government officials inside overnight.[32] Though the movement could not forestall the project, its mobilizing capacity and its potential to paralyze the government alarmed Beijing. Beijing had already been disturbed by a group of young protesters, somewhat overlapping the anti-high-speed-rail activists, who successfully broke the police line and briefly occupied the backdoor of the Liaison Office on New Year's Eve that year. These young protesters demanded universal suffrage and the release of the jailed Chinese dissident Liu Xiaobo.[33]

What worried Beijing most was that throughout the spring of 2010, this emerging group of young radicals joined hands with the LSD and the Civic Party to initiate a referendum movement amidst heated debate over the government's political reform proposal, which laid out the election method for the chief executive and the LegCo in 2012. After Beijing denied 2007–2008 universal suffrage in 2004, it further denied 2012 universal suffrage in 2007. It indicated the earliest possible dates for universal suffrage would be 2017 for the chief executive and 2020 for the LegCo.[34] Yet many in the democratic movement continued to demand universal suffrage in 2012. In fall 2009, the HKSAR government put forward a proposal for political reform for the 2012 elections that ruled out universal suffrage. In response, the LSD, later joined by the Civic Party, advocated a de facto referendum to mobilize, galvanize, and manifest the strong will of the Hong Kong people for democracy, putting pressure on Beijing to implement universal suffrage in 2012, or at least a more open election method to pave the way for full democracy in 2017–2020.[35]

The proposed referendum would be initiated by the resignation of five directly elected democratic legislative councilors, each representing one of the five geographical constituencies covering all of Hong Kong. The resigned legislator would then campaign to regain their seats in the by-election, employing the demand for universal suffrage in 2012 as their re-election platform. Each vote for any of the five candidates would then be equivalent to a vote supporting that demand, turning the by-election into a referendum. Though Hong Kong lacks a formal law that authorizes referendums as in Taiwan and other democratic countries, such a de facto referendum would set a precedent for Hong Kong citizens to express their collective will on significant issues in the future. The referendum materialized when the five democratic legislators resigned in January, and the by-election for their seats was scheduled for May 2010.

Beijing accused the referendum movement of being a road toward Hong Kong independence. The Democratic Party, for fear of angering Beijing, refused to participate in the referendum and opted for secret negotiations with Beijing in a quest to amend the government proposal.[36] On the other hand, grassroots activists and alternative online media organizations participated emphatically to help get out the vote.[37] In the end, all the resigned democrats were re-elected with nearly 90 percent of the cast votes, and half a million voters turned out to vote despite the organized boycott of the by-election by the establishment and the Democratic Party. In the aftermath of the referendum, the young radicals became ever more militant in their confrontational actions to sabotage the government public relations campaign advertising the government's reform proposal. Public opinion polls showed that popular support for the government proposal eroded after the referendum, though it had not been high to start with.[38] After the referendum, the Civic Party moderated their position and aligned themselves more closely with the Democratic Party's position. The LSD's political prowess dissipated after successive internal strife and split.

Like the 2003 mobilization that halted the Article 23 legislation, the escalating public discontent against the government's 2012 proposal for political reform forced Beijing to adapt. The demand for 2012 universal suffrage in the referendum was initially destined to go nowhere, as the moderate Democratic Party had already accepted the NPCSC 2007 decision that the earliest date for universal suffrage was 2017–2020. However, the momentum of the referendum movement put enough pressure on Beijing for it to enter into a clandestine negotiation with the Democratic Party. After rounds of negotiation, Beijing finally accepted the Democratic Party's proposal for a piecemeal modification of the 2012 LegCo election method to increase the "direct election component" of the FC legislators. The proposal designated that in the 2012 LegCo election, five directly elected seats and five new FC seats would be added. The five new FC seats would be nominated by directly elected district councilors and then put to the vote by all voters who were not eligible to vote in any other FC election. In other words, those newly added FC seats were close to directly elected seats.[39] This is yet another example of Beijing having to retreat, however reluctantly, to ensure stability in Hong Kong in the face of large-scale popular mobilization. Later in the year, rumor had it that Beijing pushed the Hong Kong government to relaunch the stalled Article 23 legislation before Donald Tsang finished his term as chief executive in 2012. But after vociferous resistance expressed by journalists, scholars, and opposition groups, Tsang finally stated in his annual policy address in October 2010 that the legislation would not be on the agenda for the remainder of his term.[40]

In the 2012 election of the chief executive, Leung Chun-ying, widely believed to be a hard-liner representing Chinese state enterprises and the hawkish cadres in Beijing, won after a split vote between him and Henry Tang, a representative of Hong Kong local tycoons, in the elitist Election Committee. After Leung was inaugurated in the spring, the HKSAR sped up policies to increase Beijing's grip on the city that hard-line nationalists had been advocating. One such policy was establishing a Moral and National Education Curriculum in all public middle schools to inculcate the Beijing version of Chinese history and political consciousness upon all schoolchildren. The government made it mandatory for all schools to implement the curriculum within three years. Such a plan invoked great resistance not only from parents but also from middle-school students themselves.

While the mainstream democrats did not express their opposition to the curriculum and only hoped to introduce more liberal content into it, a spontaneous movement against the curriculum gathered pace over the summer of 2012. At the forefront of the movement was the newly founded organization Scholarism. Its membership was made up exclusively of middle-school students, with Joshua Wong Chi-fung as the leader. The organization prepared handbills and online videos to explain why the National Education Curriculum was an attempt by Beijing to establish outright ideological and political control in schools. The curriculum included items that were familiar in mainland China but alien to Hong Kong, such as evaluating students' level of patriotism through gauging their positive affection when shown materials about PRC achievements, and mutual evaluations of patriotic feeling among students.[41]

Scholarism's call for shelving the curriculum gathered momentum over the summer of 2012. In September, Scholarism was joined by a group of social-movement activists (many of whom were veterans of the anti-high-speed-rail and referendum movements) and radical democratic politicians to launch a large-scale school boycott and rally. On September 7, just before the LegCo election, more than 100,000 students and other concerned citizens rallied in the Civic Square outside the government headquarters.[42] To prevent a long-term occupation and protect the electoral prospect of the pro-establishment legislators during the September 9 LegCo election, the government backed down and announced on the evening of September 8 that it would no longer mandate all schools to implement the National Education Curriculum within three years. It would instead let each school decide when and how to implement the curriculum. Seeing it as a win, the protesters dispersed overnight.[43]

Through the waves of mobilization, from the anti-Article 23 protests in 2003 to the anti-high-speed-rail protest and referendum movement in 2010, and the anti-National Education movement in 2012, we see that Hong Kong's contentious civil society continued to increase in size and militancy. Represented by the Democratic Party, the moderates, who advocated compromise and nonconfrontational action, no longer enjoyed a hegemonic position in the opposition movement. After 1997, each protest created a network of activists, many of whom continued their activism and helped fuel the next movements, drawing in more and younger activists along the way. On top of this increasing confrontation and scale, the opposition movement also manifested a transformation of its political consciousness in the rise of Hong Kong localism.

8 HONG KONG AS A POLITICAL CONSCIOUSNESS

While the democratic movement underwent radicalization, as evidenced by its more confrontational stances and actions in the aftermath of the 2003 protest, major politicians and activists did not depart from the mainstream democrats in their goals and programs. Both the League of Social Democrats and the young activists involved in the anti-high-speed-rail mobilization, for example, shared the vision that striving for democracy in Hong Kong was part and parcel of China's democratic movement. Besides mobilizing on Hong Kong issues, they also organized or actively participated in actions supporting the dissidents in mainland China. They included multiple demonstrations demanding the release of Liu Xiaobo, a march denouncing the death of 1989 pro-democracy labor leader Li Wangyang upon his release after more than two decades of imprisonment, and others.

As we saw in the introductory chapter, a distinct Hong Kong identity emerged before 1997, but this identity had been a cultural identity rather than a political one. This identity mainly expressed itself in movies, pop songs, and literature, but not much in politics. The opposition movement in Hong Kong had not manifested a political identity separate from the Chinese nationalist identity. It is noteworthy that the party platform of the Hong Kong Democratic Party, the flagship party of the mainstream opposition, opened stating that "the Democratic Party staunchly supports Hong Kong's return to China and opposes distancing and segmentation between Hong Kong and China" and "Hong Kongers are part of the Chinese people ... the Democratic Party supports China's democratic development."[1]

The radical wing of the democrats that emerged after 2003 was no different. The party platform of the League of Social Democrats at its founding in 2006 asserted that "any discussion about Hong Kong's future development cannot be separate from the consideration of the direction of Chinese development"; that "we oppose any other countries' interference with Chinese sovereignty in any forms, including encouragement of any regions to break away from the motherland and any economic and trade sanctions on China"; and that "the Hong Kong government should actively discuss with the central and provincial governments of China making Hong Kong complement China's holistic development ... and Hong Kong should be connected with mainland China in transportation and communication as one integrated whole."[2] These stances are indeed indistinguishable from those of any establishment party.

Underneath Chinese nationalism's apparent persistence in the opposition movement, a Hong Kong localist consciousness emerged in the 2000s. This localist political consciousness prioritized the struggle against local injustices. It protected the pre-existing local culture in Hong Kong as the foundation of asserting Hong Kong autonomy vis-à-vis Beijing. At first, for lack of a clear articulation of ideas and programs, this ambivalent and budding local political consciousness coexisted with the Chinese national consciousness in many collective actions undertaken by the radical wing of the democratic movements. But soon the localist consciousness expressed itself in more articulate ways, leading to open debates within the opposition movement. By the time of the anti-extradition protests in 2019, localism had attained hegemony in the movement, as manifested in the demands, slogans, and public-opinion findings amidst the protest.

Latent Localism in Social and Democratic Movements

In the last chapter, we saw that community movements seeking to protect historic buildings and neighborhoods against redevelopment mushroomed after the 2003 protest against Article 23. Besides pushing back against inequality and developers' domination in the economy, and fighting for the rights to public space, something deeper was lurking beneath these protests. Foreign media noticed early on that these movements manifested an assertion of Hong Kong's local identity in opposition to the Chinese identity that Beijing attempted to promote. On the eve of the first anniversary of the 2003 protest, the *New York Times* published an article titled "City of Immigrants Begins to Find an Identity of Its Own," showing that this sudden surge of community protest was about more than conservation – they also represented a yearning for local Hong Kong identity.[3]

One of the better-known examples is the 2006–2007 protest against the demolition of the Star Ferry Pier and Queen's Pier. The two piers were constructed as an integral part of the City Hall and Edinburgh Place in the high modernist architectural style in the 1950s.[4] Protesters, composed of veteran social-movement activists, progressive architects, young intellectuals, and university students, argued that the piers and the square next to them were a space where many ceremonies of significance to Hong Kong's history happened. Queen's Pier was where British royal visitors landed and from where the last British governor departed on the night of June 30, 1997. The two piers also constituted public spaces where many civic activities and protests took place, including the hunger strike against a ferry fare hike that triggered the historic 1966 riots. It carried many collective memories of Hong Kong people on which the Hong Kong local identity rested.

The protesters disseminated their message through the newly flourishing online and social media. Their efforts resulted in nearly three months of occupation of Queen's Pier in the summer of 2007, when demolition was about to begin. The occupation led to a confrontation with construction workers and the police on August 1. Many occupiers were cleared and arrested, and the demolition project moved on. Despite its failure, the movement led to a variety of similar protests that sought to preserve historic buildings and communities. Some of them succeeded in making the government or developers retrofit instead of demolishing the buildings.[5] Authors and scholars in both Hong Kong and mainland China started to debate the significance of these movements.[6] Some Chinese nationalist writers, such as Jiang Shigong, discussed in Chapter 6, denounced these movements as a pure manifestation of nostalgia for the bygone British colonial era.[7] Others saw them as a revival of a local Hong Kong identity that could benefit Hong Kong's quest for democracy against authoritarian China.[8]

There was an obvious correlation between these community movements and the rising Taiwan nationalism under the first pro-independence Democratic Progressive Party administration. On the fifty-seventh anniversary of the February 28 massacre in Taiwan in 2004, pro-independence activists organized a rally entitled "February 28 Hand-in-Hand Protecting Taiwan". Protesters held hands to form a human chain along Taiwan's coastline to protest China's targeting of Taiwan with missiles. In late March that year, Hong Kong's community activists and some democrats organized a "Hand-in-Hand Protecting Victoria Harbor" event. Protesters formed a human chain along the northern coast of Hong Kong Island to protest reclamation and construction projects that would compromise the coastline and harbor view of Hong Kong Island. The parallel in the repertoire is unmistakable.[9]

In the democrats' campaign for universal suffrage in 2007–2008, a group of pro-democrat scholars, professionals, and politicians ran a full-page advertisement in major newspapers on June 7, 2004, to publish the "Standing Firm on Hong Kong Core Values" declaration.[10] Listing "liberty, democracy, human rights, rule of law, fairness, social justice, peace and compassion, integrity and transparency, plurality, respect for individuals, and upholding professionalism" as the core values of Hong Kong, the declaration refers to Hong Kong as a "community of destiny" (*mingyun gongtongti*), a phrase the drafters directly borrowed from the Taiwan nationalists, who invented the term when they were constructing the imagined community of the Taiwan nation in the 1990s.[11]

While a Hong Kong political identity that is separate from China started to emerge in oppositional activist and intellectual circles following the 2003 protest, the de facto referendum initiated by the Civic Party and the LSD, as discussed in the last chapter, constituted a watershed moment that effectuated the idea of Hong Kong as a distinct political community. As we saw in Chapter 5, Hong Kongers were originally entitled to self-determination through a referendum under the UN Declaration on the Granting of Independence to Colonial Countries and Peoples, just like other colonial territories. After the PRC replaced the Republic of China in Taiwan to occupy China's seat in the UN, it stripped Hong Kong of this right by successfully removing Hong Kong (together with Macau) from the UN colony list. During the Sino-British Joint Declaration and the Drafting of the Basic Law, there had been groups advocating for a referendum among Hong Kong people to determine the future status and political system of Hong Kong after 1997. Beijing was always adamantly against such a proposal, as any referendum would hint at Hong Kong's right to self-determination. It is not surprising that ever since the 2009 referendum movement started, Beijing has attacked it as an attempt to move Hong Kong toward independence.[12]

Though the referendum movement itself hinted at Hong Kong's right to self-determination, its organizers and supporters never explicitly used the language of self-determination to frame their movement. Some participants might have been aware that the concept of the referendum itself was associated with self-determination. However, they must have deliberately remained silent on this matter for fear that it would provoke Beijing. But this unspoken localist political consciousness was already a departure from the traditional democratic movement, which has been heavily loaded with nationalist symbols, slogans, and aspirations for the rejuvenation of China through democracy. The referendum movement and the many conservation movements manifested the opposition's intensifying localist consciousness mostly in actions, but not yet in words.

This localist consciousness in the opposition movement leaped from an unspoken consciousness embedded in actions to one elaborated overtly with Chin Wan's (Horace Chin Wan-kan) best seller *On the Hong Kong City State* in 2011. The book drew from many vague and covert localist ideas in the radical social movements and developed them into explicit advocacy for Hong Kong–China separation. Chin's ideas and commitment to such conviction have changed since the book's publication.[13] But the book set off a chain reaction that eventually fostered demand for Hong Kong self-determination or even Hong Kong independence beyond the author's control. These ideas shaped the mass mobilization around the Occupy movement in 2014 and the anti-extradition movement in 2019, even though Chin himself has been vehemently critical of the leading activists in those protests.

On the Hong Kong City State

In *On the Hong Kong City State*, Chin conceptualizes Hong Kong as a political entity permanently separate from mainland China rather than a temporary arrangement before China's eventual democratization. The book, which has stayed on the best-seller list in major bookstores since its first publication in late 2011, triggered a fierce debate in mainstream and social media. It was selected as one of the best books of the year in 2011 by the Hong Kong Book Prize, organized by Radio and Television Hong Kong.

Chin holds a doctoral degree in ethnology from the University of Göttingen. He was the senior adviser to the HKSAR government on cultural, arts, and civic affairs from 1997 to 2007 under Patrick Ho Chi-ping. After leaving the government, he joined the faculty of the Department of Chinese at Lingnan University. During his tenure as a government adviser, he used his pen name, Chin Wan, to author cultural critiques in major newspapers. He became a leading public intellectual voice supporting the rising conservation movement, providing historical background and recommendations for the activists in their quest to save historic urban buildings and rural landscapes from development projects.

These movements had lacked a clear understanding of their own cultural and political significance, let alone a coherent ideology or program. The local consciousness expressed in these actions was vague and unspoken. Chin Wan's versatile writings gave it voice. In the early 2000s, he used his column in the *Hong Kong Economic Journal* to discuss a wide range of issues related to the movements, from Hong Kong's local histories and folk cultures to social movements' tactics and strategy. Many of these commentaries materialized into a series of best-selling collections.[14] *On the Hong Kong City State* is the first systematic reinterpretation of Hong Kong's history, a critique of Hong Kong's status quo, and an advocation for Hong Kong's opposition movement to adopt a "Hong Kong First" program.

One important starting point of Chin's view is that after the sovereignty handover, Beijing promoted the view that Hong Kong has always depended for survival on the mercy of the PRC, which supplied the colony with essential foodstuffs and water since the 1950s. Hong Kong continued to be economically dependent on

Beijing after 1997. This discourse, according to which Hong Kong's very existence is not possible without China's generosity, is psychological warfare aimed at destroying Hong Kongers' self-confidence and dignity. Chin proposes an alternative historiography proposing that China needed Hong Kong more than Hong Kong needed China during and after the Cold War.

Many scholarly works have confirmed such a view of Hong Kong's history and Hong Kong's economic relations with China.[15] Chinese supply of foodstuffs and water to Hong Kong was nearly the only path through which China could obtain foreign currency during the Cold War, and Hong Kong's purchase of Chinese water was much more expensive than securing water via other means, such as seawater desalination (which small countries like Singapore and Israel have been relying on in recent years). After China opened up for foreign investment, China enjoyed the advantage of investment from more politically reliable and economically less dominating Hong Kong entrepreneurs and did not need to rely on Western transnational corporations as many developing countries did.

According to Chin, Hong Kong was vital to the CCP regime's survival during Mao's autarkic era and the beginning of market reform. The last Soviet leader, Gorbachev, allegedly confessed to Deng Xiaoping during his visit to China in 1989 that the Soviet Union was jealous of China for the existence of Hong Kong, and that Russia's economic reform would have been easier if it had had a Hong Kong equivalent as its gateway to the world economy. Such a special role for Hong Kong persisted beyond 1997.[16]

Though Hong Kong had been a British colony before 1997, the Hong Kong government, in alliance with local British and Chinese capitalists, was not subordinate to London and enjoyed significant autonomy in policy making and implementation. Hong Kong was, therefore, already a semi-autonomous city-state, according to Chin. This is an established view in much academic writing, which illustrates that the Hong Kong government stood firm in defending Hong Kong's interests in London during the colonial period.[17] This view has been sidelined by the Chinese official discourse that emphasizes the repressive and humiliating nature of colonial rule.

Chin's theses that China's economy has been at least as reliant on Hong Kong as Hong Kong was on China, and that Hong Kong was already a city-state autonomous from both the UK and China before 1997, were not new findings. Chin's contribution was to popularize the conclusions of scholarly works by bringing them to the general public. His work unsettled the iron grip of the popular (mis)conceptions that Hong Kong has been one-sidedly reliant on mainland China and that Hong Kong never enjoyed any autonomy before 1997, as promoted by Beijing's propaganda.

Chin found that Beijing had been trying to maintain the city-state character of Hong Kong in 1997–2003, a period when the "One Country, Two Systems" arrangement was honored. But with the failure of Article 23 legislation in the wake of massive protest, Beijing changed its Hong Kong strategy. Whereas Beijing still could not resort to an outright crackdown on the opposition for fear of losing Hong Kong's special function amidst any international backlash, Beijing began to undermine the city-state autonomy of Hong Kong in the name of economic rejuvenation through Hong Kong–mainland China socioeconomic integration.[18]

One key policy under this socioeconomic integration attempt began in 2003, when Beijing turned on the green light for mainland tourists to visit Hong Kong as individuals. Before that, to maintain the social boundary between Hong Kong and mainland China, the Chinese authorities only allowed mainland tourists to visit Hong Kong in authorized groups. The authorities also strictly regulated the size and number of those groups. With the opening of tourism to individuals, the number of mainland visitors to Hong Kong soared. By 2012, the annual count of mainland Chinese visitors reached 35 million, five times the population of Hong Kong's 7 million inhabitants. Such a flood of tourists generated escalating conflict and tension between Hong Kong residents and mainlanders when shops for luxury goods and daily necessities started to prioritize mainland tourists over locals. Many mainland tourists were willing to pay higher prices for a wide range of consumer items, as they were even more expensive on the mainland because of tariffs. One consequence of mainland tourism's rise was that the mom-and-pop shops that served the locals in many neighborhoods disappeared. Tourist-oriented chain stores came to dominate the retail sector. Among the tourists were formula-milk smugglers who swept clean the shelves of groceries and pharmacies amidst the scandal of fake formula milk that would cause severe detriment to infants' development in mainland China. Such smuggling activities created an unheard-of shortage of formula milk in many Hong Kong districts. Birth tourism also rose as many pregnant women traveled to Hong Kong as tourists to give birth and ensure Hong Kong residency for their children. This strained the public hospital system's resources to an extent that even the HKSAR government and Communist news outlet could not deny.[19] According to Chin, the wave of mainland tourists, who were so numerous and so different in their social customs, were seen as threatening the livelihoods of Hong Kong locals.

Other policies that dissolved the Hong Kong–mainland boundary, according to Chin, included the expansion of the investment immigration scheme for mainlanders and rapid land development in the New Territories that catered to the investment and residential needs of wealthy mainland migrants. At the same time, the Liaison Office escalated their efforts in organizing mainland migrants, whom the Chinese government sent at a daily quota of 150 and Hong Kong had to receive without screening, into pro-establishment voting blocks (as we discussed in Chapter 6).

Between 1997 and 2012, new mainland migrants who moved to Hong Kong constituted about 10 percent of Hong Kong's total population. A former CCP affiliate in Hong Kong, Ching Cheong, wrote that the Chinese authorities have been using this migration scheme to send state agents and CCP cadres into different strata of Hong Kong's society.[20] Democratic leader Martin Lee compared such a migration process to the massive Han migration into Tibet that would eventually turn the locals into a minority group. He called it "Tibetization of Hong Kong."[21] Donald Tsang, the chief executive of Hong Kong from 2005 to 2012, and a think tank organization with close ties to him, have explicitly argued that Hong Kong needed a "population blood transfusion," replacing lowly educated and low-income locals with highly educated and high-income mainland migrants.[22]

Chin claimed that the influx of mainland tourists and migrants was the largest threat to the local institutions and social customs of Hong Kong. He asserted that the migrants should be called colonizers, as most of them were sent by the Chinese government rather than admitted by the Hong Kong authorities. He supported a redistributive policy that restricted the power of land developers and business monopolies, and advocated for the enhancement of social welfare for the citizens of Hong Kong. But he added that such policies would be meaningless and ineffective as long as Hong Kong does not maintain a clear boundary as a political community. The unlimited flow of mainland settlers, with an unscreened daily quota of 150; the unchecked inroad of Chinese capital into Hong Kong; and the bottomless demand for public health care resources and daily necessities from mainland tourists aggravated social inequality and crippled the supply of public and consumer goods in Hong Kong, warned Chin.

Chin proposed that the Hong Kong government take back the authority to screen incoming migrants from mainland China, just as it did for migrants from all other countries and as all other governments in the world do. The government should restrict the number of incoming mainland tourists, too. But to Chin's disappointment, the Hong Kong opposition movement never took these issues seriously. On the contrary, they didn't shy away from criticizing complaints about mainland tourists and migrants as "racist," "xenophobic," and "nostalgic."[23] Chin asserts that, on the contrary, the local population's sentiments toward these issues were closer to the backlash against Han settler colonization in Tibet and Xinjiang than to anti-immigrant politics in Western countries.[24]

Chin attributes the opposition's silence on the rapid dissolution of the Hong Kong–mainland border to its Chinese nationalist ideology. Since its inception, the democrats in Hong Kong have dreamed of a liberal and democratic China. Many opposition leaders started their political careers by protesting British colonial rule and supporting China's sovereignty over Hong Kong. To them, struggling for a democratic and strong China was the priority, and the fight for democracy in Hong Kong was subordinated to this larger call. Their insensitivity to the difference between Hong Kong locals and mainland Chinese made them, advertently or not, welcome the dissolution of the social and economic boundaries between Hong Kong and mainland China.[25]

This prioritization of China's liberalization and democratization over Hong Kong's was reflected not only in the democrats' framing of the Hong Kong democratic movement as part of the

Chinese democratic movement, but also in their support of closer integration between Hong Kong and mainland China. In reaction to this prioritization, Chin put forward the most controversial thesis in his book: democratization in China was hopeless. To him, if democratization finally came to China, it would only bring ultra-nationalist populism or even fascism.[26] Such a provocative view was premised on the understanding that after more than sixty years of Communist rule, in addition to more than three decades of unfettered capitalist development, both the great and small traditions of China that used to hold society together and foster trust among its people had been annihilated. Now, only the heavy-handed control of the party-state held China together. Should that control disappear, then an atomized society, lacking viable social fabric and healthy civic institutions, extreme right-wing populism, or even outright fascism would be more likely to rise from the ashes of the fallen Communist state.

Chin, therefore, advocated "Hong Kong First" and "Hong Kong–China segmentation" instead of the "China First" and "China–Hong Kong integration" stance that was so central to the Hong Kong democratic movement. To Chin, the mainstream democrats' view that Hong Kong's democratic movement was but a subordinate part of the larger Chinese democratic movement was toxic. This view would only lead to the erosion of Hong Kong people's will to fight the CCP, as well as the erosion of their passive and unrealistic hope for progressive change in China. This explains the mainstream democrats' distaste for local militant struggles and their preference for meek civil disobedience. To Chin, the democratic movement of Hong Kong needed to be more militant and more focused on the fight for more social and political separation between Hong Kong and mainland China.

Chin asserted that China's great and small traditions, though destroyed under decades of Communist rule, had been well preserved in Hong Kong, where such traditions were merged with modern institutions and values originating from the European Enlightenment. It follows that defending Hong Kong's pre-existing customs and institutions, and enhancing Hong Kong's democracy and autonomy, are a way to preserve Chinese traditions that have been lost in mainland China. In Chin's grand vision, Hong Kong would need to rebuild its city-state character and reconsolidate its border with mainland China. After that, Hong Kong could ally with other city-states or city-state-like units within the greater cultural Chinese world, like Taiwan and any other regions that break away from China in the future, to form a new Chinese Federation. This would be an important step toward the rejuvenation of cultural China that has been destroyed by Communist rule.[27]

The Dawn of Localist Politics

While Chin's ideas were deemed extremist when his *On the Hong Kong City State* was first published in 2011, they inspired a new generation of activists who were born after Tiananmen and felt distant from the Chinese democratic movement. The book directly inspired the rise of the "Liberate" (*gwong fuk*) protests, in which self-proclaimed localists organized rallies and protests against mainland Chinese tourists and smugglers. These actions often invoked brawls between localist protesters and mainland smugglers, retail owners specialized in the mainland tourist business, and pro-establishment groups. Resembling the subsistence-rights contentions like food riots in preindustrial China and Europe,[28] these "Liberate" protests often invited police intervention and escalated into larger confrontation with the authorities.[29] Many activists of these "Liberate" protests later became the core Mongkok occupiers during the Occupy movement in 2014, as I shall turn to in a moment. Some of them further evolved into the pro-independence group Hong Kong Indigenous, which invented the "Liberate Hong Kong, revolution of our times" slogan that dominated the 2019 anti-extradition movement. Chin's idea of pursuing cultural segmentation between Hong Kong and mainland China also helped inspire the movement against the Moral and National Education Curriculum in 2012, spearheaded by high-school student activists. Many activists and leaders of Scholarism, the student organization behind the movement, later admitted that Chin's ideas influenced them.[30] Chin's thesis of Hong Kong as a city-state facilitated the split and rapid fall of the League of Social Democrats, which splintered into rival political groups, some of which became keen supporters of Chin, while others feverishly opposed his ideas.

Despite the influence of *On the Hong Kong City State*, Chin himself moved toward an ever more enigmatic position of seeing Hong Kong as a bastion of a Chinese spiritual renaissance by drawing on Daoist and Buddhist mysticism. Shifting to emphasizing Hong Kong's cultural linkage to pre-Communist China, he later tried to start a Han clothing cult after the Han clothing movement in mainland China.[31] He even organized imperial rituals paying tribute to the thirteenth-century Song emperor who stayed in the Hong Kong region before committing suicide nearby, claiming to rebuild Hong Kong's central role in an orthodox cultural China.

The influence of *On the Hong Kong City State*, nevertheless, was soon overshadowed by more radical thoughts. The most significant new development was the rise of Hong Kong nationalism and separatism as advocated by the University of Hong Kong's student union magazine *Undergrad* in 2014. While Chin advocated an autonomous Hong Kong under a Chinese Federation, the special feaure of the *Undergrad*, entitled "Hong Kong Nation, Self-Determination of Destiny," followed the theory of Taiwan nationalism and asserted that the only path toward freedom in Hong Kong was to build an independent Hong Kong nation-state separate from China.[32]

Drawing heavily on Benedict Anderson's notion of the nation-state as an imagined community with utopian and liberational potential,[33] the student radicals asserted that Hong Kong could be constructed from the ground up through shared experiences of national struggle and the exercise of the right to self-determination among the people. Such construction did not need to resort to linkage to a bygone cultural China, as suggested by Chin. Regardless of its feasibility, this separatist idea has gained ground among the younger generation in Hong Kong ever since the publication of the special issue. Such slogans as "Hong Kong independence," "China, get out of Hong Kong," "Hong Kong is not China," and "Hong Kong self-determination" frequently appeared in the seventy-nine-day Occupy movement in 2014 and its aftermath.[34]

Recurrent opinion surveys documented this rising localist consciousness. One of the most credible surveys was the one conducted by the University of Hong Kong's public-opinion program, which became the independent Hong Kong Public Opinion Research Institute in 2019. The institute regularly conducts opinion surveys on the identity of Hong Kong people. One question asks respondents whether they identify themselves as Chinese or as Hong Kongers.

The relative prevalence of the two has changed over the years. Self-identification as Chinese peaked in 2008, the year of the Beijing Olympics, and the Hong Kong identity reached its bottom in the same year. But the percentage of respondents identifying themselves as Hong Kongers has kept rising, while those identifying themselves as Chinese has kept falling. By December 2019, 55 percent of respondents identified themselves solely as Hong Kongers, compared to 10.9 percent identifying themselves as Chinese, as seen in Figure 8.1.

This contrast was more prominent among younger respondents. In the 18–29 age group, Hong Konger versus Chinese identity was at a staggering 81.8 versus 1.8 percent in December 2019.[35] Another public-opinion poll, conducted in the summer of 2016, shows that 17 percent of Hong Kong residents supported Hong Kong independence. For the 15–24 age group, nearly 40 percent supported Hong Kong independence, in contrast to 26 percent opposing it.[36] This number is striking, given the perceived infeasibility of independence and the fact

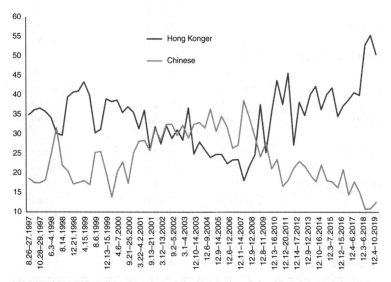

Figure 8.1 Respondents identifying themselves as Hong Kongers versus Chinese, 1998–2020
Source: Hong Kong Public Opinion Research Institute, People's Ethnic Identity Survey (Random Sample ~1,000)

that Hong Kong independence was a taboo subject that even the radical democrats were reluctant to talk about.

Analysis of voters' preferences in the 2016 LegCo election reveals that candidates with localist orientations were particularly popular among the unpropertied and younger voters. Propertied, older voters are more attracted to establishment candidates.[37] The result of the analysis is shown in Table 8.1.

This illustrates how the rise of localist politics cut across class politics and generational conflicts in Hong Kong. It also shows how the distributive effects of the mainlandization of the Hong Kong

Table 8.1 *Correlates of political identification in a voter survey conducted in 2016*

	Favor traditional democrats	Favor establishment	Favor localist
Homeowner	−0.092	0.430[*]	−0.635[***]
	(0.214)	(0.254)	(0.235)
Income	0.001	−0.024	0.067
	(0.063)	(0.071)	(0.068)
Young (age ≤ 30)	0.014	−0.614[***]	0.777[***]
	(0.181)	(0.222)	(0.206)
Female	−0.325	−0.436[*]	−0.019
	(0.209)	(0.229)	(0.227)
Married	−0.506[**]	0.984	−0.266
	(0.208)	(0.252)	(0.246)
Education	0.016	−0.032	0.046
	(0.042)	(0.046)	(0.046)
Hong Kong-born	0.669[*]	−0.612[*]	0.020
	(0.371)	(0.365)	(0.340)
Constant	4.717[***]	4.483[***]	3.810[***]
	(0.520)	(0.530)	(0.508)
No. of observations	1677	1689	1660
R squared	0.02	0.08	0.05

Estimation strategy is ordinary least squares. Standard errors are in parentheses. * $p < 0.1$, ** $p < 0.05$, *** $p < 0.01$.
Source: Wong and Wan 2018

economy shaped politics. As we saw in the last chapter, the influx of Chinese capital and both professional and unskilled migrants in Hong Kong drove up housing prices, rent, and the cost of living while keeping wages stagnant. Therefore the mainlandization of the economy drove a wedge between its beneficiaries (the older propertied class) and its victims (unpropertied youngsters), pushing the latter to localist politics opposing Hong Kong–mainland integration.

The class politics behind the radicalization of the democratic movement amidst rising inequality in the 2000s made Hong Kong's business elite, above all real-estate developers, and the FC system protecting their interests the target of radical social movements, as we saw in the last chapter. When the mainlandization of the business elite in Hong Kong became more apparent in the 2010s, localists who resented the Hong Kong–China integration became ever more dominant in the democratic and social movements. These were the social and ideational forces underlying Hong Kongers' confrontation with Beijing from the Occupy movement in 2014 to the 2016 Fishball Uprising and the 2019 anti-extradition protest.

The Occupy Movement

Since Beijing dictated in 2007 that the earliest date for universal suffrage would be 2017 for the election of the chief executive and 2020 for the LegCo, the democrats had been readying for the political battle over electoral reform in 2017–2020. They expected that Beijing was not likely to offer Hong Kong genuine universal suffrage in elections for the chief executive, and just how much Beijing would allow Hong Kong's citizens to freely elect their leader hinged on the nomination process of the candidates for chief executive.

As the universal-suffrage method adopted for the 2017–2020 elections would be seen as the ultimate form of Hong Kong's political system designated in the Sino-British Joint Declaration and the Basic Law, the opposition had been clear from the outset that they would not accept any symbolic universal suffrage. They were aware that if they accepted such a proposal, the international community would suppose that Beijing had met its obligation in fulfilling the promise of universal suffrage to Hong Kong. In such a case, the hope for genuine democracy in Hong Kong would be gone forever. The democrats feared that Beijing would maintain full control of the nomination process so that only candidates absolutely loyal to Beijing would have the chance to run in the election. It would be just like many village elections in mainland China, where the CCP organization nominated candidates for villages to vote for.[38]

The democratic movement in Hong Kong was not without victories. The 2003 mass protest successfully fought off the Article 23 antisubversion legislation. The 2010 referendum movement successfully pressured Beijing to accept moderate proposals to gradually increase democratic representation in the LegCo election in 2012. The student-led movement against the National Education Curriculum in 2012 managed to force the government to shelve the program. Encouraged by these wins, the democrats started in 2013 to contemplate mobilizing the city to put maximum pressure on Beijing to allow an electoral reform proposal that was as close to genuine universal suffrage as possible.

In January 2013, pro-democrat legal scholar Benny Tai Yiu-ting, an associate professor at the School of Law at the University of Hong Kong, floated the idea of "Occupy Central" to pressure the authorities when the discussion about electoral reform was set to start in 2014. The idea was to mobilize democratic activists and leaders, and their supporters, to occupy the busiest areas in the central business district of Hong Kong and threaten to paralyze the city's financial and administrative heart. As an act of civil disobedience, the occupation itself and the mass arrests that would follow would generate wide international attention, just like Occupy Wall Street did in the US in 2011.

After Tai coined this idea, he started to contact and deliberate with opposition and social-movement leaders to put the plan into practice. Pro-democratic media and online platforms debated the idea enthusiastically. The plan for an occupation movement gained traction instantly, and most democratic and social leaders endorsed the idea and pledged participation when the occupation occurred. An Occupy Central with Love and Peace Secretariat was established in April. The secretariat hosted deliberation days to discuss the tactics and strategy of the movement. It hosted training sessions to prepare the activists for confrontation with the police. Fund-raising for the movement started. Leaders involved in the prolonged deliberation later admitted that they expected that merely talking about an upcoming occupation of Hong Kong's financial and administrative centers would create enough pressure for the Hong Kong government and Beijing to come to the negotiation table, just like the referendum movement in 2010 brought Beijing into negotiation with the Democratic Party. One of the scholars who endorsed the Occupy idea early on and became the core leader of the movement, Chan Kin-man, an associate professor of sociology at the Chinese University of Hong Kong, was also a key participant of the Democratic Party's negotiation with Beijing concerning the 2010 political reform.[39]

In the meantime, the Democratic Party and other opposition parties formed an "Alliance for Genuine Universal Suffrage." They formulated a political reform proposal according to which the election of the chief executive in 2017 and beyond would include candidates nominated by voters and political parties. The Hong Kong Federation of Students (HKFS) and Scholarism jointly put forward a more radical proposal according to which only candidates nominated by voters and LegCo councilors could run for election as chief executive. The Occupy Central Secretariat put these two proposals to an unofficial referendum on June 22, 2014, in which 790,000 voters participated. The alliance's proposal won by a small majority.[40]

It turned out that the discussion and the threat of an occupation did not suffice to pressure Beijing to negotiate with the democrats. In response to the Occupy Central plan, Beijing's propaganda machine attacked the movement as a sinister plot to blackmail Beijing and attempt to move Hong Kong toward independence. Beijing also accused foreign powers of being behind the plan. The movement was called a "Color Revolution," like those in the former Soviet republics in the early 2000s, when the US allegedly masterminded the opposition movements to topple Moscow-friendly governments.[41]

While Beijing was stepping up its attack on the Occupy Central movement and showing no sign of negotiating with the democrats, the planning for Occupy Central was well underway in the spring and early summer of 2014. On June 10, Beijing issued the "One Country Two Systems" White Paper discussed in Chapter 6. The White Paper reinstated the hard-line position that One Country was more central than Two Systems, and that all the rights and autonomy enjoyed by the HKSAR government and residents of Hong Kong were not pre-existing but were granted by Beijing. Such a hard-line position was not new, but it had hitherto only circulated in unofficial and scholarly publications. The White Paper, with Jiang Shigong as one of the key authors, enshrined such a hard-line view as the foundation of Beijing's official Hong Kong policy.

The White Paper presaged a final denial of genuine universal suffrage in Hong Kong. This only helped fuel the preparations of the Occupy movement. The HKFS and Scholarism started planning for a class boycott in universities and high schools at the beginning of the fall semester. Over the summer of 2014, a showdown between Beijing and the opposition in Hong Kong was brewing. On August 31, the National People's Congress Standing Committee (NPCSC) issued an interpretation of the Basic Law that set out the 2017–2020 universal-suffrage constraint. Concerning universal suffrage for the 2017 chief executive election, it dictated that:

> When the selection of the Chief Executive of the Hong Kong Special Administrative Region is implemented by the method of universal suffrage:
>
> (1) A broadly representative nominating committee shall be formed. The provisions for the number of members, composition and formation method of the nominating committee shall be made in accordance with the number of members, composition and formation method of the Election Committee for the Fourth Chief Executive.
>
> (2) The nominating committee shall nominate two to three candidates for the office of chief executive in accordance with democratic procedures. Each candidate must have the endorsement of more than half of all the members of the nominating committee.
>
> (3) All eligible electors of the Hong Kong Special Administrative Region have the right to vote in the election of the chief executive and elect one of the candidates for the office of chief executive in accordance with law.
>
> (4) The chief executive-elect, after being selected through universal suffrage, will have to be appointed by the Central People's Government.[42]

As such, the existing elitist and exclusionary Election Committee, which elected the chief executive every five years, would effectively morph into a nomination committee for the election of the chief executive. Each candidate for election as chief executive would need to have the votes of more than half of the committee members. As the future nomination committee would mostly be populated by Beijing loyalists and its tycoon allies, just as the Election Committee has been, this decision by the NPCSC showed that Beijing left no room for any opposition candidates to enter the election of the chief executive.

The democrats saw the August 31 decision as a death sentence to genuine universal suffrage in the election of the chief executive. This triggered an uproar. The students initiated a five-day class boycott and organized a large rally on the campus of the Chinese University of Hong Kong on September 22. After the class boycott ended on September 26, students gathered in front of the government headquarters in Admiralty near Central. As the rally continued to grow, an occupation of the Civic Square in front of the government's headquarters unfolded. Benny Tai declared in the early morning of September 28 that Occupy Central had started. After sunrise, riot police were dispatched to disperse the rallying crowd with tear gas. The television images of riot police battling protesters drew more people to the streets, and the crowd soon spilled over onto the main roads near the government building complex. A sit-in started and disrupted traffic. Protesters continued to swamp the streets in many other areas that night, initiating the Occupy Mongkok, the central commercial district of Kowloon, and a few other commercially central places. It opened the door to the seventy-nine-day occupation.[43]

Once Occupy started in a way very different from what Tai had envisioned, the movement took on a life of its own. It evolved beyond the planning and control of the original leaders, including Benny Tai.[44] As many protesters spontaneously protected themselves from police tear gas and pepper spray with umbrellas, journalists started to call the movement the Umbrella Revolution or Umbrella Movement. Very soon, Occupy consolidated into two main locations, one in Admiralty near the government headquarters and the other in Mongkok. While the moderate democrats, the original Occupy leaders, the HKFS, and Scholarism were influential in Admiralty's Occupy site, the Mongkok site was soon dominated by the more militant localists, including Chin Wan, his allies and followers, and many "Liberate" movement activists.

Alex Chow Yong-kang, the leader of the HKFS and central in leading the Occupy movement in Admiralty, later recollected the differences between Admiralty and Mongkok. He described the "urban commons" emerging in Admiralty, where the plurality of artistic expressions and intellectual deliberations flowered under the co-ordination of the main stage run by moderate democrats and student leaders. Chow also delineated the more militant and localist Mongkok, where protesters developed fighting tactics in street battles over the seventy-nine days of routine skirmishes with pro-establishment thugs and the police force. Chow correctly predicted that the "emergence of these two approaches to social change in Hong Kong ... would outlive the Umbrella Movement."[45] The resurgence and amalgamation of these two approaches in the 2019 uprising vindicate Chow's prediction.

Ethnographic and survey research of the protesters at the two sites found that participants in Mongkok and Admiralty were not very different in socioeconomic and demographic backgrounds. Their difference lay mainly in political and action orientation. Mongkok protesters transgressed many pre-existing protest norms in Hong Kong, such as the insistence on nonviolent civil disobedience. They elevated militancy, the principles of self-organizing and violent self-defense, to new levels of legitimacy.[46] These transgressions traveled well beyond 2014 Occupy. For example, the hit-and-run tactics that the occupiers developed to deal with police illuminate the well-known militant and leaderless "be water" guerrilla protest in the 2019 uprising.[47]

Throughout the Occupy movement, the leaders in control of the Admiralty Occupy zone constantly tried to end the occupation early for fear of Tiananmen-style bloodshed. They envisioned a mass arrest of peaceful activists as the endgame of the civil-disobedience movement. Mongkok occupiers, however, showed no consideration of an endgame, as they constantly battled waves of attacks by police and pro-establishment thugs through the fall.[48] This created a conflictual coexistence of the Admiralty and Mongkok occupations. So long as the Mongkok occupiers fought on and effectively defended their territory, the leaders in Admiralty did not end their more peaceful occupation for fear that it would hand the leadership of the whole movement to the Mongkok militants. Leaders from Admiralty attempted to establish leadership in the Mongkok site, but were constantly repelled by the militants. After Mongkok's occupation was worn out and cleared by an elite police unit in a bloody battle on November 25–7, the Admiralty occupiers staged a sit-in of notable activists and pro-democrat celebrities who were cleared by police without any struggle. All occupation ended on December 11, 2014.[49]

The Militants, the Separatists, and Hong Kong Self-Determination

After the occupation ended, activists of all stripes started to reorient their energy in preparation for the 2016 LegCo election, hoping that the energy generated by the Occupy movement would lead to a larger electoral victory of the democrats. While the localist Hong Kong consciousness expressed in Occupy was not dominant, it continued to rise and radicalize into a separatist ideology among youngsters, who felt frustrated by the futile end of the Occupy protests.[50] As we saw earlier, a poll conducted on the eve of the 2016 LegCo election in September by the Chinese University of Hong Kong School of Journalism and Communication found that 17 percent of Hong Kongers supported Hong Kong independence. Moreover, in the 15–24 age group, respondents "for" Hong Kong independence constituted 40 percent vis-à-vis 26 percent opposed. Given that Hong Kong independence is widely perceived as nearly impossible, such a high percentage of support is surprising.

The rising support for a separatist ideology among youngsters led to the rise of explicitly pro-separatist groups like Hong Kong Indigenous, formed in 2015. Hong Kong Indigenous was formed mainly of young, new political activists who became active through participating in Occupy. After the end of Occupy, this group carried on the "Liberate" protests and organized a series of rallies to interfere with smuggling activities by mainland tourists in neighborhoods near the Hong Kong–mainland border.[51]

On the night of February 8, 2016, the group set out to protect the Lunar New Year street hawkers (street food vendors) in

Mongkok, who faced harassment and prosecution by government sanitation officers and the police. While Hong Kong Indigenous saw the street hawkers as a representation of Hong Kong's local culture and the resilience of lower-income Hong Kongers, the involvement of veteran Occupy protesters in this action in Mongkok was seen as a provocation from the police standpoint. Riot police arrived and the confrontation soon escalated into violent conflict. Protesters from Hong Kong Indigenous defended themselves with homemade shields, construction workers' safety helmets, eye goggles, face masks, and other protective gear inherited from the Occupy street battles. They charged toward the police line and started to throw bricks dug up from the ground into the crowd of police. They even set up fire barricades on the street. The battle continued until sunrise on February 9, with nearly 100 protesters and police wounded and more than sixty protesters arrested. This episode, commonly known as the Fishball Revolution or Fishball Uprising, named after the most popular street food sold by the hawkers that night, was the most confrontational protest that Hong Kong had seen since the 1966–1967 unrest. In retrospect, it was a prelude to what was to come in 2019.[52]

The activists and leaders of the Fishball Uprising were seen as heroes by many young radicals. One of its leaders, Edward Leung Tin-kei, was running for a by-election for a suddenly vacant seat in the LegCo in March. Leung was a mainland Chinese immigrant who had settled in Hong Kong as a young child. He was an athletic and popular but apolitical student at the University of Hong Kong, majoring in philosophy. His first participation in politics was joining Occupy with his classmates. He admitted later that he was inspired by Chin Wan's *On the Hong Kong City State*, and then further radicalized under the influence of the *On the Hong Kong Nation* special issue of the Hong Kong University student magazine *Undergrad*. By the time he joined Hong Kong Indigenous in 2015, he had become an advocate of Hong Kong independence and militant direct action, quickly rising to be one of the leaders of the organization.[53]

He did not win the by-election, but gathered 66,000 votes, or 15 percent of the vote, in a crowded field of seven candidates. This number could comfortably have got him elected in the regular LegCo election in September that year. The result of that by-election showed that the radical localists were popular among young voters. Having a significant number of them elected into the LegCo was suddenly plausible. More significantly, the main slogan of Leung's by-election campaign, "Liberate Hong Kong, the revolution of our times," became a rallying cry of the localists in the years to come. It became the most popular slogan chanted in the anti-extradition movement in 2019.

Encouraged by the results of the by-election, it became clear that dozens of radical young localists openly advocating Hong Kong independence, including Leung himself, would run for the LegCo election. To prevent their victories, the Hong Kong authorities disqualified Leung and a slate of localist candidates from the LegCo election in August, citing their support of Hong Kong independence as a violation of the Basic Law. Edward Leung then threw his support behind a number of less well-known activists, who were allies of the Hong Kong Indigenous, to run as surrogates. As their surrogates were mostly low-profile personalities having no track record of advocating Hong Kong's independence, they managed to get on the ballot without disqualification.[54]

Besides the radical localists, several prominent leaders in the Occupy Movement, including former leaders of HKFS and Scholarism, coalesced to form a new political party, Demosisto. They ran in the election on a self-determination platform. They did not support Hong Kong's independence, but they advocated that the future status of Hong Kong after 2047 and the political system of Hong Kong had to be decided through a referendum under the principle of self-determination.[55]

The election result showed that the basic 60–40 percent split of voters between the democrats and the establishment did not change much. Under the LegCo structure that divided the seventy seats into thirty-five directly elected seats and thirty-five others elected in FCs easily manipulated by Beijing, the opposition's seats increased incrementally from twenty-seven to twenty-nine, still falling far short of gaining the majority. But the election also showed that the political landscape in Hong Kong had shifted in the form of rising radicalism in both the opposition camp and the pro-establishment camp. There were the retirements or election losses of some long-term legislators on both sides. Many younger, more confrontational candidates from both camps won.

In the opposition camp, six successful localist candidates departed from the opposition's tradition of never questioning Chinese sovereignty over Hong Kong. Their rise is attributable to the Occupy movement and the Fishball Uprising.[56] Among the six, three support the right to self-determination of Hong Kong's people. However, they remain elusive about how self-determination can be achieved and reluctant to express their support of the independence option. The other three elected localists advocated formal independence of Hong Kong or asserted the de facto independence of Hong Kong under the Basic Law (two were candidates endorsed by Edward Leung). However, they have been careful not to openly advocate independence in their campaigns for fear of disqualification by the government. Together with their like-minded comrades who failed to win seats, all localists mustered about 19 percent of total votes in the direct election.[57]

In the election, the establishment camp saw the rise of a group of hard-line conservative professionals who were believed to be cultivated and favored by the Liaison Office. Over the years, Beijing has been relying on the "old patriots," who originated from the local underground CCP under British rule, and local business magnates to govern Hong Kong in the form of indirect rule. But ever since the competition between Leung Chun-ying and Henry Tang and the winning of the former in the 2012 election of the chief executive, the cleavage between Beijing's business allies and Chief Executive Leung Chun-ying, as well as the Liaison Office allegedly behind him, has been growing. Establishment business and political leader James Tien and senior "old Patriot" Jasper Tsang Yok-sing openly and repeatedly criticized Leung Chun-ying's hard-line approach. Many saw this cleavage as an extension of the rivalry between Hong Kong and mainland China business elites. In the 2016 LegCo election, six new underlings of the Liaison Office won seats with a 100 percent success rate, in some cases at the expense of Beijing's old business allies, who lost or were forced to quit under repeated intimidation before the election by some invisible hands.[58]

The election results showcased that the establishment's monopoly in the semi-democratic legislature remains unchanged. The rising hard-liners and radicals from the establishment and opposition camps were set to clash in the legislative chamber and beyond. In October, when the elected LegCo members were sworn in, some of the democrats, including both veteran LegCo democrats and the new localists, added political slogans to the oath. The two surrogate candidates supported by Edward Leung even chanted

"Hong Kong is not China" and added "Hong Kong nation" to the oath.[59] This performance of opposition in the swearing-in ceremony had been a routine over the years. But in early November, the NPCSC reinterpreted the Basic Law and dictated that any legislators who disrespect the swearing-in process would be in violation of the Basic Law and could be disqualified. The HKSAR government took action swiftly and eventually disqualified six elected legislators. Among them, five happened to be pro-independence or pro-self-determination candidates.[60] This move is widely seen as showing Beijing's determination to root out the rise of localists and radicals at the expense of the election's integrity. It also shows that the new generation's institutional route to politics is blocked.

Following the 2014 Occupy movement and the 2016 election, the draconian crackdown on Hong Kong's civil society accelerated. It included the prosecution and imprisonment of Occupy leaders and activists, as well as the Fishball leaders and activists. Edward Leung was sentenced to six years in prison for his leadership role in the Fishball conflicts.[61] At the same time, Chinese security personnel allegedly kidnapped several booksellers who published books deemed embarrassing to Beijing. They were kidnapped in Hong Kong or a third country (Thailand) and transferred to mainland China in late 2015.[62] The HKSAR government expelled a senior foreign journalist moderating a forum at the Foreign Correspondents' Club featuring a pro-independence speaker.[63] These attest to Beijing's increasingly hard-line policy over Hong Kong.

The attempt to pass the extradition bill in 2019 was just a further step in this direction. What Beijing, and nearly everyone in the world, did not anticipate was the explosion of sustained militant resistance that successfully killed the bill, but which led to Beijing's imposition of the National Security Law on Hong Kong. As it turned out, the post-Occupy crackdown did not stifle Hong Kong civil society's discontent or protest capability. On the contrary, the crackdown fueled the anger and determination of the younger generation of Hong Kongers who came of age during the Occupy movement. Edward Leung, the separatist, deemed the first political prisoner facing a heavy sentence in Hong Kong, became the spiritual leader of angry, young localists in 2019.[64] Their rage, in conjunction with the increasingly visible dissent in Hong Kong's business elite circles, eventually precipitated the conflict and crisis of 2019 and beyond.

9 CONCLUSION
Endgame or New Beginning?

We have seen in the previous chapters that Hong Kong has never been a tranquil place. Its settlers have never been submissive communities since the major settlements developed in the region centuries ago. Empires or nation-states attempting to absorb the territory, subjugate its communities, and assimilate its population always faced a dilemma between establishing full political control at the expense of its economic function and maintaining its utility by tolerating its autonomy.

As we saw in Chapter 2, Hong Kong's location at the southern periphery of a continental empire and the eastern end of a maritime commercial world centered in the West has placed it at the interstices of empires. Its existence in this global liminal space has been marked by its precarity, creativity, and recalcitrance. The mix of communities originating from the core of different empires created a hybrid and contentious space, difficult to reach and control by the state. We revisited the uprising of fishers and salt producers in 1197 against the Song empire; the local gentry's support of the Ming loyalists in Taiwan against the Qing empire in the mid-seventeenth century; wars between old and new agrarian settlers in the nineteenth century; the waves of anti-British uprisings in the twentieth century; and the opposition movements that sought democracy, autonomy, and social justice under the late colonial and Communist regimes. This long history of resistance shows that Hong Kong's transformation from an agrarian to an industrial–commercial–financial center does not alter its geohistorical character as a vibrant economic hub at the edge of empires. This character underlines Hong Kong's long-term economic prosperity as much as its unrest through the ages. Hong Kong is just like a fertile, productive, and earthquake-prone land which sits on the fault lines between tectonic plates.

This understanding of Hong Kong's geohistoric legacies helps us make sense of the city's post-handover development as the clashing of large geopolitical and geo-economic forces at the turn of the twenty-first century. In Chapter 3, we saw how the tension rose between Beijing's urge to integrate China into the global economy and the party-state's imperative to maintain absolute control of its economy by delaying financial liberalization after China's accession to the WTO in 2001. Beijing's remedy to this tension was perpetuating Hong Kong's role as China's offshore financial center beyond the sovereignty handover. To sustain Hong Kong's independent judicial and financial system, which is so indispensable to its financial centrality, Beijing needed the international community to certify Hong Kong's autonomous status and renew the many special trading privileges extended to Hong Kong in colonial times. This led to Beijing's tolerance of Hong Kong's freedom and the international community's continuous involvement in Hong Kong after 1997.

The Hong Kong solution to China's economic dilemma created a new challenge for Beijing's governance of Hong Kong. Hong Kong's function as China's offshore financial center and China's global rise as a capitalist powerhouse led to the influx of politically well-connected Chinese business elites into Hong Kong. I showed in Chapter 3 that these elites used Hong Kong as a platform to raise global capital or as a springboard to seek investment opportunities abroad. This mainlandization of Hong Kong's business monopoly accelerated after 2010, when Chinese companies were ever more eager to export their excess capacity and monetary wealth overseas using China's monetary stimulus, and when China's economic rebound following the 2008 global financial crisis faltered. In Chapter 4, we traced how the rising political influence of the mainland Chinese elites led to new conflict between these elites and the local business elites, who had been Beijing's allies in governing Hong Kong. The rise of mainland corporations at the expense of the US and other foreign interests in the financial market changed foreign powers' calculation in continuing to recognize Hong Kong's autonomous status and the corresponding trade privileges. This created a new dilemma for Beijing between the expansion of

Beijing's direct control of Hong Kong and the imperative of maintaining Hong Kong's internationally recognized autonomy by restraining such control.

Chapter 5 showed that Beijing always saw Hong Kong in light of the historical precedents of absorbing other pre-existing states in its frontier regions, like Tibet. Beijing's official scholars have grown increasingly outspoken in using the empire's language to advocate the urgency of establishing direct rule and cultural assimilation in Hong Kong after 1997. They saw "One Country, Two Systems" as no more than a transient arrangement to buy time for the final and full absorption of Hong Kong into China, just like Beijing did to Tibet after 1959. Many Chinese official texts on the Hong Kong question pointed to the parallel between its political imperative in Hong Kong and the history of assimilating other ethnic frontiers from the old Chinese empire to the PRC.

The political urge to establish direct rule and cultural assimilation in Hong Kong, as shown in Chapter 6, led Beijing to tighten the screw on all aspects of Hong Kong politics and society after 2003. Though the practical need of maintaining Hong Kong's global financial centrality restrained the expansion of Beijing's direct rule, Beijing's increasing anxiety about losing Hong Kong urged it into taking increasingly bold steps of imposing full control, even at the risk of jeopardizing the international recognition of Hong Kong's autonomy. These steps include the increasingly active role of the Central Government Liaison Office in Hong Kong's politics and society. The attempted introduction of an extradition bill resulted precisely from this imperial instinct. It invoked an unprecedently large-scale conflict between Beijing and the majority of the Hong Kong population in 2019.

The explosion of militant protests in 2019 did not come out of nowhere. We saw in Chapter 7 that it was rooted in a long evolution of opposition movements. These movements originated in colonial times and adapted to the changing political context of the territory after 1997. In the late colonial period and the early years of Beijing's rule, Beijing was restrained from direct political intervention. The democratic and social movements favored a nonconfrontational approach that sought compromise and dialogue with Beijing. But as Beijing became more aggressive in exerting direct rule in Hong Kong, polarization between the disenfranchised propertyless class and the business elite (Beijing's governing allies) intensified, leading to the emergence of the more radical, confrontational wing of the social and democratic movements. The radical activists sought a rapid and fundamental undoing of Hong Kong's business monopoly and the oligarchic political system that protected their privileges.

Chapter 8 showed that the radicalization of the opposition movement after 1997 was evidenced not only in the tactics or immediate demands, but also in the manifestation of a Hong Kong identity as a new political consciousness. When class polarization combined with the mainlandization of business monopolies, the confrontational wing of the social and democratic movements witnessed the growth of an increasingly explicit localist consciousness. Their demand for greater autonomy under the Chinese nation-state rapidly mutated into more explicit demands for self-determination or even independence.

While the older generation's opposition leaders would not see 2047 in their lifetimes, the new generation of Hong Kongers, who came of age after the sovereignty handover, was well aware of the imminent formal expiration of "One Country, Two Systems." They saw it as a new peril to already diminishing freedom in Hong Kong. They also saw it as a new opportunity to reimagine and renegotiate the future status of Hong Kong beyond 2047. To them, Hong Kong's democratic movement was not part of the pursuit of a democratic China, but a quest for larger institutional and cultural separation between China and Hong Kong. This autonomist or separatist turn of the opposition heightened Beijing's anxiety that Hong Kong was following Taiwan's footsteps on a path toward entrenched separatist politics. This localist consciousness manifested itself fully in the 2019 unrest. The anxiety pushed Beijing to attempt to muffle these voices once and for all by imposing the National Security Law on Hong Kong in July 2020, effectively bringing an end to "One Country, Two Systems" twenty-seven years before its time.

The Early Arrival of 2047

When the anti-extradition-bill protest of 2019 exploded and grew more confrontational, it was quite obvious that Beijing had resorted to the old playbook to deal with it. The playbook offered an immediate soft retreat to let the protest fizzle out, then waiting for the public opinion to turn against the protesters. In the meantime, establishment forces could regroup and look for the appropriate time to push back on the opposition.

This playbook seemed to work in dealing with the 2003 protest against the anti-subversion legislation. The government announced that they would shelve the bill indefinitely after the Half-Million People March on July 1, avoiding imminent bloodshed on July 9, the scheduled date of the vote, when the opposition had planned a rally outside the legislative chamber. Then Beijing let Chief Executive Tung Chee-hwa resign in March 2005 to be replaced by Donald Tsang, who was regarded as more pragmatic and friendly with the democrats and Western countries. In retrospect, Beijing used this tactical retreat to buy time to establish tighter control of the electoral process, the media, and education, getting ready for a new offensive.

Such a one-step-backward–two-steps-forward approach was repeated in Beijing's response to the anti-National Education protest in 2012. In response to a big rally opposing the education reform, the government scrapped the plan. In 2014, though Beijing was adamant not to yield to the demands for genuine universal suffrage by the Occupy movement, the authorities restrained themselves. They did not resort to serious force to clear the occupation, but simply waited for the movement to wane and for the public backlash against protesters to grow. After the 2014 Occupy, Leung Chun-ying, the chief executive responsible for handling the crisis, decided not to run for another term. Many believed it was because of pressure from Beijing. He was replaced by Carrie Lam, who traced her career to the British colonial government and presented a softer image than Leung initially.

After the clash over the extradition bill on June 12, 2019, the government announced it would suspend the bill. It must have thought that this would be sufficient for the protest and its public support to diminish. On the contrary, the protest was sustained and became ever more confrontational. The authorities tried to mobilize pro-establishment thugs, most notoriously mobsters from original inhabitant villages in the Yuen Long area, to attack protesters. But this tactic failed to intimidate the rebels and only made them more militant. The escalation continued even after the government formally withdrew the bill on September 4. The government used all the legal tools that it inherited from the British colonial government to crack down on the protest. The police rounded up protesters and charged them with unlawful assembly or rioting. These charges were on the books in colonial times and were inherited by the HKSAR but had rarely been used since during the last two decades of colonial rule. The HKSAR government even invoked the colonial-era emergency law to legislate a face-mask ban. The decree empowered the police to pre-empt protests by arresting anyone wearing a face mask, which was part of the anti-extradition black bloc protesters' outfit.

The government's strategy was to crack down on protesters while backing down on their demands selectively. It fully expected that public opinion would turn around over time. However, in the end, public support for the increasingly militant protesters was consistently high into the fall. The result of the district council elections on November 24, 2019, confirmed the protest's wide popularity. In the election, many newbie democrat candidates openly supportive of the protests won in landslide victories against establishment candidates, many of whom were senior incumbents with deep connections in the local districts. In the district council elections in 2015, pro-Beijing candidates won nearly 70 percent of the seats. This had always been the norm, and even the Occupy movement in 2014 did not break this norm. In the 2019 election, however, the democrats won 86 percent of the seats. This must have shocked Beijing.

The landslide emboldened the democrats and protesters, who started to eye a similar landslide victory in the LegCo election scheduled for September 2020. Though protest activities were interrupted by the COVID-19 pandemic, the opposition devised a strategy to win a majority in the LegCo. In March, Occupy Central leader Benny Tai started to explore the road map to attain a Legislative majority in the upcoming election.[1] Though half of the seats are reserved as conservative FC seats, attaining a majority became feasible given the local business and professional elites' increasingly visible discontent with the authorities during the 2019 unrest. The democrats envisioned that if they won the majority of the LegCo, they would threaten to veto all government bills and bring the government to a halt. Such a threat could force the government to negotiate with the democrats over their demands to revamp the police force and restart the political transition toward universal suffrage.

In the early spring of 2020, it became clear that Beijing was pushing for a revival of Article 23 to respond to the 2019 protests. Chinese official media and Hong Kong establishment politicians, including Chief Executive Carrie Lam, started reiterating Hong Kong's constitutional responsibility to fight back against subversive activities.[2] While Beijing was drumming up the call for a return of Article 23 in March and April, the opposition's plan to seek legislative majority gained momentum as the voter registration drive for different FC sectors gathered steam. Fearing that a democratic majority in the LegCo was within reach, Beijing's official media started to express its concern about a brewing "color revolution" and the "opposition's seizure of power" in Hong Kong. Beijing was anxious that they were on the verge of losing Hong Kong like they lost Taiwan.[3]

Pressed by this anxiety about losing the lever of power in Hong Kong in the upcoming LegCo election, Beijing shifted its tone on national security legislation. While CCP media and Hong Kong establishment figures spent most of March and April pushing for a return of Article 23, official media stopped mentioning Article 23 in May. In its place was talk about legislating a National Security Law in the National People's Congress Standing Committee and directly imposing it on Hong Kong. Beijing's plan to bypass the HKSAR's legislative process and directly impose the National Security Law was confirmed when the National People's Congress convened on May 22. Apparently, Beijing was so worried about the opposition's takeover of the Hong Kong LegCo that it no longer trusted that the council would be able to legislate on Article 23. The National Security Law was rushed through the National People's Congress Standing Committee in June. It became effective on July 1, 2020. The law outlawed any activities and expression deemed sympathetic to separatism, subversive to the Hong Kong or Beijing authorities, collusive with foreign forces, and conducive to terrorism, with vague definitions of all those offences. Beijing sent national security officials to Hong Kong to work with law enforcement in creating a National Security Committee to implement the law. Special courts could be set up to try cases under the new law. Those cases could be tried in secret, and they could also be transferred to mainland Chinese courts. Anybody suspected of violating the law could have their assets frozen and passport confiscated.

This is a drastic move in two senses. First, Beijing no longer feels that British colonial-era laws targeting protest and organizations are sufficient to keep Hong Kong under its control and that new tools to outlaw speech and opinions are needed. The definition of the offenses falling under the law's purview is as vague and as harsh as can be. The National Security Law spells the end of freedom of expression, information, and association that Hong Kong has enjoyed for a long time. Second, the law's imposition directly from Beijing without even the pretension of respecting Hong Kong's autonomy is unprecedented. The introduction of mainland law enforcement into Hong Kong, the establishment of secret trials, and the possibility of transferring the accused to mainland China trample on the rule of law in Hong Kong.

The surprising imposition of the National Security Law manifests Beijing's deep anxiety about losing Hong Kong. Alerted by the example of Taiwan, where the pro-independence political party took control of the government through elections, Beijing fears the imminent seizure of power by a Hong Kong opposition sympathetic to self-determination or independence. Beijing is determined that this path has to be closed off forcefully at all costs. Whether this move is going to be able to stifle the unrest in Hong Kong for good remains to be seen. However, Beijing has provoked a serious international backlash. The legislation's process and content are already sufficient for the US, the UK, and many other countries to rethink their Hong Kong policy. Moreover, the law contains Article 38, which effectively put everyone in the whole world under its jurisdiction: "This Law shall apply to offences under this Law committed against the Hong Kong Special Administrative Region from outside the Region by a person who is not a permanent resident of the Region."[4] Article 38 of the National Security Law is the first time any Chinese law has been extended to include non-Chinese nationals residing outside China, and opened the possibility for them to be indicted and tried in Chinese courts.

Just one month after the law was implemented, the Hong Kong National Security Committee issued a global "Wanted" list. Most of the wanted individuals were Hong Kong activists or politicians currently residing outside Hong Kong. Among them is Samuel Chu, a US citizen heading a lobby group called Hong Kong

Democracy Council in Washington, DC. Beijing apparently could not wait to prove that Article 38 is not just for show.

It is well-known that by Beijing's standard, reporting a new epidemic, researching accounting fraud by state enterprises, and investigating corruption can all be considered subversive of the state. How similar laws have been applied in mainland China shows that the National Security Law jeopardizes not only dissidents and activists, but also journalists, financial analysts, and apolitical businesses, who are now vulnerable to persecution or blackmail by the authorities or politically connected business rivals.

In March 2021, the National People's Congress went further, to decide on overhauling the election methods for Hong Kong's LegCo and chief executive, significantly compressing the proportion of directly elected seats and setting up a new committee composed of senior government officials to vet all candidates at all elections on the ground of national security. The reform significantly reduced the directly elected seats in the LegCo to only 20 percent of all LegCo seats. Even the share of FC seats is compressed to make room for new seats generated in the Election Committee. Categories in FC seats and the Election Committee were reshuffled to increase Beijing's direct grip and close off the path of the opposition's inroads.[5] As such, Beijing obliterated any democratic progress in Hong Kong electoral systems since the 1990s.

Financial Centrality on the Line

Beijing's overreach unleashed an international outcry. The US, which has already been on a collision course with China over many other issues – including the South China Sea, the responsibility for causing the global pandemic, tariffs, sensitive hi-tech, and many more – reacted strongly to the National Security Law. On May 27, 2020, on the eve of the law's passing, the US State Department announced that it no longer certified Hong Kong as sufficiently autonomous from China and that it would stop treating Hong Kong as separate from mainland China in its law and policy.[6] As then Secretary of State Michael Pompeo put it, "To the extent the Chinese Communist Party treats Hong Kong as just another Communist-run city, the United States will do the same. We're not going to allow Beijing to benefit from the harm they're imposing on the people of Hong Kong."[7] On June 29, the State Department ceased to exempt Hong Kong from the US export control regime. This means that China can no longer rely on Hong Kong as the backdoor to access equipment and software with US components carrying sensitive technology.[8]

At about the same time, the US Congress swiftly passed the Hong Kong Autonomy Act, with a unanimous bipartisan vote in both the Senate and the House. The Act authorized the US government to put financial and immigration sanctions on identified Hong Kong and Chinese officials responsible for suppressing Hong Kong's freedom and financial institutions doing business with them. On July 14, the White House issued the President's Executive Order on Hong Kong Normalization. The order detailed how the US would stop treating Hong Kong as a separate entity from mainland China in trade, investment, and visas.[9] More extreme measures of cutting off Hong Kong access to the international US dollar transaction system were reportedly discussed. Though the White House decided not to pursue such a nuclear option at the time, the mere discussion of it added grave uncertainty to Hong Kong's status as China's offshore financial center.[10] The possibility of sanctions for doing business with officials sanctioned by the US alerts Hong Kong's foreign banks, which have reportedly already started auditing their clients for sanction risk.[11] On August 7, the US Treasury Department leveled financial sanctions on eleven of the top officials in Hong Kong and mainland China involved in Hong Kong policy. These sanctions were at the same level of severity as the sanctions applied to terrorists and genocidal war criminals. The sanctions barred the targeted individuals from entering the US and also froze their US assets. Any entities in the world found providing service to them and doing business with them will face US secondary sanctions.[12]

Many countries are likely to follow suit to revamp their relations with Hong Kong and stop treating Hong Kong as a separate entity from mainland China. Many democratic countries maintain an extradition treaty with Hong Kong, though they do not have such an arrangement with mainland China. After implementing the National Security Law, the US, the UK, Australia, New Zealand, Canada, Germany, France, and Finland have suspended their extradition agreement with Hong Kong.[13] Many of these countries also adopted a policy of offering political asylum to Hong Kong citizens facing prosecution under the National Security Law. The UK even started granting residency rights and pathway to citizenship to Hong Kong residents born in Hong Kong before 1997, together with their families. It will open the UK door to up to 3 million Hong Kong migrants.[14] Japan, Singapore, and Taiwan are all starting to lure talent and investment from Hong Kong.[15] Beijing strongly denounced these reactions from democratic countries. It knows very well that an exodus of Hong Kong residents with their wealth could drain the city of resources and hurt China economically. Those who seek an exit from Hong Kong will include not only Hong Kong residents but also mainland tycoons who store their wealth in Hong Kong as a safe haven.

Even without Western countries' reformulation of their Hong Kong policy, the National Security Law's threat to freedom of information, the rule of law, and protection of property rights is sending a chill through the international business community in Hong Kong. The American Chamber of Commerce in Hong Kong conducted a survey of its members after the law's details became clear. It found that 40 percent of businesses surveyed and 53 percent of individuals had developed a plan to leave Hong Kong. Seventy-five percent of respondents expressed pessimism about Hong Kong's business prospects under the National Security Law.[16] In July, the New York Times announced that it would divert part of its Hong Kong office to Seoul, explicitly citing the deteriorating environment for journalists under the National Security Law as the reason. Deutsche Bank also announced that it would move its Hong Kong office to Singapore.[17]

China's decision to impose the National Security Law as a pre-emptive strike against a perceived revolutionary situation in Hong Kong amounts to the premature end of "One Country, Two Systems" twenty-seven years before the 2047 deadline. The cost of this move for China could be grave. The international backlash could make China lose Hong Kong as a technological backdoor and off-shore financial center. It adds a significant challenge to China at a time when the US is tightening the siege of China's hi-tech sector through its sanctions on Huawei and other hi-tech companies. The US is also tightening its regulation of Chinese companies trading on the US stock market, potentially expelling many large Chinese enterprises from the US.[18] The international backlash comes at a time when China needs Hong Kong most. The economic fallout of the international backlash against the National Security Law will take time to materialize, but China is well aware of the economic price they may pay for it. Beijing has been reviving the discussion about developing new onshore financial centers like Shanghai, Shenzhen, and Hainan Island to replace Hong Kong. But the lack of a separate monetary system fully integrated with the global financial system without any capital control, as well as the lack of an independent judicial system, in those places would make such a vision little more than a distant dream.[19]

The question is, would China succeed in stifling the political threat from Hong Kong once and for all? Looking at the perseverance of the resistance seeking autonomy or independence in Tibet and Xinjiang more than five decades after Beijing established full direct control, the prospect of a tranquil Hong Kong under the National Security Law is dim in the long run. The international community's concerted efforts to offer an exit option for persecuted Hong Kong citizens and the growth of Hong Kong diasporic activism in the course of the 2019 protest created an international support network and escape route for the resistance. All these point to a protracted conflict, even though the conflict might be less manifest until opportunities for another eruption appear. In the aftermath of the 2014 Umbrella Movement, a close observer of Hong Kong notes that "Hong Kong as a place defined by liberties was disappearing, but the fight for its identity and to preserve treasured aspects of its civil society had gone largely unnoticed."[20] This persistence, with ups and downs of overt conflict, becomes clearer if we put Hong Kong's conflict in comparative and global perspective.

Hong Kong's Future in Comparative and Global Perspective

Hong Kong's quest for autonomy from Beijing after the sovereignty handover is by no means unique. Since the rise of the Westphalia system of sovereign nation-states in the seventeenth century, the world's political space has never been perfectly organized in contiguous nation-states. In the long history of the breakup of empires (such as the Austro-Hungarian Empire, the Ottoman Empire, and the Dutch empire in Southeast Asia) or the formation of unitary nation-states from smaller units (such as the formation of Great Britain, Indonesia, and Japan), there were often territorial units whose belonging to definite nation-states was disputed. If significant populations inhabited such units, the populations' will to break away or join another state often fostered significant and persistent contention.

How the belonging of such territorial units is addressed and resolved is never a purely legal–constitutional issue. As in all other matters of international politics, any legal–constitutional resolution of conflicts is no more than a reflection of the balance of political forces at the particular moment when such resolution was attained. How long such a resolution holds when the original balance of forces changes depends on how much all parties involved follow the rule of law. Whether these disputes are resolved, are at least contained in a peaceful framework, or lead to deadly conflict or even war is determined by the nation-state claimants' approach to the political demands from the inhabitants of the territorial units. The international communities' dispositions also shape the course and form of conflicts. Table 9.1 shows the many cases in which a significant proportion of a territory's inhabitants demanded autonomy or separation from the larger nation-state that exercised or claimed sovereignty over the territory.[21]

Previous studies have shown that if the overarching sovereign state offers constitutional autonomy to the territorial unit concerned, the inhabitants there would be content and would not manifest strong motivation for confrontational mobilization against the sovereign state.[22] Other studies suggest that international involvement and support of the inhabitants' movement for autonomy is essential to the movement's success in the long run.[23] Built on these works, I classify the cases along two dimensions. The first dimension classifies these cases by whether the dominating nation-state offers or tolerates constitutional liberty and autonomy in the territory. This concerns how the central government of the nation-state and the territory are related. It is not necessarily tied to the governmental form of the dominating nation-state. A nation-state can be a constitutional democracy but still adopt a coercive approach

Table 9.1 *Path of resistance of territory seeking larger autonomy or separation from a dominating sovereign state*

	Authoritarian coercion by the dominating state	Constitutional liberty offered by the dominating state
External support by major powers	IV. **Confrontational resistance** Kosovo, Tibet, Hong Kong (*c.* 2003–), South Sudan, East Timor	I. **Autonomy achieved** Gibraltar, Hong Kong (1997–*c.* 2003), Åland
Little support by major powers	III. **Extreme violence** Chechnya, Northern Ireland (before 1998), Basque country	II. **Ongoing negotiation** Quebec, Scotland, Northern Ireland (after 1998) Puerto Rico, Okinawa

to maintaining control of the territory. One classic example is London's handling of Northern Ireland in the 1970s. On the other hand, a nation-state can be authoritarian, but its state can still relate to the territory on the principle of constitutional liberty. The second dimension classifies the cases by whether the claimant of autonomy or independence secures major international powers' support.

In all of the cases in Table 9.1, the demand for autonomy or separation persists regardless of whether the dominating nation-state offers the territory constitutional liberty or tries to coerce it into submission. Whether the demand receives major international support also does not matter to the persistence of the demand. Persistence of demands is more the rule than the exception. Throughout world history, the quest for autonomy or separation, once established in a significant portion of the population, does not go away easily if the population concerned is not wiped out or resettled altogether through different forms of genocide. The demand might be stifled for a period under draconian repression, but it could easily flare up again with greater ferocity.[24] The kind of prolonged authoritarian quiescence after a major crackdown resembling what mainland China experienced after Tiananmen is less likely to happen in this context of struggle for autonomy or independence, as the repressing regime could not employ nationalist pride to legitimate itself once the repressed population develops its own political identity separate from or even antagonistic to the majority population that the regime claims to represent.

While the demand for autonomy or separation is constant, the variation shown in the table is about whether the demand leads to a peaceful resolution (or non-resolution), confrontational mobilization, or extreme violence. One major determinant of whether the demand is expressed peacefully is whether the dominating nation-state relates to the territory in question on the principle of constitutional liberty, offering the territory certain constitutional rights to liberty. All cases under which the nation-state resorts to coercive measures end up in confrontational resistance.

When the inhabitants whose refusal to be absorbed by the dominating nation-state (like Gibraltar refusing "return" to Spain from Britain, and Swedish-speaking Åland residents refusing Finland's control) was handled with tolerance and constitutional rights were offered by the dominating nation-state, and when their causes obtained significant support from major powers (Britain for Gibraltar, Sweden and other European nations for Åland),[25] they could often maintain their autonomy or separation in peace. If they enjoyed the constitutional right of liberty, but their causes for larger autonomy or separation received little international support, they would usually accept the status quo and continue negotiating with the political center via peaceful, constitutional means, like election and referendum, as in the cases of Quebec and Scotland.[26]

Cases in which the dominating nation-state attempted to strip the territory of its autonomy through coercion often resulted in overt conflict. The form of conflict varied depending on the international community's disposition. When the inhabitants' demands for autonomy or separation received support from major international powers, the conflicts would largely be confined to nonviolent resistance (as in Tibet and East Timor) or conventional warfare (as in Kosovo and South Sudan).[27] Support by major powers allowed those powers to exert a restraining influence on the resistance, preventing it from sliding toward terrorism. On the other hand, resistance that faced international isolation and brutal repression (as in the case of the IRA and Chechnya separatists) was easily tempted by extreme and desperate tactics like targeting civilians of the occupying nation.[28]

The case of Hong Kong straddles quadrants I and IV, shifting from I to IV over time. In the late colonial era and the early years following the handover, most Hong Kong inhabitants first preferred to stay under British rule and then aspired to uphold local autonomy from Beijing. In the 1980s through the early 2000s, Beijing adopted a pragmatic line of more or less addressing the Hong Kong question with constitutional liberty. The effort to create and then legitimize the Basic Law as a mini-constitution of the HKSAR and the restraint that Beijing exercised in the early days after the handover were remarkable compared to the style of governance in mainland China. Hong Kong's path of sovereignty handover and autonomy after 1997 has been supported by the British in the form of the Sino-British Joint Declaration and by the US in the US–Hong Kong Policy Act. Hong Kong was, therefore, in quadrant I in the beginning. The democrats co-operated with Beijing to maintain the "One Country, Two Systems" status quo in Hong Kong even though they are oppositional on many specific policy issues.

What we see throughout this book is the movement of Beijing's posture toward Hong Kong from constitutional liberty to authoritarian coercion, or what Michael Davis recently described as a transition from a "liberal constitutional order" to an "authoritarian national security order."[29] The imposition of the National Security Law on July 1, 2020, concludes this movement. At the same time, international support of Hong Kong's quest for autonomy persists and strengthens over time. Hong Kong is now solidly in quandrant IV, in the league with Tibet and pre-independence East Timor. It is too early to tell whether the new political equilibrium in Hong Kong will rest in that quadrant after the dust settles from the 2019–2020 unrest. Besides remaining in quadrant IV for a long-simmering conflict, could Hong Kong possibly move to other quadrants in the scheme?

A public-opinion poll released two months after imposition of the National Security Law showed that support for universal suffrage and for all demands of the 2019 protests had become even stronger.[30] This suggests that Hong Kongers' resistance will remain constant. One possible scenario is that Hong Kong moves back to quadrant I. As unlikely as it sounds, it is not impossible. If, in the long run, the National Security Law does not manage to stifle unrest, and if, over time, the international sanctions it invoked sufficiently hurt

Chinese elite interests in Hong Kong, given Hong Kong's unique and not yet replaceable role as China's offshore global financial center, Beijing could backpedal. A formal revocation of the law would be almost impossible, but Beijing might choose to slacken its implementation. This has already happened to the anti-face-mask law that the HKSAR government legislated by decree in October 2019. The protesters just ignored the law. The arrival of the COVID-19 pandemic made wearing a face mask universal. The law remains in place, and the government even successfully beat back a judicial review of it by opposition lawyers. But the government has ceased its enforcement after an initial flurry of arrests. It is possible that the National Security Law will end up like this, but it is far from guaranteed. It is also very possible that the new equilibrium will stay in quadrant IV, and Hong Kong could see a prolonged, low-intensity resistance against Chinese rule that will occasionally flare up into more open conflict when opportunities emerge.

Another possibility is that Hong Kong could slowly slide toward quadrant III. This could happen if major world powers, most importantly the US, decide that Hong Kong is a lost cause, like South Vietnam in 1975. Suppose the US and the international community withdraw support from any remaining resistance in Hong Kong and seek rapprochement with Beijing. In that case, the Hong Kong resistance, thrown into isolation and freed from any restraint instilled by supportive international powers, could well move toward a more extreme and unconventional form of violent resistance. We have already seen, at the height of the 2019 protests, the use of poorly made improvised explosive devices in a few instances. But so far, this tactic is the exception and does not garner widespread support.[31]

The scenario of Hong Kong moving to quadrant III is not yet very likely. Continued support for the Hong Kong resistance and the sanctioning of China have been consistent with the shift of the US and its allies to a more confrontational China policy. From the 1990s through the 2000s, the US sought an active engagement with China. Ever since Nixon's visit to China in 1972, the US has been in a quasi-alliance with Beijing to contain Soviet expansion in Asia. Right after the 1989 Tiananmen massacre and the collapse of the Soviet bloc in the early 1990s, the US shifted to human rights diplomacy toward China for a brief moment. However, Beijing managed to woo and mobilize politically influential US corporations by promising them access to the Chinese market. This move shifted Washington to a more conciliatory approach to China. From 1994 on, the policy of pursuing full trade liberalization with China became the priority of US–China policy, culminating in the US support of China's accession to the WTO in 2001.[32]

The policy of economic engagement continued for about fifteen years. In those fifteen years, all other concerns regarding US–China relations – including South China Sea territorial disputes, Taiwan, Tibet, human rights, and others – were subjugated to the goal of integrating China fully into the global free market. The vested interests that benefited from China's opening were the main force behind this policy orientation. They have been keen on lobbying for a China-friendly policy and have blocked any move that would damage US–China amity.[33] In this context, Washington continuously certified Hong Kong's autonomy from China and maintained Hong Kong's special trading status despite Beijing's increasing intervention in Hong Kong until 2020. Washington also ignored Beijing's use of Hong Kong as a backdoor to access sensitive advanced technology or to aid authoritarian allies in breach of US sanctions.

This overall preference for US–China amity in the US corporate sector started to change over the 2000s when Beijing started re-empowering state companies and offered them financial and policy preferences to help them compete with foreign enterprises in the Chinese market. This trend accelerated after 2010, when the US and Western economies were battered by the global financial crisis while the Chinese economy rebounded strongly under a large-scale monetary stimulus program. Beijing's leaders judged that the global financial crisis spelled the end of US leadership in the world, and that it was China's turn to lead. From then on, Beijing became ever more aggressive in squeezing US corporations in the Chinese market and harvested their trade secrets and technology. China became bolder in employing its economic leverage to penalize other countries in political disputes with Beijing.[34] US corporations' loss vis-à-vis Chinese companies worsened after Beijing launched its Belt and Road Initiative in 2013. The project was to create external demand that helped absorb China's industrial overcapacity and alleviate its economic slowdown. US corporations started to feel squeezed out of developing-world markets.[35]

In this context, US corporate lobbyists became much less enthusiastic about lobbying for US–China amity. Sometimes, they would even lobby for a policy that was outright hostile to China. From 2015 on, the US Congress managed to pass many laws that would irritate Beijing with bipartisan and unanimous (or near-unanimous) support. Such a high level of bipartisanship was unusual for the times, given the polarized political environment in the US today. Laws to irritate Beijing include the Hong Kong Human Rights and Democracy Act of 2019, the Taiwan Travel Act of 2018, the Uyghur Human Rights Policy Acts of 2020, and the Hong Kong Autonomy Act of 2020. The Hong Kong Human Rights and Democracy Act and the Hong Kong Autonomy Act warrant more proactive action from Washington to sanction China over the loss of freedom in Hong Kong. From an embargo on Chinese hi-tech companies to more support of South China Sea claimants against China, Washington's confrontation with Beijing continues to escalate. Other countries, such as the UK, Australia, and Japan, have faced intensified conflict of interest with China that increases in tandem with the US's more confrontational approach.[36]

The rising tension between China and the US and its allies will not reverse any time soon, as such escalation stems from the structural intensification of rivalry between Chinese and Western corporate interests and receives broad political support. In this context, the US and its allies' support of the resistance in Hong Kong will not subside anytime in the near future. Given all this, the key variable that would shape Hong Kong's path in uncharted territory under the National Security Law is whether Beijing would contain its coercive impulse and retreat into the original pragmatic constitutional restraint over Hong Kong. This will be, in turn, shaped by the contentious interaction between the Hong Kong resistance and elite politics within the CCP regime. Hong Kong's continuous financial centrality to China, a centrality that most other cases in Table 9.1 did not enjoy, warrants that Hong Kong would enjoy more advantages as compared with other regions seeking to break away from dominant nation-states.

The tension and tectonic shifts that have been simmering under the surface for a long time precipitated the turmoil in 2019. The 2019 uprising is not only an uprising by the grassroots society in Hong Kong. It is also superimposed on the increasing tension among the local business elite, foreign capital, and the mainland Chinese financial elite. In 2020, the National Security Law and the US decision to decertify Hong Kong's status as a separate customs territory has connected the turmoil of Hong Kong to greater US–China rivalry. The volatility of Hong Kong spilled into other aspects of world politics – the Pandora's box of local and global turbulence is open.

Hong Kong has defied predictions of its demise many times before, showing its intransigent will to fight for greater autonomy. This time around, the report about Hong Kong's death is again greatly exaggerated. The future of the city is becoming as uncertain as ever, but as other times in Hong Kong's history and struggles in other places of the world repeatedly show, this uncertainty and the suffocating repression that Hong Kong society faces will not stop its fearless dwellers from struggling for their destiny. There will be a period of apparent tranquility, but resentment will continue to grow underneath the surface, waiting for any cracks in the regime to break open into overt resistance again. The struggle for the future of Hong Kong did not end in the 2019 unrest and the crackdown afterward. It has just begun.

GLOSSARY

Anhui 安徽
Bao'an 寶安
Beijing 北京
Bo Xilai 薄熙來
Cao Erbao 曹二寶
Cao Juren 曹聚仁
Cha Shih May-lung 查史美倫
Chan Fang On-sang 陳方安生
Chan, Ka-keung Ceajer 陳家強
Chan Kin-man 陳健民
Chan Shung-fai 陳崇輝
Chan Wai-yip 陳偉業
Chan Wan 陳雲
Chan Wan-kan 陳雲根
changqi dasuan 長期打算
chongfen liyong 充分利用
Chaozhou 潮州
Che Kung 車公
Chen Qing 陳晴
Chen Jianwen 陳健文
Chiang Ching-kuo 蔣經國
Chiang Kai-shek 蔣介石
Chen Lin 陳林
Chen Shuang 陳爽
Chen Wei 陳蔚
Chen Zixiang 陳子翔
Chen Zuo'er 陳佐洱
Ching Cheong 程翔
Choi Yuen 菜園
Chow Yong-kang 周永康
Deng Xiaoping 鄧小平

Diao Tong 刁潼
diguode jiyi 帝國的技藝
Dong Qiwu 董其武
Dong Zhe 董喆
Dushu 讀書
Fang Fang 方方
Fung E 馮愉敏
Fok Ying Tung 霍英東
gaitu guiliu 改土歸流
Gansu 甘肅
Gu Kailai 谷開來
Guangdong 廣東
Guangzhou 廣州
Guo Pei 郭沛
Guo Qifei 郭齊飛
gwong fuk heung gong 光復香港
si doi gak ming 時代革命
Hakka 客家
Han 漢
Han Shuxia 韓淑霞
hanjian 漢奸
Hau 侯
Heung Yee Kuk 鄉議局
Ho Chi-ping 何志平
Ho Tsu-kwok 何柱國
Hua Jing 華菁
Huang Haibo 黃海波
Huang Henan 黃赫男
Huang Zheng 黃錚
Hu Jintao 胡錦濤
Hung, Benjamin 洪丕正
Hung Man 熊敏
Hung Shing 洪聖
jiandu quan 監督權
Jiang Shigong 強世功
Jiang Zemin 江澤民
Jiangsu 江蘇
Kam Tin 錦田
Kowloon 九龍
Kuan Hsin-chi 關信基
Kwan, Edward 關百忠
Kwok Chung 郭松

Ng Ngoi-yee 吳靄儀
Ngai, Joseph 倪以理
Ni Mu 倪木
Pang 彭
Pu Zefei 濮澤飛
Punti 本地
Qianhai 前海
Qin Jing 秦靖
Qin Lisheng 秦力生
Qin Xiao 秦曉
Qin Yang 秦陽
Qing 清
Qinghai 青海
Rao Guizhu 饒桂珠
Ren Shanshan 任珊珊
Sai Kung 西貢
Shaanxi 陝西
Shanghai 上海
Shatin 沙田
Shenzhen 深圳
Sheung Shui 上水
shijie diguo di'erban 世界帝國第二版
shudian wangzu 數典忘祖
Sichuan 四川
Song Renqiang 宋任強
Szeto Wah 司徒華
Song 宋
Song Xin 宋欣
Su Xiaopeng 蘇曉鵬
Ta Kung Po 大公報
Taiping 太平
Tai Yiu-ting 戴耀廷
Tang 鄧
Tang Hsiang-chien 唐翔千
Tang Ying-yen 唐英年
Tanka 蛋家
Tian Bin 田斌
Tianjin 天津
Tiananmen 天安門
Tien Pei-chun 田北俊
Tien Puk-sun 田北辰
Tien Yuan-hao 田元灝

yuek 約
Zeng Xiaosong 曾曉松
Zeng Yu 曾昱
Zhan Sheng 詹勝
Zhang Jingwu 張經武
Zhang Leping 張樂平
Zhang Shengqiao 張聖橋
Zhang Yi 張毅
Zhang Yue 張玥
Zhao Bing 趙昺
Zhao Jiayin 趙佳音
Zhao Yang 趙暘
Zhou Enlai 周恩來
Zhou Xiaochuan 周小川
Zhou yuanzhi 周遠志
Zhu Rongji 朱鎔基
Zhu Yunlai 朱雲來

NOTES

1 Introduction

1 For a detailed account of the siege, see "The Longest Day" (special report on Hong Kong Police siege of Hong Kong Polytechnic University) (理大圍城特備專頁), *The Stand News*, at thestandnews .com/%E7%90%86%E5%A4%A7%E5%9C%8D%E5%9F% 8E/.

2 For a detailed account of the battle of CUHK, see "Battle of CUHK Part I: Defending the University Community on the Hill" (中大之戰. 上:捍衛 山城的共同體), *The Stand News*, November 15, 2019, at https://bit.ly/ 3qeftAp; Battle of CUHK Part II: Conflicts and Misunderstandings among Mountain Community Activists before Retreat (中大之戰. 下: 退場前後; 山城抗爭者的矛盾與誤解), *The Stand News*, November 16, 2019, at thestandnews.com/politics/r-%E4%B8%AD%E5%A4% A7%E4%B9%8B%E6%88%B0-%E4%B8%8B-%E9%80%80% E5%A0%B4%E5%89%8D%E5%BE%8C-%E5%B1%B1%E5%9F %8E%E6%8A%97%E7%88%AD%E8%80%85%E7%9A%84% E7%9F%9B%E7%9B%BE%E8%88%87%E8%AA%A4%E8% A7%A3/

3 "Chronicle of the Hong Kong Anti-extradition Movement in One Chart: Summary of the Roaring 285 Days in Hong Kong" (香港反送 中大事記:壹張圖看香港人怒吼的285天), *The Reporter*, November 25, 2019, at twreporter.org/a/hong-kong-extradition-law-events.

4 "Listen to the Song That Hong Kong's Youthful Protesters Are Calling Their "National Anthem'," *TIME*, September 12, 2019, at https://time.com/5672018/glory-to-hong-kong-protests-national-anthem.

5 "Report on Anti-extradition Law Protest: 100 Days into the Protest, Barrister Laments Abusive Arrests as Only 189 of 1,400 Arrested Were Officially Charged" (逆權運動:抗爭百日逾1,400人被捕 僅189人被控

大狀:警方濫捕) *Apple Daily*, September 16, 2019, at https://hk
.appledaily.com/local/20190916/ED54EYSICU7356ENKSN
PLITDUM/.

6 "*Mingpao* Survey Shows 68.8% of Respondents Support Massive
Restructuring of HK Police Force and 50% Gave Zero Credibility to
Police" (明報民調:68.8%市民支持大規模重組警隊; 五成人評對警方
信任度0分), *Ming Pao*, October 15, 2019, at https://bit.ly/3BV6JBk;
see also Centre for Communication and Public Opinion Survey, the
Chinese University of Hong Kong 2020.

7 "Landslide Victory for Hong Kong Pro-democracy Parties in De
Facto Protest Referendum," *CNN*, November 25, 2019, at cnn
.com/2019/11/24/asia/hong-kong-district-council-elections-intl
/index.html.

8 "As Extradition Law Amendments Spark Worries, Charles Ho Tsu-
kwok hopes Businessmen Could Feel Comfortable Going Back to
Hong Kong" (《逃犯條例》修訂惹商界憂慮 何柱國:讓商人返港如沐
春風), *Sing Tao Daily* (USA), March 26, 2019, at singtaousa.com
/home/19-%E5%8D%B3%E6%99%82%E6%B8%AF%E8%81%
9E/2268949-%E3%80%8A%E9%80%83%E7%8A%AF%E6%
A2%9D%E4%BE%8B%E3%80%8B%E4%BF%AE%E8%A8%
82%E6%83%B9%E5%95%86%E7%95%8C%E6%86%82%E6%
85%AE%E3%80%80%E4%BD%95%E6%9F%B1%E5%9C%8B
%EF%BC%9A%E8%AE%93%E5%95%86%E4%BA%BA%E8%
BF%94%E6%B8%AF%E5%A6%82%E6%B2%90%E6%98%
A5%E9%A2%A8/?fromG=1.

9 "Extradition Law Amendments: Pro-establishment Businessmen
Worries Impact on Business Environment; Business and Professionals
Alliance Hesitant on Voicing Support" (逃犯條例:建制商界憂修例影響
營商環境 經民聯未決定是否支持), *HK01*, March 7, 2019, at https://
bit.ly/3qdVd1L.

10 "Chinese Official Media Blasts Li Ka-shing with Little Reservation in
Their Language" (中國官媒齊轟李嘉誠言語激烈不留情面), *Radio
Free Asia*, September 16, 2019, rfa.org/mandarin/yataibaodao/gang
tai/ql1-09162019063433.html.

11 "Report on Extradition Law Amendments Protests: Various
Organizations Urge Establishment of Independent Inquiry Commission
(List Updating)" (逃犯條例: 各界促成立獨立調查委員會 (列表不斷更
新)), *Ming Pao*, July 26, 2019, at https://news.mingpao.com/ins/%
E6%B8%AF%E8%81%9E/article/20190726/s00001/
1564126660759/%E3%80%90%E9%80%83%E7%8A%AF%E6%
A2%9D%E4%BE%8B%E3%80%91%E5%90%84%E7%95%8C%

E4%BF%83%E6%88%90%E7%AB%8B%E7%8D%A8%E7%AB
%8B%E8%AA%BF%E6%9F%A5%E5%A7%94%E5%93%A1%
E6%9C%83%EF%BC%88%E5%88%97%E8%A1%A8%E4%
B8%8D%E6%96%B7%E6%9B%B4%E6%96%B0%EF%BC%89.

12 "Fears of Capital Flight as Beijing Tightens Grip on Hong Kong," *Financial Times*, July 19, 2019, at ft.com/content/79dbc0b6-91bb-11e9-b7ea-60e35ef678d2.

13 "Extradition Law Amendments – International Chamber of Commerce – HK Issues Stern Opposition: The Risk of Losing Freedom, Property and Life" (引渡修例: 國際商會措辭強硬反對:面臨失去自由、財產、生命風險), *HK Citizen News*, at https://bit.ly/3F1kSit.

14 "The International Front: One-Year Summary of Overseas Pro-HK Groups" (國際戰線:海外撐港組織壹年結), *The Stand News*, June 15, 2020, at thestandnews.com/politics/%E5%9C%8B%E9%9A%9B%
E6%88%B0%E7%B7%9A-%E6%B5%B7%E5%A4%96%E6%
92%90%E6%B8%AF%E7%B5%84%E7%B9%94%E4%B8%
80%E5%B9%B4%E7%B5%90.

15 Hughes 1968: 13, 16.

16 Bush 2016: Chapter 1.

17 Hung and Ip 2012.

18 See Szeto 2011; see also "Xia Ming: Hong Kong's Movement for Democracy Will Have Broader, More Globalized Impact" (夏明:香港的民主運動一定會走向更大的全球化格局), *RFI Chinese*, June 30, 2020, at rfi.fr/tw/%E4%B8%AD%E5%9C%8B/20200630-%E5%A4%8F%
E6%98%8E-%E9%A6%99%E6%B8%AF%E7%9A%84%E6%B0%
91%E4%B8%BB%E9%81%8B%E5%8B%95%E4%B8%80%E5%
AE%9A%E6%9C%83%E8%B5%B0%E5%90%91%E6%9B%B4%
E5%A4%A7%E7%9A%84%E5%85%A8%E7%90%83%E5%8C%
96%E6%A0%BC%E5%B1%80.

19 Zheng and Chiew, eds., 2013: Part I.

20 Hamilton, ed., 1999; Chow 1993; Mathews et al. 2007; Wong 1996.

21 Mathews 2000; Siu 1996.

22 Abbas 1997.

23 E.g., Krarr, Louis and Joe McGowan, "The Death of Hong Kong," *CNN Money*, June 26, 1995, at https://money.cnn.com/magazines/fortune/fortune_archive/1995/06/26/203948/index.htm.

24 See a review of these views in Wong 2000.

25 Ngo, ed., 1999.

26 Yeh et al. 2006; Karreman and Knaap 2009.

27 Ma 2007; Sing 2004.

28 Lee and Chan 2011; Sing 2009; Dapiran 2017.

29 Hung and Ip 2012.

30 Dapiran 2017.
31 Chan et al., eds., 2000; Tam 2012; Lo 2014.
32 Chu 2017; Ku and Pun, eds., 2004; Ip 2019.
33 See Chapter 5 below.
34 See Chapters 5, 6 below.
35 Abu-Lughod 1989; Braudel 1992 [1979]: Chapters 2, 3; Arrighi 1992: Chapter 2; Weber 1966 [1921].
36 Tilly 1990; Tilly and Blockmans, eds., 1994; Spruyt 1996; Braudel 1992 [1979]: Chapter 4; Arrighi 1994: Chapter 3.
37 Machiavelli 1992 [1513]: 14–15.
38 Sassen 2001; Taylor and Derudder 2015.
39 Brenner 2004; Calder 2021.
40 See Moberg 2017.
41 Tilly 1989; Sewell 1996.
42 Marx 1978 [1852].
43 Foucault 1980: 75–7.
44 Marx 1978 [1852]: 437.

2 At Empires' Edge, 1197–1997

1 For a critical review of this dominant historiography, see Wong 2000, Tsui 2017.
2 It was named Bao'an county before the Qing.
3 Siu 1985a; Chan 1993.
4 Jao 1959.
5 The Che Kung Temples in Sai Kung and Shatin are good examples, so are the several Yeung Hau Temples in the area.
6 Scott 2009.
7 Duara 2016.
8 Meacham 1984; Solheim 2006; Hung 1998; Anderson 1972; Cheung 1991.
9 Hung 1998.
10 Hung 1998; see also Siu and Liu 2006; He and Faure, eds., 2016.
11 Lin 1985.
12 Lin 1985; Chan 1993.
13 Hung 1998; Siu and Liu 2006; Rowe 2002.
14 Carroll 1997: 16–18, 2005: Chapter 1.
15 Carroll 2005: 23, 31–2.
16 Yen 2013: 448–54; "Once Eschewed, Henry Fok Secures Place in Hong Kong," *Wall Street Journal,* June 26, 1997, at wsj.com/articles/SB867265427339421500.
17 Cheung 1984.

18 Cheung 1984: 42–4.
19 Hung 1998, 2001.
20 Ho 2019; Ng 2017; "40th Anniversary of Boat Household Struggle: the Past and Present of Unlawful Assembly" (艇戶抗爭40年 非法集結罪的前世今生) *U-Beat Magazine* (大學線), March 6, 2018, at http://ubeat.com.cuhk.edu.hk/134_hk_history/4.
21 See Faure 1986.
22 Watson 1975, 1983; Baker 1966.
23 Siu 1985b.
24 Grant 1962.
25 See Kamm 1977.
26 Hong Kong Government 1948: 47.
27 Faure 1986.
28 Topley 1964; Palmer 1987; Lockhart 1899.
29 Faure 1986.
30 Eitel 1882: 132.
31 Chun 1987.
32 Groves 1969; Lockhart 1899.
33 Chun 1987.
34 Freedman 1966: 5–6; Lockhart 1899: 57.
35 Grove 1964.
36 Chiu and Hung 1999.
37 Bristow 1984.
38 Schiffer 1991.
39 Chiu and Hung 1999.
40 CO 1030/1033; Chiu and Hung 1999.
41 Chiu and Hung 1999.
42 Aijmer 1980, 1986.
43 See Chiu and Hung, 1999.
44 "Hong Kong's 'Indigenous' Villages Mirror Tensions of an Increasingly Divided City," *NPR*, October 17, 2019, at npr.org/2019/10/17/769228499/hong-kongs-indigenous-villages-mirror-tensions-of-an-increasingly-divided-city.
45 Sinn 2003; Chan 1991.
46 Carroll 2006; Chan 1975; Tsai 1993; Tsang 2007: Chapter 7.
47 Hamashita 2008: Chapter 8; Kuo 2014.
48 Ngo 1999; Kuo 2014.
49 Snow 2004: Chapter 6; Tsang 2007: Chapters 9–10.
50 Tsang 2007: Chapters 11–12; Chiu 1996.
51 Chiu 1996.

52 "Once Eschewed, Henry Fok Secures Place in Hong Kong," *Wall Street Journal*, June 26, 1997, at wsj.com/articles/SB867265427339421500.
53 Loh 2010; Jiang 2012.
54 Zhou 2002, 2009; see also Chapter 7 below.
55 Hong Kong Government 1957.
56 Scott 1989: Chapters 3–4.
57 Mark 2004, 2007; Smart 1992.
58 Scott 1989: Chapter 3; see also Chapter 7 below.
59 Scott 1989: Chapter 3; see also Chapter 7 below.
60 Lui 2017; Scott 1989: Chapter 4; Chan 2011: Chapters 9–10.
61 Hamilton 2018; Chiu and Lui 2009.
62 Chiu and Lui 2009: Chapter 3; Lui and Wong 1998.
63 Law 2009: Chapter 7; Leung 2012; Loh 2010.
64 So 1999.
65 See Yep, ed., 2013.

3 The Making of China's Offshore Financial Center

1 For example, former chief executive of Hong Kong Tung Chee-hwa was one of the commentators most keen to remind Hong Kong citizens that Hong Kong's increasing dependence on China rendered Hong Kong little bargaining power on all matters with Beijing: "Economically Dependent on China and Contributions Falling Drastically, How Much Bargaining Power Does Hong Kong Have?" (經濟依賴中國 貢獻比例大減 香港有幾多牙力?), *Mingpao*, May 10, 2015, at mingpaocanada.com/tor/htm/News/20150510/thb_r.htm.
2 Louis 1997.
3 See Schenk 2001, 2011; Lui and Chiu 2009: Chapters 2, 3; Guo 2009.
4 Hamilton 2018.
5 Hung 2015, 2020a.
6 Hung 2015.
7 Han 1998.
8 García-Herrero 2011.
9 Lady 2019; Cheung et al. 2017.
10 Pauly 2011.
11 US–HK Policy Act 1992.
12 US–HK Policy Act 1992, Title I, Section 103(4).
13 "Communication from Hong Kong," World Trade Organization document, June 3, 1997, WTO WT/L/218, at https://docs.wto.org/dol2fe/Pages/SS/directdoc.aspx?filename=Q:/WT/L/218.pdf.

14 "WTO Successfully Concludes Negotiations on China's Entry," World Trade Organization, September 17, 2001, at wto.org/english/news_e/pres01_e/pr243_e.htm.

15 ChinaAg 2015.

16 Huang 2019.

17 Murphy et al. 2017; Mayer Brown 2008; Grimmer 2019.

18 Hung 2015; Lardy 2019; Liu 2020.

19 Hung 2020b.

20 "All About the Money: Why Hong Kong Matters So Much to China," *Wall Street Journal*, October 22, 2019, at wsj.com/articles/all-about-the-money-why-hong-kong-matters-so-much-to-china-11571736607.

21 "China's Elite – Including Xi Jinping – Are Linked to Offshore Deals That Hid Millions of Dollars," *Quartz*, April 4, 2016, at https://qz.com/653836/chinas-elite-including-xi-jinping-are-linked-to-offshore-deals-that-hid-millions-of-dollars; "Scandal Ensnares Relatives of Fallen Chinese Leader," *Wall Street Journal*, April 26, 2012, at wsj.com/articles/SB10001424052702304723304577365603131112294.

22 "Luxury Homes Tie Chinese Communist Elite to Hong Kong's Fate," *New York Times*, August 12, 2020, at nytimes.com/2020/08/12/business/china-hong-kong-elite.html.

23 "Niche Auction Houses Thrive in Hong Kong," *New York Times*, October 4, 2013, at nytimes.com/2013/10/04/arts/international/niche-auction-houses-thrive-in-hong-kong.html.

24 "Bankers' Exits and Zombie Accounts: China's Shanghai Free Trade Zone Sputters," *Reuters*, September 1, 2019, at reuters.com/article/us-china-shanghai-ftz/banker-exits-zombie-accounts-chinas-shanghai-free-trade-zone-sputters-idUSKCN1VN01V; "China's Economic Zone Fails to Draw HK Property Tycoons," *Reuters*, August 16, 2013, at https://uk.reuters.com/article/us-property-china/chinas-new-economic-zone-fails-to-draw-hk-property-tycoons-idUKBRE97F07520130816.

25 Guo 2009: Chapter 2.

26 Walter and Howie 2012: 159.

27 Eichengreen and Xia 2019; Bénassy-Quéréa and Capelleb 2014.

28 Boughton 2001: Chapter 18.

29 Zhou 2009; Murphy and Yuan 2009.

30 IMF, "Special Drawing Right (SDR)," at imf.org/en/About/Factsheets/Sheets/2016/08/01/14/51/Special-Drawing-Right-SDR.

31 Fung et al. 2014.

32 Ma and Xu 2012.

33 Eichengreen and Kawai 2014; Cohen 2012; Frankel 2012; Minkis and Lau 2012.

34 Hung 2020a; Hung 2018.

4 The Mainlandization of Business Monopolies

1 Fong 2014.
2 Lui and Chiu 2009; Chan 1991.
3 Jing 2018; Goodstadt 2000; Bush 2016: Chapter 3.
4 Hung 2010; see Chapter 7 below.
5 Ma 2015; Fong 2016.
6 "Pan-Democrat Voter Share Slips in Hong Kong Elections since 1997," *South China Morning Post*, July 3, 2017, at scmp.com/news/hong-kong/politics/article/2100963/pan-democrat-voter-share-slips-hong-kong-elections-1997.
7 Currently there are eighteen district councils in Hong Kong. Every directly elected councilor is elected in a small district comprising about 17,000 citizens. The district councils generated by the 2007 election comprised 534 councilors, of which 405 were directly elected and the rest were mostly appointed by the government.
8 Kwong 2010: Chapter 6; Cheng 2004; Wong 2014.
9 Lui and Chiu 2009; see also Wong 2015.
10 "Chinese Capital Floods to Hong Kong from All Directions, Set to Surpass Local Chinese Capital in Ten Years" (中資湧港全方位布局10年後參與度超華資), *Hong Kong Commercial Daily*, January 11, 2016; "Chim Pui-chung Plans to Run for LegCo, Hong Kong Financial Center Is an Exaggeration as It Declines to Become a Playground of Chinese Capital" (詹培忠擬參選立會 "港金融中心只係吹噓" 淪中資玩意), *Apple Daily*, July 30, 2019; "Chinese Securities Association of Hong Kong 12th Anniversary and the Inauguration Ceremony of the Seventh Board of Directors" (香港中資證券業協會十二周年暨第七屆董事會就職典禮), *Wen Wei Po*, May 2, 2019.
11 "Central People, Hong Kong People" (中環人·香港人), *Ming Pao*, December 11, 2019.
12 "Hong Kong Bankers Are Losing Their Jobs to China Rivals," *Bloomberg*, October 12, 2020, at bloombergquint.com/china/hong-kong-bankers-are-losing-their-jobs-to-mainland-china-rivals.
13 "Chinese Investment Banks Strength Increases, Expanding Aggressively in Hong Kong in Recent Years, Took Close to 60 Percent Consulting Fees in Asia" (中資投行實力升市佔勁 近年積極來港發展 搶亞洲六成咨詢費) *Wen Wei Po*, October 11, 2016.
14 "Chinese Capital Snatches up All of Residential Lands, Hong Kong Capital Dominates Commercial Lands" (中資盡攬住宅地 港資包攬商業地), *Wen Wei Po*, June 26, 2017.
15 "Aggressively Seizing Land at High Price, Hong Kong Land Shrinks in Supply, Chinese Capital Outcompetes Hong Kong Local Tycoons"

(高價瘋搶 港地買少見少 中資"挾爆"大孖沙) *East Week*, March 8, 2017.

16 "China's HNA Pays $960 mln for 4th Land Purchase in Hong Kong," *Reuters*, March 16, 2017.

17 "Buying up Hong Kong – Acquisition 2: Chinese Capital favors Large and Expensive Commercial Buildings, the Most and Second Most Expensive Property Belongs to Chinese Capital" (買起香港–收購 (2): 中資偏愛大型高價商廈, 已包辦最貴商廈第一二名), *852 Post*, July 26, 2017, at post852.com.

18 "Chinese Capital No Longer Snatching Land, Hong Kong Capital Regain Dominance" (中資搶地不再 港資重奪主導權), *Hong Kong Economic Times*, August 10, 2018.

19 Pang 2018.

20 "James Tien: If Chinese Capital Controls Everyday Life, One Country Two Systems Can Be Ignored"(田北俊:倘中資控制民生 不用理一國兩制), *Mingpao*, June 16, 2014.

21 "Business Environment in Hong Kong Deteriorated, Michael Tien: Worrying Chinese Capital Will Replace Hong Kong Capital" (香港營商環境嚴峻 田北辰: 恐中資取代華資). *Economic Digest*, Oct 19, 2019.

22 "Former Chief of JPMorgan's China Unit Is Arrested," *New York Times*, May 21, 2014, at https://dealbook.nytimes.com/2014/05/21/former-top-china-jpmorgan-banker-said-to-be-arrested-in-hong-kong.

23 "Chinese Banks' Hong Kong Ranks on Track to Outnumber Global Rivals," *Financial Times*, August 15, 2020, at ft.com/content/abbbfcec-736c-47ba-b106-b1bdafebd099.

24 Financial Services Development Council, at fsdc.org.hk/en/about/mission.

25 Leung 2012; see also "CY Leung: The troubles of Hong Kong's unloved leader," *BBC*, July 6, 2013, at https://www.bbc.com/news/world-asia-23193421.

26 "How Leung Chun-ying Became the Chief Executive" (梁振英是怎樣當上行政長官的), *Hong Kong Economic Times*, February 1, 2013, at https://bit.ly/3mWC6Y8; Lian 2017; "Song Lin Supported Leung Chun-ying to Run for Chief Executive" (宋林支持梁振英參選特首), *Oriental Daily*, June 2, 2017, at https://orientaldaily.on.cc/cnt/news/20170602/00176_002.html.

27 Lian 2017.

28 "Election Committee War: If Pan-Democrats Join Hands with the Business Sector, John Tsang Votes Could Approach 601" (【選委戰】泛民商界若聯手 曾俊華潛在票源直逼601票), *HK01*, December 12, 2016, at https://bit.ly/3wr8PYn.

29 Wang-Kaeding and Kaeding 2019.

30 "[Internet Article 23] Five Liberal Party Members and James Tien Are against the Bill" (網絡23條：5自由黨議員　田北俊個人反對草案), *Mingpao*, December 7, 2015, at https://news.mingpao.com/ins/%
E6%B8%AF%E8%81%9E/article/20151207/s00001/
1449471350468/%E3%80%90%E7%B6%B2%E7%B5%A123%
E6%A2%9D%E3%80%915%E8%87%AA%E7%94%B1%E9%
BB%A8%E8%AD%B0%E5%93%A1-%E7%94%B0%E5%8C%
97%E4%BF%8A%E5%80%8B%E4%BA%BA%E5%8F%8D%
E5%B0%8D%E8%8D%89%E6%A1%88.

31 "James Tien: Leung Chun-ying Should Consider Resignation" (田北俊:梁振英應考慮辭職), *Mingpao*, October 24, 2014, at https://news.mingpao.com/ins/%E6%B8%AF%E8%81%9E/article/20141024/s00001/1414140526680/%E7%94%B0%E5%8C%97%E4%BF%8A-%E6%A2%81%E6%8C%AF%E8%8B%B1%E6%87%89%E8%80%83%E6%85%AE%E8%BE%AD%E8%81%B7.

32 "Pro-mainland Chinese financiers based in Hong Kong Launch New Bauhinia Party Aimed at Reforming Legco, Restraining 'Extremist Forces'," *South China Morning Post*. December 6, 2020, at scmp.com /news/hong-kong/politics/article/3112771/mainland-born-hong-kong-based-financiers-launch-new.

33 "Abandoning High Salary to Come Back to China to Found His Business, Founding Shoufang Web Became Talk of the Town" (棄高薪回國創業　夥辦搜房網譜佳話), *Takungpao*, September 16, 2020, at takungpao.com.hk/finance/236131/2020/0916/498134 .html.

34 "Chairman of Bauhinia Party Li Shan: The Realistic Dimension of the Path of Hong Kong Governance" (紫荊黨主席李山:香港治理路徑的現實向度), *Zhijing*, December 9, 2020, at http://hk.zijing.org/2020/1209/837691.shtml.

35 "Pro-mainland Chinese Financiers Based in Hong Kong Launch New Bauhinia Party Aimed at Reforming Legco, Restraining 'Extremist Forces'," South China Morning Post. December 6, 2020. scmp.com /news/hong-kong/politics/article/3112771/mainland-born-hong-kong-based-financiers-launch-new.

36 "The Inside Story of the Liaoning: How Xu Zengping Sealed Deal for China's First Aircraft Carrier," *SCMP*, January 19, 2015, at scmp.com /news/china/article/1681755/how-xu-zengping-became-middleman-chinas-deal-buy-liaoning.

37 Muller 2019.

38 US–HK Policy Act 1992, Section 103(8).

39 Gettinger 2016.

40 "U.S. Export Controls Update: Why Hong Kong Dominates the New Unverified List," *Corporate Compliance Insights*, July 30, 2014, at corporatecomplianceinsights.com/us-export-controls-update-why-hong -kong-dominates-the-new-unverified-list.

41 Song 2014.

42 "Patrick Ho, Former Head of Organization Backed by Chinese Energy Conglomerate, Sentenced to 3 Years in Prison for International Bribery and Money Laundering Offenses," US Department of Justice, March 25, 2019, justice.gov/usao-sdny/pr/ patrick-ho-former-head-organization-backed-chinese-energy-con glomerate-sentenced-3.

43 "Patrick Ho, Former Head of Organization Backed by Chinese Energy Conglomerate, Sentenced to 3 Years in Prison for International Bribery and Money Laundering Offenses," US Department of Justice, March 25, 2019, at justice.gov/usao-sdny /pr/patrick-ho-former-head-organization-backed-chinese-energy-con glomerate-sentenced-3.

44 "Chinese Telecommunications Conglomerate Huawei and Huawei CFO Wanzhou Meng Charged with Financial Fraud," US Department of Justice, January 28, 2019, at justice.gov/opa/pr/chinese-telecommunications-conglomerate-huawei-and-huawei-cfo-wanzhou-meng-charged-financial.

45 "Chinese Telecommunications Conglomerate Huawei and Huawei CFO Wanzhou Meng Charged with Financial Fraud," US Department of Justice, January 28, 2019, at justice.gov/opa/pr/chinese-telecommunications-conglomerate-huawei-and-huawei-cfo-wanzhou-meng-charged-financial.

46 "Justice Department Statement on the Request to Hong Kong for Edward Snowden's Provisional Arrest," US Department of Justice, June 26, 2013, at justice.gov/opa/pr/justice-department-statement-request-hong-kong-edward-snowden-s-provisional-arrest; "Hong Kong Hurt 'Trust' with U.S. by Letting Snowden Go, W.H. Says," *CBS News*, June 24, 2013, cbsnews.com/news/hong-kong-hurt-trust-with-us-by-letting-snowden-go-wh-says.

47 "How Tensions with the West Are Putting the Future of China's Skynet Mass Surveillance System at Stake," *South China Morning Post*, September 23, 2018, at scmp.com/news/china/science/article/ 2165372/how-tensions-west-are-putting-future-chinas-skynet-mass.

48 "US Security Concerns Force Cosco-Owned Orient Overseas to Sell Long Beach Port in California," *South China Morning Post*, April 30,

2019, at scmp.com/business/companies/article/3008324/us-security-concerns-force-cosco-owned-orient-overseas-sell-long.

49 "UPDATE 1 – Australia Set to Block Hong Kong-Based CK Group's $9.4 bln Bid for APA," *Reuters*, November 7, 2018, at reuters.com/article/apa-ma-ck-infra/update-1-set-to-block-hong-kong-based-ck-groups-9-4-bln-bid-for-apa-idUSL4N1XI2TK.

5 "One Country, Two Systems" before Hong Kong

1 Deng Xiaoping's conversation with the British foreign minister, 1981, cited in Qi 2004: 216, my translation.
2 Norbu 1991.
3 Harris 2008.
4 Qi 2004; Du 2011.
5 Li 1997: 68.
6 Choi 2017.
7 Lee 2012.
8 Hung 2016.
9 E.g., Chen et al. 2003.
10 See Duara 2011.
11 Duara 1997; Chow 2001; Zhao 2004.
12 E.g., Crossley 1999; Crossley et al., eds., 2006; Perdue 2001, 2005; Shepherd 1993.
13 E.g., Bovingdon 2010; Barnett, ed., 1994; Goldstein: 1997, 2007; Smith 1996.
14 See Blumenthal 2020.
15 Herman 1997.
16 Di Cosmo 1998.
17 The Republic of China recognized Mongolia as an independent country only in 2002, after the KMT was unseated by the opposition party in the Republic of China in Taiwan.
18 Constitution of the Soviet Republic, Jiangxi, 1931, cited in Schein 2000: 58; see also Liu 2003.
19 CCP Central Committee Department of United Front Work 1991: 495–6, translation mine.
20 Kuo 2014.
21 Snow 1968: 100.
22 Mullaney 2011.
23 Chen 2009.
24 See Starr, ed., 2004.

25 Brophy 2017.

26 Petech 1973; Goldstein 1973.

27 Stein 1972, Chapter 2; Goldstein 1997: 1–29; Michael 1986; Wang 1998: 14–54.

28 Goldstein 1989: 186–212, 449–63; Stoddard 1986: 90–1.

29 Stoddard 1986: 88–93; Takla 1969; Wangye 2004: 41–128; Goldstein 1989: Chapter 8.

30 Wangye 2004: 129–63.

31 Goldstein 1989: Chapter 20; Wangye, 2004: 129–63; Wang 1998: 148–99.

32 Excerpted in CCP Central Documents Research Office et al., ed., 2001: 93, 114, my translation.

33 Goldstein 2007: 23–5, 301–5, 422–53; Wang 1998: 267–89.

34 Wang 1998: 168.

35 Goldstein 1997: 53; Goldstein 2014: Chapter 9.

36 Dalai Lama 1990: 119; Wang 1998: 166.

37 Grunfeld 1987: 111–15; Goldstein 1997: 55–6.

38 Dalai Lama 1990: 90.

39 Goldstein 2007: 314–27.

40 Norbu 1979; Grunfeld 1987: 120–2, 127–9; Wang 1998: 171–84; Goldstein 2019.

41 "Commentary on the So-Called 'The Essence of Nationalities Question Is the Question of Class'" (評所謂"民族問題的實質是階級問題") *People's Daily*, April 7, 1980.

42 Goldstein 2007: 184–239; Grunfeld 1987: 127–46; Goldstein et al. 2004; Chen et al. 2003: 156–8.

43 Goldstein 2019: Chapters 12–15; Smith 1994: 57–68; Smith 1996: 387–450; Norbu 1979.

44 Goldstein 1997: 61–99; Wang 1998: 234; 404–11; 482–93; 529–34; Barnett, ed., 1994.

45 Mao Zedong's conversation with Cao Juren, 1958, cited in "Relation between Mao Zedong and Chiang Kai-shek after the Establishment of the New China" (新中國成立後毛澤東與蔣介石的關係) *News of the Chinese Communist Party* (中國共產黨新聞網), May 24, 2007 at http://cpc.people.com.cn/GB/64162/64172/64915/5775867.html; Xia 1997: 83–4; Hung and Kuo 2010.

46 "Zhou Enlai and the Solution to the Taiwan Question" (周恩來與解決台灣問題), *News of the Chinese Communist Party* (中國共產黨新聞網), at http://cpc.people.com.cn/BIG5/85037/8627785.html.

47 Qing China ceded today's core urban area of Hong Kong to Britain under the Treaty of Nanking (Nanjing) in 1842, then leased what

became today's New Territories, which constituted Hong Kong's rural hinterland, to Britain for ninety-nine years in 1898. At first it was not clear whether Beijing would reclaim all of Hong Kong or just the New Territories.

48 "Deng Kept His HK Options open in 1979," *South China Morning Post*, January 2, 2010, at scmp.com/article/702556/deng-kept-his-hk-options-open-1979.

49 Louis 1997.

50 Tsang 1988.

51 Miners 1986: 167.

52 "Beijing's Hong Kong Disinformation: Declassified Records Show China Always Opposed Democracy, Even When Hong Kong Was a Colony," *Wall Street Journal*, October 27, 2014, at wsj.com/articles/gordon-crovitz-beijings-hong-kong-disinformation-1414366413.

53 Amberg 1985; Head 1998.

54 "為什麼說香港不是殖民地 (香港基本法問答)" (Why Hong Kong Was Not a Colony (Q & A on Hong Kong Basic Law), *People's Daily*, March 17, 1997, 2.

55 For an overview of the process of Sino-British negotiation over Hong Kong's future in the early 1980s, see Yahuda 1993.

6 From Autonomy to Coercive Assimilation

1 Ma 1997.

2 Hong Kong Observer Society 1982.

3 Cited in Cheng 1984: 202.

4 "Behind the Sins of Meeting Point: Foreword – Rise and Fall of a Democratic Movement" (匯點:原罪背後 1:前言—場民主運動的誕生與落幕), *Stand News*, May 13, 2015, at thestandnews.com/politics/%E6%A6%82%E8%A7%80%E6%B0%91%E4%B8%BB%E9%BB%A8-%E6%BB%B2%E9%80%8F-2-%E4%B8%80%E9%BD%8A%E9%AC%A5%E8%B5%B0%E5%8C%AF%E9%BB%9E%E6%B4%BE; "A Look at the Democratic Party – Infiltration Part II: 'Let's Cast Out the Meeting Point Faction!'" (概觀民主黨. 滲透 2:「一齊鬥走匯點派！」), *Stand News*, May 13, 2016, at thestandnews.com/politics/%E5%8C%AF%E9%BB%9E-%E5%8E%9F%E7%BD%AA%E8%83%8C%E5%BE%8C-%E4%B8%80%E5%A0%B4%E6%B0%91%E4%B8%BB%E9%81%8B%E5%8B%95%E7%9A%84%E8%AA%95%E7%94%9F%E8%88%87%E8%90%BD%E5%B9%95.

5 So 1999: 58–72; Cheng 1984: 121–4.

6 January 1983, cited in Cheng 1984: 123–4.

7 "On Rightly Assessing and Handling Class Struggle in the Current Stage" (正確地估量和處理現階段的階級鬥爭), *People's Daily* editorial, November 6, 1982, my translation.

8 Cited in Choi 2007, my translation.

9 Sino-British Joint Declaration, Annex I, 6–7.

10 Lee 1996: 236.

11 Deng Xiaoping, cited in Qi 2004: 185–6.

12 Sino-British Joint Declaration, 5 (3).

13 Zhao 2004; Cabestan 2005; Modongal 2016.

14 So 1999: 118–54; Xu 1993: 151–92.

15 So 1999: 118–54, 2000; Xu 1993: 151–92.

16 So 1999: 118–54, 2000; Xu 1993: 151–92, 414–15.

17 Xu 1993: 363–424; So 1999: 155–82.

18 Szeto 2011.

19 Full text of the Basic Law, Chapter 4, Article 45, at basiclaw.gov.hk/en/basiclawtext/chapter_4.html.

20 Full text of the Basic Law, Chapter 4, Article 68, at basiclaw.gov.hk/en/basiclawtext/chapter_4.html.

21 Xu 1993: 363–424; So 1999: 155–216; Yuan 1997: 71–100.

22 Billeter 1998.

23 E.g., Tse Wai-Mo, "Solid Evidence: Martin Lee Is a Traitor" (謝緯武:李柱銘當漢奸的鐵證), *Wen Wei Po*, January 31, 2004, at http://paper.wenweipo.com/2004/01/31/PL0401310002.htm; "Martin Lee Not Shameful of Betraying His Nation, Reveals Typical Traitorous Logic" (中國評論新聞:李柱銘做漢奸不以為恥 典型漢奸邏輯), *CRNTT News*, October 30, 2007, at http://hk.crntt.com/doc/1004/8/0/6/100480632.html?coluid=2&kindid=0&docid=100480632; "When Scolded as a Traitor and Running Dog on the Street, Anita Chan Cowardly Escaped the Scene" (新浪網:陳方安生遭市民當街唾罵漢奸走狗 灰溜溜逃離現場), *Sina News*, September 2, 2019, at https://news.sina.com.cn/c/2019-09-02/doc-iicezzrq2792111.shtml.

24 Inscription on the memorial for Hong Kong's reunion with China, July 1, 1997, translation mine.

25 Ma 2017.

26 "Law Wai-Kwong: HK Association of Banks Discusses Article 23 of the Basic Law and Expresses Their Worries" (羅偉光:銀行公會討論23條表憂慮), *Apple Daily*, December 4, 2002, at https://hk.appledaily.com/local/20021204/YO724CMZW7IQ52FUVEFDKPD2CE.

27 US Department of State, *Statement on Hong Kong: Article 23 of the Basic Law*, May 2, 2003, at https://2001-2009.state.gov/r/pa/prs/ps/2003/20157.htm.

28 "People's Daily Overseas: One Country Is the Precondition and Foundation of Two Systems" (人民日報海外版: "一國"是"兩制"的前提和基礎), *Sina News*, February 23, 2004, at http://news.sina.com.cn /o/2004-02-23/05431869560s.shtml.

29 See Mingpao editorial office, ed., 2004, *passim*; Yiu-chong Wong 2004.

30 Standing Committee of the National People's Congress of the PRC, "Decision of the Standing Committee of the National People's Congress on Issues Relating to the Methods for Selecting the Chief Executive of the Hong Kong Special Administrative Region in the Year 2007 and for Forming the Legislative Council of the Hong Kong Special Administrative Region in the Year 2008," April 26, 2004, at basiclaw.gov.hk/en/basiclawtext/images/basiclawtext_doc21.pdf.

31 See Chapter 7 below for more details.

32 National People's Congress of the PRC, *Decision on Hong Kong's Constitutional Development*, at fmcoprc.gov.hk/eng/syzx/tyflsw/ t944943.htm.

33 See Lilla 2010.

34 Jiang 2008: 187–8.

35 Gross 2007.

36 Jiang 2008.

37 Jiang 2008: 142–45.

38 Jiang 2008: 31.

39 "Jiang Shigong: 'One Country, Two Systems' Needs to Move Out of the Deng Xiaoping Era" (強世功:「一國兩制」亟須走出「鄧小平時代」), *Duo Wei News*, December 1, 2016, at https://duoweicn.dwnews.com /CN-2016%E5%B9%B416%E6%9C%9F/10003099.html.

40 Jiang 2019.

41 "'National Education' Raises Furor in Hong Kong," *CNN*, July 30, 2012, at cnn.com/2012/07/30/world/asia/hong-kong-national-education-controversy/index.html.

42 "The High School Course Beijing Accuses of Radicalizing Hong Kong," *New York Times*, September 1, 2019, at nytimes.com/2019/09/01/world/ asia/hong-kong-protests-education-china.html; "How a History Exam Question Stirred Up Controversy over China, Japan and Hong Kong's Education System," *South China Morning Post*, May 16, 2020, at scmp .com/news/hong-kong/education/article/3084674/how-history-exam-question-stirred-controversy-over-china; "China Pushes to Integrate Hong Kong through Patriotic Education, Security Overhauls," *Wall Street Journal*, November 1, 2019, at wsj.com/articles/china-pushes-to-integrate-hong-kong-through-patriotic-education-security-overhauls -11572617038.

43 Cao 2008.

44 Cao 2008.

45 "Article by a Beijing Official Stationed in Hong Kong Sparks Criticism" (北京駐港官員文章引發批評), *Voice of America* (Chinese), April 28, 2008, at voachinese.com/a/a-21-w2009-04-28-voa59-61340857/1025199.html.

46 "Basic Law's Article 22 'Does Not Apply' to Beijing's Liaison Office, Hong Kong Justice Secretary Says," *South China Morning Post*, April 27, 2020, at scmp.com/news/hong-kong/politics/article/3081816/basic-laws-article-22-does-not-apply-beijings-liaison.

47 Lo et al. 2019; Cheng 2010; Lam and Lam 2013; Yuen 2020.

48 Lee 2020.

49 "Hong Kongers Shocked by the Central Government's Interference of Chief Executive Election" (李子木:中央干擾選舉, 港人驚呼"狼來了"), *Deutsche Welle* (Chinese), March 23, 2012, at dw.com/zh/%E4%B8%AD%E5%A4%AE%E5%B9%B2%E6%89%B0%E9%80%89%E4%B8%BE%E6%B8%AF%E4%BA%BA%E6%83%8A%E5%91%BC%E7%8B%BC%E6%9D%A5%E4%BA%86/a-15833065.

50 Lee 2020.

51 Wong et al. 2018; Wong et al. 2020; "New Immigrants, New Voters Part II: Who's Diluting Whom?", *Stand News* (新移民. 新選民2:是誰溝淡誰?), November 18, 2015, thestandnews.com/politics/%E6%96%B0%E7%A7%BB%E6%B0%91-%E6%96%B0%E9%81%B8%E6%B0%91-2-%E6%98%AF%E8%AA%B0%E6%BA%9D%E6%B7%A1%E8%AA%B0.

52 "As Single Entry Permit Holders from Mainland Soar, Legislator Urge HKSAR Government to Retain Screening Power" (持單程證來港內地人暴增 議員促香港取回審批權) *Radio Free Asia*, November 29, 2017, at rfa.org/cantonese/news/htm/hk-permit-11292017061103.html; Ching 2012.

53 "Buying Hong Kong – Population (2): Twenty Years after Handover, Hong Kong Residency Grew 850,000 but 'Hong Konger' May Have Zero Increase" (買起香港 人口 (2):回歸廿年居港人口增85萬 惟"香港人"或處於"零增長"?), *852 Post*, July 18, 2017, at post852.com.

54 "Jiang Shigong on Further Summarizing and Enhancing the Theoretical Foundation of the Central Government's Governance of Hong Kong" (強世功-進一步總結強化中央治港的理論基礎), *People's Daily*, June 13, 2014, at http://theory.people.com.cn/n/2014/0613/c40531-25143583.html.

7 The Class Politics of Democratic Movements

1 Lau and Kuan 1988; Lau 1984.

2 Chiu and Lui 2000; So 1999.

3 Wong and Lui 1992, 1993.

4 Zhou 2002, 2009.

5 Loh 2010; Smart 1992.

6 "The Truth of the 1967 Riots Has Been Suspended for 50 Years, and Eight Unsolved Mysteries" (六七暴動真相懸空50年, 八大待解之謎), *The Initium*, May 9, 2017, at https://theinitium.com/article/20170509-hongkong-67-myth; Zhou 2002; Cheung 2009; Cooper 1970.

7 Yep and Lui 2010; Lui 2017.

8 DeWolf, Christopher, "Sir Murray MacLehose, the Unexpected Father of Modern Hong Kong," *Zolima City Magazine*, at https://zolimacity mag.com/sir-murray-maclehose-unexpected-father-of-modern-hong-kong; Scott 1989.

9 Law 2009; Chan 2015; Leung 2000; HKFS 1982.

10 Leung 2000.

11 Lui and Wong 1998.

12 Scott 1989.

13 The LegCo expanded from twenty-six members in 1967 gradually to fifty in 1980 and sixty in 1991, then its size remained unchanged until 2012, when it increased to seventy.

14 See Choi et al., eds., 1998; Lee 2019.

15 Li 2012; "Thirtieth Anniversary of the Basic Law: A Summary of Its Origins and When the Word 'Referendum' Emerged" (基本法30年: 壹文總覽基本法來龍去脈 「普選」二字何時出現?), *HK01*, March 25, 2020, at https://bit.ly/3H4I9BF.

16 Lo 2013.

17 Szeto 2011; for a questioning of this account of the event, see "Thirtieth Anniversary of the June 4 Massacre: Middle-Aged Generation Picks up Their Memory of the Ignored 'June 7 Mongkok Riot'" (「六四」三十年 中生代重組記憶碎片:「六四」後三天 消失了的「六. 七旺角騷動) *Ming Pao Weekly*, June 3, 2019, at https://bit.ly/3BUS1KD.

18 Chan and Lee 2010; Hung and Ip 2012.

19 Szeto 2011.

20 "Interview with Prof. Johannes Chan Man-mum: Article 23 and National Security" (專訪陳文敏:二十三條與國家安全), *Amnesty International Hong Kong*, July 22, 2020, at amnesty.org.hk/%E5% B0%88%E8%A8%AA%E9%99%B3%E6%96%87%E6%95%8F %EF%BC%9A%E4%BA%8C%E5%8D%81%E4%B8%89%E6% A2%9D%E8%88%87%E5%9C%8B%E5%AE%B6%E5%AE% 89%E5%85%A8.

21 Ma 2005.

22 Ma 2005; Fu et al., eds., 2005.

23 Lee and Chan 2011: Part I.

24 Lee and Chan 2011: Part II.
25 Chan 2009; Ip 2018.
26 Hung 2010; Cartledge 2017.
27 Lam 2010.
28 Choi and Yan 2010; Ku 2012; Hung 2010; Veg 2007; Veg 2017.
29 Chu 2014.
30 Hong Kong Journalists Association, 2007a, 2007b; see also Lee and Chan, 2008; Chan and Lee 2011.
31 Hung and Ip 2012; Lee and Chan 2018: Chapter 4.
32 Tse 2010.
33 "On New Year's Day, Nearly Ten Thousand Hong Kongers Rally for Democracy on the Streets" (香港上萬民眾元旦遊行爭民主), *BBC News* (Chinese), January 1, 2010, at bbc.com/zhongwen/simp/china/2010/01/100101_hongkong_rally.
34 See the previous chapter.
35 Hung 2010.
36 "A Summary of the 'Five District Referendum' in Hong Kong" (綜述:香港的"五區總辭"), *BBC News* (Chinese), January 26, 2010, at bbc.com/zhongwen/trad/china/2010/01/100126_ana_hongkong_democracy.
37 For a discussion about the role of alternative online media on the radicalization of the democratic movement, see Leung 2015.
38 "Opinion Poll: Support for Government Political Reform Proposal Dropped below 50 Percent" (民調:政改支持跌破一半), *Mingpao*, June 15, 2010.
39 Chen 2010.
40 "Government of HKSAR: CE Targets Housing, Inequality and Other Livelihood Issues in *Policy Address*" (香港特區政府:行政長官的《施政報告》優先處理房屋政策、貧富差距等民生問題), October 13, 2010, at info.gov.hk/gia/general/201010/13/P201010130158.htm.
41 Lin 2012.
42 "Hong Kong Anti-National Education Rally Organizers Claimed 120 Thousand Participants" (港反國教集會 大會稱12萬人參加) *BBC News* (Chinese), September 7, 2012, at bbc.com/zhongwen/trad/chinese_news/2012/09/120907_hk_demo_education?MOB.
43 "HK Government Yields to Public Outcry, Cancels 3-Year Deadline on Moral and National Education" (港府讓步 取消國民教育三年死限), *BBC News* (Chinese), September 8, 2012, at bbc.com/zhongwen/trad/chinese_news/2012/09/120908_hk_education.

8 Hong Kong as a Political Consciousness

1 Platform of the Democratic Party (民主黨政策總綱), at dphk.org/index
   .php?route=information/category&cid=6.

2 "The League of Social Democrats Advocate 'Connecting with the
   Mainland as One'; Avery Ng: Part of the Expression Is Outdated and
   We Are Working Hard to Modify It" (社民連倡「與内地交通聯為一
   體」 吳文遠:部分表述過時正落力修改), *852 Post*, March 5, 2016, at
   post852.com.

3 "Hong Kong Journal; City of Immigrants Begins to Find an Identity of Its
   Own," *New York Times*, June 9, 2004, at nytimes.com/2004/06/29/
   world/hong-kong-journal-city-of-immigrants-begins-to-find-an-identity-
   of-its-own.html.

4 Ku 2012; Dewolf 2019.

5 Veg 2007.

6 E.g., Long 2011; Chan 2007.

7 Jiang 2008: Chapter 6.

8 Choi 2011; Ting 2013.

9 Hung 2011b; "Human Chain Extends from Central to Wanchai as
   20,000 Join Hands to Protect Victoria Harbor" (人鏈由中環延至灣仔
   兩萬人手牽手護維港), *Apple Daily*, March 22, 2004, at https://hk
   .appledaily.com/local/20040322/57LF3XPWXVTY3GEQPXXUL
   YUI5Q.

10 "Push to Defend City's Core Values," *South China Morning Post*,
    June 7, 2004, at scmp.com/article/458500/push-defend-citys-core-
    values; Jones 2015: Introduction.

11 See also Keading 2014.

12 The Central People's Government of the People's Republic of
    China, "Statement of the Hong Kong Macau Affairs Office on
    'Five-District Referendum' Initiated by Certain Organizations in
    Hong Kong" (中國中央人民政府:港澳辦就香港個別社團"五區公投
    運動"事發表談話), January 15, 2010, at gov.cn/jrzg/2010-01/15/
    content_1511742.htm.

13 In the sequel to *On the Hong Kong City State*, Chin published *On
    Hong Kong as China's Survivors* (Chin 2013), in which he claimed that
    Hong Kong kept the authentic Chinese culture destroyed by
    Communism in China, and that Hong Kong should be the new center
    of China's cultural revival.

14 E.g. Chin 2008.

15 See Chapter 3 above.

16 Chin 2011: 112–27; 135–40.

17 See Yep, ed., 2013.

18 Chin 2011: 145–63.

19 "Expecting Influx of 'Birth Tourists', Medical Professionals Urge Strong Measures to Stop It" (料雙非衝關增 醫療界促強堵), *Wen Wei Po*, April 22, 2012, at http://paper.wenweipo.com/2012/04/22/HK1204220022.htm.

20 Ching 2012.

21 Lee 2012.

22 Hu 2007.

23 See Lowe and Tsang 2017; Ip 2015.

24 Chin 2011: 150–63.

25 Chin 2011: 175–9; 51–4.

26 Chin 2011: 36–6.

27 Chin 2015.

28 See Hung 2011b.

29 "How Chinese Milk Smugglers Are Fueling Hong Kong Protests," *Huffington Post*, October 1, 2014, at huffpost.com/entry/hong-kong-smugglers-china_n_5909876.

30 Joshua Wong, "The Spirit of Christ Brings Me to the Street" (黃之鋒:基督精神帶我走上街頭), *Parenting TW*, January 1, 2013, at parenting.com.tw/article/5046548-; for the localist identity expressed in the movement, see Chan 2013; Lee et al. 2013; Morris and Vickers 2015.

31 For China's Han clothing cult movement, see Carrico 2017.

32 Undergrad Editorial Board, ed., 2014.

33 Anderson 1983.

34 See Hui 2015; Veg 2017; Wu 2016; Steinhardt et al. 2018; Yew and Kwong 2014; Yuen and Chung 2018.

35 Hong Kong Public Opinion Research Institute (PORI), *Survey on People's Ethnic Identity in Hong Kong*, at pori.hk/opinion-charts-3.

36 "Surveying Hong Kong Residents' Opinions on the City's Future by 2047: A CUHK Poll Found That Nearly 40% of Youth Aged 15–24 Supported HK Independence" (探討市民對2047香港前途看法 中大民調:15至24歲青年近四成支持港獨), *Ming Pao*, July 24, 2016, at https://bit.ly/3H4efxk; https://hongkongfp.com/2016/07/25/17-hongkongers-support-independence-2047-especially-youth-cuhk-survery.

37 Wong and Wan 2018; see also Keliher 2020; Augustin-Jean and Cheung 2018.

38 Kennedy 2002.

39 "Background Introduction: The Occupy Central Movement" (時事背景：「佔領中環"運動」), *BBC Chinese*, June 18, 2014, at bbc.com

/zhongwen/trad/china/2014/06/140618_hk_occupy_central_back
ground; "Benny Tai Said Occupy Central Failed to Make Central
Government Budge; Movement's Secretariat Issued a Late-Night
Statement Pledging Continuation of Movement and There Is No
Reduction of Support" (戴耀廷:佔中逼中央讓步"失敗" 秘書處夜發聲
明: 佔中必行 支持沒減), *Ming Pao*, at https://news.mingpao.com/pns/
%E8%A6%81%E8%81%9E/article/20140903/s00001/
1409679668737/%E6%88%B4%E8%80%80%E5%BB%B7-%
E4%BD%94%E4%B8%AD%E9%80%BC%E4%B8%AD%E5%
A4%AE%E8%AE%93%E6%AD%A5%E3%80%8C%E5%A4%
B1%E6%95%97%E3%80%8D.

40   Wilfred Chan and McKirdy Euan, "Hong Kong's Occupy Central
Democracy 'Referendum': What You Should Know," *CNN*, June 30,
2014, cnn.com/2014/06/24/world/asia/hong-kong-politics-explainer
/index.html.

41   "Chen Zuo'er, Chairman of Chinese Association of Hong Kong &
Macau Studies, Commented That Even USA Would Not Allow
a Terrorist to Become Governor" (港澳研究會會長陳佐洱:美國也不
會讓恐怖分子當州長), *Guancha News*, August 30, 2014, at guancha
.cn/local/2014_08_30_262282.shtml.

42   The Central People's Government of the People's Republic of China,
"Decision of the Standing Committee of the National People's
Congress on Issues Regarding Universal Suffrage of the Hong Kong
Chief Executive and the Election of the Legislative Council in 2016"
(全國人大常委會關於香港行政長官普選問題和2016年立法會產生辦
法的決定), August 31, 2014, at gov.cn/xinwen/2014-08/31/con
tent_2742923.htm.

43   "Thousands of Hong Kong Students Start Week-Long Boycott," *BBC
News*, September 22, 2014, at bbc.com/news/world-asia-china
-29306128; "Occupy Central – The First 12 Hours: Full Report as
Events Unfolded," *South China Morning Post*, September 2014, at
scmp.com/news/hong-kong/article/1602958/live-occupy-central-kicks
-hundreds-classroom-boycott-students-leave; "Hong Kong Activists
Start 'Occupy Central' Protest," *Washington Post*, September 27,
2014, at washingtonpost.com/world/asia_pacific/hong-kong-activists-
start-occupy-central-protest/2014/09/27/95f4051c-468c-11e4-b437
-1a7368204804_story.html; see also Sing 2019; Hui 2015.

44   Some characterized the evolution of the movement as an act of impro-
visation (Ho 2019), and others used the concept of "eventfulness" to
describe the dynamics of its development (Lee and Sing, eds., 2019).

45   Chow 2019: 41; see also Pang 2020; Ku 2019.

46 Yuen 2019.

47 Dapiran 2019.

48 Cheng 2019; Yuen 2020.

49 "Hong Kong Protests: Timeline of the Occupation," *BBC News*, December 11, 2014, at bbc.com/news/world-asia-china-30390820.

50 Ortmann 2016; Wu 2016; Lo 2018; Kwong 2016; Lam and Cooper 2018.

51 Yuen and Chung 2018.

52 "Hong Kong's 'Fishball Revolution' Is about a Lot More Than Just Street Food," *QUARTZ*, February 8, 2016, at https://qz.com/612813/hong-kongs-fishball-revolution-is-about-a-lot-more-than-just-street-food; "Hong Kong's Mong Kok Clashes: More than Fish Balls," *BBC News*, February 9, 2016, at bbc.com/news/world-asia-china -35529785; "A Not-Understood Fight of a Mong Kok Youth" (旺角少年,不被理解的戰鬥), *The Initium*, September 21, 2015, at https://theinitium.com/article/20150921-hongkong-occupycentraloneyear02.

53 Lam 2017.

54 Lam 2017.

55 "Hong Kong Legislative Elections Have Given Voice to a New Political Generation," *Time*, September 5, 2016, at https://time.com/4478978/hong-kong-legislative-council-election-legco; "Localists and Self-Determinists Snatch 390,000 Votes and Scholar Believes Democratic Self-Determination Could Be an Important Agenda for Hong Kong" (本土自決派共得39萬選票　學者:民主自決成香港重要議題), *The Initium*, September 5, 2016, at https://theinitium.com/article/20160905-hongkong-legco-analysis.

56 For a discussion of the localist consciousness expressed in the election, see Kaeding 2017.

57 Choi and Chan 2016; "Data of the Legislative Council Election: From Bipolar to Tripolar as Localist and Self-Determinists Grab 20% of Votes" (立會選戰·數據: 二營對立變三分天下　本土和自決派奪兩成票), *HK01*, September 5, 2016, at https://bit.ly/2ZY5aVY.

58 Wang-Kaeding and Kaeding 2019; Lian 2017; "'Bad boy' of Hong Kong politics accuses liaison office of interference, but his party says relations with Beijing intact," *South China Morning Post*, September 14, 2016, at https://www.scmp.com/news/hong-kong/politics/article/2019297/credibility-hong-kong-elections-stake-liberal-party; "Pro-Beijing camp slights CY Leung following sudden 'resignation' of loyalist," *Hong Kong Free Press*, July 24, 2015, at https://hongkongfp.com/2015/07/24/pro-beijing-camp-slights-cy-leung-following-sudden-resignation-of-loyalist/; see also Chapter 4 above.

59 "At Hong Kong Swearing-In, Some Lawmakers Pepper Their Oath with Jabs," *New York Times*, October 13, 2016, at nytimes.com /2016/10/13/world/asia/hong-kong-legislative-council.html.

60 "Hong Kong Pro-democracy Legislators Disqualified from Parliament," *The Guardian*, July 14, 2017, at theguardian.com /world/2017/jul/14/hong-kong-pro-democracy-legislators-disqualified -parliament.

61 "Hong Kong Activist Edward Leung Given Six Years for Police Clash," *New York Times*, June 11, 2018, at nytimes.com/2018/06/11/world/ asia/hong-kong-edward-leung-prison-sentence.html#:~:text=Hong% 20Kong%20Activist%20Edward%20Leung%20Given%206% 20Years%20for%20Police%20Clash,-The%20pro% 2Ddemocracy&text=HONG%20KONG%20%E2%80%94%20A% 20Hong%20Kong,during%20the%20Lunar%20New%20Year.

62 "The Case of Hong Kong's Missing Booksellers," *New York Times*, April 3, 2018, at nytimes.com/2018/04/03/magazine/the-case-of-hong-kongs-missing-booksellers.html.

63 Ngo 2018.

64 "The Leader of Hong Kong's Leaderless Protest Movement Is a Philosophy Student behind Bars," *Quartz*, July 30, 2019, at https://qz.com/1678104/jailed-activist-edward-leung-is-hong-kong-protesters-spiritual-leader.

9 Conclusion

1 Tai 2020a, 2020b.

2 "Rao Geping: The Later [Hong Kong] Finishes National Security Legislation, the Higher the Price [Hong Kong] Will Pay" (饒戈平:愈遲完成國安立法　付出代價愈大), *RTHK*, March 29, 2020, at https://news.rthk.hk/rthk/ch/component/k2/1517598-20200329 .htm; "People from Across the Board in Hong Kong: National Security Is Important to People's Livelihood and Happiness, Should Finish the Relevant Legislation as Soon as Possible" (香港各界人士:國家安全關乎香港市民安居樂業　應盡快完成相關立法) *Xinhua News*, April 16, 2020, at xinhuanet.com/gangao/2020-04/ 16/c_1125866828.htm; "When the State Is Safe, Hong Kong Is Safe" (國家安,香港安) *People's Daily*, April 16, 2020, at http:// paper.people.com.cn/rmrbhwb/html/2020-04/16/content_1982071 .htm; "China's Top Official in Hong Kong Pushes for National Security Law," *The Guardian*, April 15, 2020, at theguardian.com

/world/2020/apr/15/china-official-hong-kong-luo-huining-pushes-national-security-law.

3 "Protecting Hong Kong: Don't Let the Opposition's Plot to Seize Power Succeed" (守護香港勿讓反對派奪權圖謀得逞), *Wen Wei Po*, March 26, 2020, at http://paper.wenweipo.com/2020/03/26/PL2003260002.htm; "Will LegCo Change Hands? If It Does, What Should We Do?" (立法會會變天嗎?變了怎辦?), *AM 730*, February 24, 2020, at am730.com.hk/column/%E6%96%B0%E8%81%9E/%E7%AB%8B%E6%B3%95%E6%9C%83%E6%9C%83%E8%AE%8A%E5%A4%A9%E5%97%8E%EF%BC%9F-%E8%AE%8A%E4%BA%86%E6%80%8E%E8%BE%A6%EF%BC%9F-208540.

4 "Hong Kong National Security Law Full Text," *South China Morning Post*, July 2, 2020, at scmp.com/news/hong-kong/politics/article/3091595/hong-kong-national-security-law-read-full-text.

5 "Beijing Cuts Hong Kong's Directly Elected Seats in Radical Overhaul," *The Guardian*, March 30, 2021, at theguardian.com/world/2021/mar/30/hong-kong-china-brings-in-voting-system-changes.

6 "P.R.C. National People's Congress Proposal on Hong Kong National Security Legislation," US Department of State, May 27, 2020, at state.gov/prc-national-peoples-congress-proposal-on-hong-kong-national-security-legislation.

7 "Secretary Michael R. Pompeo with Matt Schlapp, Chairman of the American Conservative Union for CPAC," US Department of State, August 10, 2020, at state.gov/secretary-michael-r-pompeo-with-matt-schlapp-chairman-of-the-american-conservative-union-for-cpac.

8 "U.S. Government Ending Controlled Defense Exports to Hong Kong," US Department of State, June 29, 2020, at state.gov/u-s-government-ending-controlled-defense-exports-to-hong-kong.

9 "Executive Orders: The President's Executive Order on Hong Kong Normalization," The White House, July 14, 2020, at whitehouse.gov/presidential-actions/presidents-executive-order-hong-kong-normalization.

10 "Trump Rejects Ending Hong Kong Dollar Peg as Penalty to China," *Bloomberg*, July 13, 2020, at bloomberg.com/news/articles/2020-07-13/trump-aides-rule-out-ending-hong-kong-dollar-peg-as-punishment.

11 "Banks in Hong Kong Audit Clients for Exposure to US Sanctions," *Financial Times*, July 9, 2020, at ft.com/content/7b2b593e-5029-48b5-9c27-ff7f5473d66e.

12 "Treasury Sanctions Individuals for Undermining Hong Kong's Autonomy," US Department of the Treasury, August 7, 2020, at https://home.treasury.gov/news/press-releases/sm1088.

13 "US Suspends Extradition Treaty with Hong Kong Due to Concerns over City's Eroding Autonomy," *CNN*, August 19, 2020, at cnn.com/2020/08/19/asia/us-hong-kong-extradition-treaty-intl-hnk/index.html.

14 "Hong Kong: UK Makes Citizenship Offer to Residents," *BBC News*, July 1, 2020, at bbc.com/news/uk-politics-53246899.

15 "Hong Kong Security Law Sparks Race for Asia's Next Financial Capital," *Nikkei Asian Review*, August 19, 2020, at https://asia.nikkei.com/Spotlight/The-Big-Story/Hong-Kong-security-law-sparks-race-for-Asia-s-next-financial-capital; "Hong Kong Bankers Get Courted by Taiwan after Security Law," *Japan Times*, July 2, 2020, at japantimes.co.jp/news/2020/07/02/asia-pacific/politics-diplomacy-asia-pacific/hong-kong-bankers-taiwan-security-law.

16 "Some Four in Ten AmCham Members Considering Leaving Hong Kong over National Security Law Fears, Survey Finds," *Yahoo! Finance*, August 13, 2020, at https://sg.finance.yahoo.com/news/four-10-amcham-members-considering-105533525.html.

17 "New York Times Will Move Part of Hong Kong Office to Seoul," *New York Times*, July 14, 2020, at nytimes.com/2020/07/14/business/media/new-york-times-hong-kong.html; "Deutsche Bank Asia CEO Picks Singapore in Snub to Hong Kong," *Bloomberg*, July 15, 2020, at bloomberg.com/news/articles/2020-07-15/deutsche-bank-asia-ceo-picks-singapore-base-in-snub-to-hong-kong.

18 "Why 200 Chinese Companies May Soon Delist from the U.S. Stock Exchange," *Forbes*, August 19, 2020, at forbes.com/sites/kenrapoza/2020/08/19/why-200-chinese-companies-may-soon-delist-from-the-us-stock-exchange/#34ea6ac3fe71.

19 "China Envisions a New Hong Kong, Firmly under Its Control," *New York Times*, November 3, 2020, at nytimes.com/2020/11/03/business/china-hong-kong-hainan-island.html; "Shanghai's Quest to Be Global Financial Centre Gains Impetus from Hong Kong Troubles but Big Obstacles Remain," *South China Morning Post*, July 2, 2020, at scmp.com/economy/china-economy/article/3091526/shanghais-quest-be-global-financial-centre-gains-impetus-hong.

20 Wasserstrom 2020: 29.

21 Cf. Woodman and Ghai 2013.

22 Siroky and Cuffe 2015.

23 Woodman and Ghai 2013.

24 See Siroky and Cuffe 2015.

25 Hannum 1990: Chapter 17; Suksi 2013.

26 Keating 2013; Himsworth 2013; Simeon and Turgeon 2013.

27 Serwer 2019; Downie 2019; Muizarajs 2019; Barnett 2013.

28 Hannum 1990: Chapter 11; Pavkovic 2013.

29 Davis 2020: Ch. 6.

30 "Exclusive: HK Survey Shows Increasing Majority Back Pro-democracy Goals, Smaller Support for Protest Movement," *Reuters*, August 29, 2020, at reuters.com/article/us-hongkong-security-poll-exclusive-idUSKBN25Q00U?fbclid=IwAR2hW5F8sQYGGRxDZXl0jjMCNOj-zhLiSDxZNkXzqo9LKO7q9bhGA1Q6WPM.

31 "Homemade Bomb Detonated for First Time in Hong Kong Protests," *New York Times*, October 14, 2019, at nytimes.com/2019/10/14/world/asia/hong-kong-bomb-ied.html.

32 Hung 2021.

33 Hung 2020c, forthcoming.

34 Hung 2020a, forthcoming.

35 Hung 2020a, 2020c, forthcoming.

36 Hung forthcoming.

REFERENCES

Abbas, Ackbar, 1997. *Hong Kong: Culture and the Politics of Disappearance.* Minneapolis: University of Minnesota Press.

Abu-Lughod, Janet L., 1989. *Before European Hegemony: The World System A.D. 1250–1350.* Oxford: Oxford University Press.

Aijmer, Goran, 1980. *Economic Man in Sha Tin: Vegetable Gardeners in a Hong Kong Valley.* London: Curzon Press.

Aijmer, Goran, 1986. *Atomistic Society in Sha Tin: Immigrants in a Hong Kong Valley.* Gothenburg: Acta Universitatis Gothoburgensis.

Amberg, Eric M., 1985. "Self-Determination in Hong Kong: A New Challenge to an Old Doctrine." *San Diego Law Review.* Vol. 22, No. 4. 839–58.

Anderson, Benedict, 1983. *Imagined Communities: Reflections on the Origin and Spread of Nationalism.* London: Verso.

Anderson, E.N., 1972. *Essays on South China's Boat People.* Taipei: Orient Cultural Service.

Arrighi, Giovanni, 1994. *The Long Twentieth Century: Money, Power, and the Origins of our Time.* New York and London: Verso.

Augustin-Jean, Louis and Anthea H.Y. Cheung, 2018, *The Economic Roots of the Umbrella Movement in Hong Kong: Globalization and the Rise of China.* London: Routledge.

Baker, H., 1966. "The Five Great Clans of the New Territories." *Journal of Hong Kong Branch of Royal Asiatic Society.* Vol. 11. 25–47.

Barnett, Robert, ed., 1994. *Resistance and Reform in Tibet.* Bloomington: Indiana University Press.

Barnett, Robert, 2013. "Language Practices and Protracted Conflict: The Tibet–China Dispute." In Jean-Pierre Cabestan and Aleksandar Pavkovic, eds., *Secessionism and Separatism in Europe and Asia: To Have a State of One's Own.* London: Routledge. 196–219.

Bénassy-Quéréa, Agnès and Damien Capelleb, 2014. "On the Inclusion of the Chinese Renminbi in the SDR Basket." *International Economics.* Vol. 139, 133–51.

Billeter, Térence, 1998. "Chinese Nationalism Falls Back on Legendary Ancestor." *China Perspectives*. No. 18, 44–51.

Blumenthal, Dan, 2020. *The China Nightmare: The Grand Ambitions of a Decaying State*. Washington, DC: American Enterprise Institute.

Boughton, James M., 2001. *Silent Revolution: The International Monetary Fund 1979–1989*. Washington, DC: International Monetary Fund.

Bovingdon, Gardner, 2010. *The Uyghurs: Strangers in Their Own Land*. New York: Columbia University Press.

Braudel, Fernand, 1992 [1979]. *Civilization and Capitalism: 15th–18th Century*. Vol. III. *The Perspective of the World*. Berkeley and Los Angeles: University of California Press.

Brenner, Neil, 2004. *New State Spaces: Urban Governance and the Rescaling of Statehood*. Oxford: Oxford University Press.

Bristow, M.R., 1984. *Land Use Planning in Hong Kong*. Hong Kong: Oxford University Press.

Brophy, David, 2017. "The 1957–58 Xinjiang Committee Plenum and the Attack on 'Local Nationalism'." Washington, DC: Wilson Center, History and Public Policy Program. At www.wilsoncenter.org/blog-post/the-1957-58-xinjiang-committee-plenum-and-the-attack-local-nationalism.

Brown, Mayer, 2008. "Arbitration of Disputes in China and Hong Kong: Challenges and Opportunities." At www.mayerbrown.com/public_docs/Event_FinalBook.pdf.

Bush, Richard, 2016. *Hong Kong in the Shadow of China: Living with the Leviathan*. Washington, DC: Brookings Institution.

Cabestan, Jean-Pierre, 2005. "The Many Facets of Chinese Nationalism." *China Perspectives*. No. 59. At https://journals.openedition.org/chinaperspectives/2793.

Calder, Kent E., 2021. *Global Political Cities: Actors and Arenas of Influence in International Affairs*. Washington, DC: Brookings Institution.

Cao, Erbao, 2008. "Governance Force of Hong Kong Under 'One Country, Two Systems'" (曹二寶: "一國兩制"條件下香港的管治力量), *Learning Times*, January 29, 2008. At www.legco.gov.hk/yr08-09/chinese/panels/ca/papers/ca0420cb2-1389-2-c.pdf.

Carrico, Kevin, 2017. *The Great Han: Race, Nationalism, and Tradition in China Today*. Berkeley: University of California Press.

Carroll, John M., 1997. "Colonialism and Collaboration: Chinese Subjects and the Making of British Hong Kong." *China Information*. Vol. 12, Nos. 1–2. 12–33.

Carroll, John M., 2005. *Edges of Empire: Chinese Elites and British Colonials in Hong Kong*. Cambridge, MA: Harvard University Press.

Cartledge, Simon, 2017. *A System Apart: Hong Kong's Political Economy from 1997 till Now*. London: Penguin Books.

CCP Central Committee Department of United Front Work (中共中央統戰部), 1991. *Collected Documents for Nationalities Questions, July 1921–September 1949* (民族問題文獻匯編) Beijing: Central Party School of the CCP Press (中共中央黨校出版社).

CCP Central Documents Research Office (中共中央文獻研究室), CCP Committee of the Tibet Autonomous Region (中共西藏自治區委員會), China Center of Tibetan Studies (中國藏學研究中心), eds., 2001. *Selected works of Mao Zedong on Tibet* (毛澤東西藏工作文獻) Beijing: Central Party Literature Press (中央文獻出版社).

Centre for Communication and Public Opinion Survey, the Chinese University of Hong Kong, 2020. "Research Report on Public Opinion during the Anti-Extradition Bill (Fugitive Offenders Bill) Movement in Hong Kong." Hong Kong: Chinese University of Hong Kong School of Journalism and Communication. At www.com.cuhk.edu.hk/ccpos/en/pdf/202005PublicOpinionSurveyReport-ENG.pdf.

Chan, Chak-Kwan, 2011. *Social Security Policy in Hong Kong: From British Colony to China's Special Administrative Region.* Lanham, MD: Rowman and Littlefield.

Chan, Chi-Tat, 2013. "Young Activists and the Anti-Patriotic Education Movement in Post-colonial Hong Kong: Some Insights from Twitter." *Citizenship, Social and Economics Education.* Vol. 12, No. 3. 148–62.

Chan, Joseph M. and Francis L.F. Lee, 2010. "Why Can't Hong Kong Forget the June 4th Incident? Media, Social Organization, Nation-State and Collective Memory." *Mass Communication Research.* Vol. 103. 215–59.

Chan, Joseph M. and Francis L.F. Lee, 2011. "The Primacy of Local Interests and Press Freedom in Hong Kong: A Survey Study of Professional Journalists." *Journalism.* Vol. 12, No. 1. 89–105.

Chan, K.C., 1993. "History." In P.K. Choi and L.S. Ho, eds., *The Other Hong Kong Report 1993.* Hong Kong: Chinese University of Hong Kong. 455–83.

Chan, King-Fai (陳景輝), 2007. "From Protecting Star Ferry Pier to Localist Politics" (從天星保衛運動到本土文化政治). *Inmediahk*, January 4, 2007. At www.inmediahk.net/node/181258.

Chan, M.M. Johannes, H. L. Fu, and Yash Ghai, eds., 2000. *Hong Kong's Constitutional Debate: Conflict Over Interpretation.* Hong Kong: Hong Kong University Press.

Chan, Man-hung (陳文鴻), 2009, "CEPA and the Hollowization of Hong Kong Industry and Economy" (CEPA與香港產業經濟空心化), *Taiwan Journal of National Policy* (臺灣國家政策學刊). Vol. 3, No. 7. 39–44.

Chan, Man-hung (陳文鴻), 2015. "Storms of the Hong Kong Social Movements: From the Riots of the Two Factions to Meeting Point" (風起雲湧的香港社運史—由兩派暴動到匯點), *Master Insight*, August 23,

2015. At www.master-insight.com/%E9%A2%A8%E8%B5%B7%
E9%9B%B2%E6%B9%A7%E7%9A%84%E9%A6%99%E6%B8%
AF%E7%A4%BE%E9%81%8B%E5%8F%B2-%E7%94%B1%E5%
85%A9%E6%B4%BE%E6%9A%B4%E5%8B%95%E5%88%B0%
E5%8C%AF%E9%BB%9E.

Chan, Ming-Kuo, 1975. "Labor and Empire: The Chinese Labor Movement
in the Canton Delta, 1895–1927." Unpublished dissertation, Department
of History, Stanford University.

Chan, Wai-Kwan, 1991. *The Making of Hong Kong Society: Three Studies
of Class Formation in Early Hong Kong.* Oxford: Clarendon Press.

Chang, Bin-Leung (張炳良), 1988. "The Emergence and Political Influence
of the New Middle Class." In Chang Bin-Leung and Ma Kwok-Ming (馬
國明), *Class Analysis and Hong Kong* (階級分析與香港). Hong Kong:
Twilights Books.

Chen, Albert H.Y., 2010. "An Unexpected Breakthrough in Hong Kong's
Constitutional Reform in 2010." *Hong Kong Law Journal.* Vol. 40,
Part 2. 260–70. At https://hub.hku.hk/bitstream/10722/135145/1/con
tent.pdf?accept=1.

Chen, Guoxin (陳國新), Xie Xuhui (謝旭輝), and Yang Haodong (楊浩東),
2003. *The Development of Marxist Theory of Nationalities by the Three
Generations of CCP leaders* (中共三代領導人對馬克思主義民族理論的
繼承發展). Guiyang: Guizhou People's Press (貴州人民出版社).

Chen, Yangyong (陳揚勇), 2009. "The Common Program and the Formation
of the Nationalities Regional Autonomy System: Also on the Formation of
the Nationalities Regional Autonomy Policy in New China" (《共同綱
領》與民族區域自治制度的確立─兼談新中國民族區域自治政策的形
成) *Studies of the History of CCP* (中共黨史研究). No. 8. 13–20.

Cheng, Edmund W., 2010. "United Front Work and Mechanisms of
Countermobilization in Hong Kong." *China Journal.* Vol. 83, 1–33.

Cheng, Edmund W., 2019. "Hong Kong's Hybrid Regime and Its
Repertoires." In Ching Kwan Lee and Ming Sing, eds., *Take Back Our
Future: An Eventful Sociology of the Hong Kong Umbrella Movement.*
Ithaca, NY: Cornell University Press. 167–92.

Cheng, Joseph C., 2004. "The 2003 District Council Elections in Hong
Kong." *Asian Survey.* Vol. 44, No. 5, 734–54.

Cheng, Joseph Y.S., 1984. Hong Kong in Search of a Future. Oxford:
Oxford University Press.

Cheung, Gary Ka-wai, 2000. *Inside Story of the 1967 Riot in Hong Kong* (香
港六七暴動內情). Hong Kong: Pacific Century Publishing (太平洋世紀出
版社).

Cheung, Gary Ka-wai, 2009. *Hong Kong's Watershed: The 1967 Riots.*
Hong Kong: University of Hong Kong Press.

Cheung, S.K. (張壽祺), 1991. *The Tankas* (蛋家人). Hong Kong: Zhonghua Book Company (中華書局).

Cheung, S.W., 1984. "Fishing Industry in Tai O: Natural Environment, Technology, Economy and Society." Unpublished M.Phil. thesis. Chinese University of Hong Kong.

Cheung, Yan-leung, Cheng Yuk-Shing, and Woo Chi-keung, 2017. *Hong Kong's Global Financial Centre and China's Development: Changing Roles and Future Prospects.* London: Routledge.

Chin, Angelina Y., 2014. "Diasporic Memories and Conceptual Geography in Post-colonial Hong Kong." *Modern Asian Studies.* Vol. 48, No. 6, 1566–93.

Chin, Wan (陳雲), 2008. *Farmers Heart and Craftsmen's Affection: Remembering Urban and Rural Customs in Old Hong Kong* (農心匠意—香港城鄉風俗憶舊) Hong Kong: Arcadia Press Ltd (花千樹出版有限公司).

Chin, Wan (陳雲), 2013. *On Hong Kong as China's Survivors* (香港遺民論). Hong Kong: Subculture Publishing (次文化出版).

Chin, Wan (陳雲) 2011. *On the Hong Kong City State* (香港城邦論). Hong Kong: Enrich Publishing (天窗出版社有限公司).

Chin, Wan, 2015. "A Federation for Hong Kong and China." *New York Times* op. ed., June 14, 2015. At www.nytimes.com/2015/06/15/opinion/a-federation-for-hong-kong-and-china.html.

China Ag., 2015 "Gateway to China: Hong Kong Re-exports of Agricultural Goods." *Agriculture and Food in China.* June 30, 2015. At http://chinaag.org/2015/06/30/gateway-to-china-hong-kong-re-exports-of-agricultural-goods.

Ching Cheong (程翔), 2012. "Assessing the Size of Underground CCP Organizations in Hong Kong from the Perspective of the 18th Party Congress" (從十八大看香港地下黨規模), *Mingpao*, November 28, 2012. At https://life.mingpao.com/general/article?issue=20121128&nodeid=1508242340650.

Chiu, Stephen W. K., 1996. "Unravelling Hong Kong's Exceptionalism: The Politics of Laissez-Faire in the Industrial Takeoff." *Political Power and Social Theory.* Vol. 10. 229–56.

Chiu, Stephen W. K. and Ho-fung Hung, 1999. "State Building and Rural Stability." In Tak-Wing Ngo, ed., *Hong Kong's History: State and Society under Colonial Rule.* London: Routledge. 74–100.

Chiu, Stephen W. K. and Tai-lok Lui, 2009. *Hong Kong: Becoming a Chinese Global City.* London: Routledge.

Chiu, Stephen W.K. and Lui Tai-lok, eds., 2000. *Dynamics of Social Movements in Hong Kong.* Hong Kong: Hong Kong University Press.

Choi, Dong Ho (蔡東豪) and Yim Kim Ho (嚴劍豪), 2010. *Seven Warriors: Battle for Tai Long Sai Wan* (七俠四義: 大浪西灣保衛戰). Hong Kong: Up Publications (上書局).

Choi, Ivan Chi-Keung (蔡子強), 2007. "Letters from the Premier" (總理的來信). *Mingpao*, June 15, 2007. At http://hktext.blogspot.com/2007/06/blog-post_7831.html.

Choi, Ivan Chi-Keung (蔡子強), Chang Yiu Kong (莊耀洸), Choi Yiu Cheong (蔡耀昌) and Paul Wong (黃昕然), eds., 1998. *Same Path, Different Destinations: Hong Kong Student Movement Since the [Sino-British] Negotiation about Hong Kong's Future* (同途殊歸:前途談判以來的香港學運). Hong Kong: Hong Kong Publisher of Humanities and Sciences (香港人文科學出版社).

Choi, Ivan Chi-Keung (蔡子強) and Chan Kun Man (陳雋文), "Comments on LegCo Election: Initial Analyses of the Legislative Council Election" (立會選舉評論: 立法會選舉結果初步評析), *Ming Pao*, September 6, 2016. At https://bit.ly/3H1788W.

Choi, Wing-Mui (蔡詠梅), 2011, "Hong Kong's New Generation Breaks the Anti-Communism Taboo" (香港新壹代打破反共禁忌), *Open Magazine*, March 1, 2011. At www.open.com.hk/old_version/1002p28.html.

Choi, Wing-Mui (蔡詠梅), 2017. "Will Hong Kong Become Another Tibet?" (香港會成為第二個西藏嗎?). *Citizen News* (眾新聞), September 18, 2017. At https://bit.ly/3EWGY5C.

Chow, Alex, 2019. "Prefigurative Politics of the Umbrella Movement." In Ching Kwan Lee and Ming Sing, eds., *Take Back Our Future: An Eventful Sociology of the Hong Kong Umbrella Movement*. Ithaca, NY: Cornell University Press. 34–51.

Chow, Kai-wing, 2001. "Narrating Nation, Race, and National Culture: Imagining the Hanzu Identity in Modern China." In Kai-wing Chow, Kevin M. Doak, and Poshek Fu, eds. *Constructing Nationhood in Modern East Asia*. Ann Arbor: University of Michigan Press. 47–83.

Chow, Rey, 1993. *Writing Diaspora: Tactics of Intervention in Contemporary Cultural Studies*. Indianapolis: University of Indiana Press.

Chu, Eddie Hoi-dick (朱凱迪), "Preservation of Rural New Territory and Hong Kong's Democratic Movement" (保育新界鄉郊與香港民主運動), *InMedia HK*, June 7, 2014. At www.inmediahk.net/node/1023425.

Chu, Stephen You-Wai, 2013. *Lost in Transition: Hong Kong Culture in the Age of China*. Albany: SUNY Press.

Chun, A., 1987. "The Land Revolution in Twentieth Century Rural Hong Kong." *Bulletin of the Institute of Ethnology Academia Sinica*. No. 61. 1–40.

CO 1030/1033. *Heung Yee Kuk*. London: Public Record Office.

Cohen, B.J., 2012. "The Yuan Tomorrow? Evaluating China's Currency Internationalisation Strategy." *New Political Economy*. Vol. 17, No. 3. 361–71.

Congress of the United States of America, 1992. US–HK Policy Act 1992 (Enrolled as Agreed to or Passed by Both House and Senate). At http://hongkong.usconsulate.gov/ushk_pa_1992.html.

Cooper, John, 1970. *Colony in Conflict: The Hong Kong Disturbances, May 1967–January 1968.* Hong Kong: Swindon.

Crossley, Pamela Kyle, 1999. *A Translucent Mirror: History and Identity in Qing Imperial Ideology.* Berkeley and Los Angeles: University of California Press.

Crossley, Pamela Kyle, Helen F. Siu, and Donald S. Sutton, eds., 2006. *Empire at the Margins: Culture, Ethnicity, and Frontier in Early Modern China.* Berkeley and Los Angeles: University of California Press.

Dalai Lama, 1990. *Freedom in Exile: The Autobiography of the Dalai Lama.* New York: Harper Collins.

Dapiran, Antony, 2017. *City of Protest: A Recent History of Dissent in Hong Kong.* London: Penguin.

Dapiran, Antony, 2019. "'Be Water!' Seven Tactics That Are Winning Hong Kong's Democracy Revolution." *New Statesman,* August 1, 2019. At www.newstatesman.com/world/2019/08/be-water-seven-tactics-are-winning-hong-kongs-democracy-revolution.

Davis, Michael C., 2007. "The Quest for Self-Rule in Tibet." *Journal of Democracy.* Vol. 18, No. 4. 157–71.

Davis, Michael C., 2020. *Making Hong Kong Chinese: The Rollback of Human Rights and the Rule of Law.* Ann Arbor, MI: Association for Asian Studies.

Dewolf, Christopher, 2019. "Hong Kong Modern Heritage VI: City Hall." At https://zolimacitymag.com/hong-kongs-modern-heritage-part-vi-city-hall.

Di Cosmo, Nicola, 1998. "Qing Colonial Administration in Inner Asia." *International History Review.* Vol. 20, No. 2. 287–309.

Downie, Richard, 2019. "South Sudan: The Painful Rise and Rapid Descent of the World's Newest Nation." In Jon B. Alterman and Will Todman, eds., *Independence Movements and Their Aftermath: Self-Determination and the Struggle for Success.* Lanham, MD: CSIS/Rowman and Littlefield. 100–16.

Du, Yufang (杜玉芳), 2011. "Choice of Path of Unification of the Motherland: Formation of the 'Tibet model' and Its Influence" (祖國統一的路徑抉擇—"西藏模式"的形成及影響). *Journal of the Central Party School of the Communist Party of China* (中共中央黨校學報). No. 2, At www.zgzydxxb .cn/index.php?m=content&c=index&a=show&catid=51&id=799.

Duara, Prasenjit, 1997. *Rescuing History from the Nation: Questioning Narrative of Modern China.* Chicago: Chicago University Press.

Duara, Prasenjit, 2011. "The Multi-national State in Modern World History: The Chinese Experiment." *Frontiers of History in China*. Vol. 6, No. 2. 285–95.

Duara, Prasenjit, 2016. "Hong Kong as a Global Frontier: Interface of China, Asia, and the World." In Priscilla Roberts and John M. Carroll, eds., *Hong Kong in the Cold War*. Hong Kong: Hong Kong University Press. 211–30.

Eichengreen, Barry and Guangtao Xia, 2019. "China and the SDR: Financial Liberalization through the Back Door." *Quarterly Journal of Finance*. Vol. 9, No. 3, 1950007.

Eichengreen, Barry and Masahiro Kawai, 2014. "Issues for Renminbi Internationalization: An Overview." Asian Development Bank Institute Working Paper 454, At www.adb.org/sites/default/files/publication/156309/adbi-wp454.pdf.

Eitel, E.J., 1895. *Europe in China: The History of Hong Kong from the Beginning to 1882*. Hong Kong: Kelly and Walsh Ltd.

Faure, David, 1986. *The Structure of Chinese Rural Society: Lineage and Village in the Eastern New Territories, Hong Kong*. Hong Kong: Oxford University Press.

Fong, Brian, 2014. "The Partnership between the Chinese Government and Hong Kong's Capitalist Class: Implications for HKSAR Governance, 1997–2012." *China Quarterly*. Vol. 217, 195–220.

Fong, Brian, 2017. "In-between Liberal Authoritarianism and Electoral Authoritarianism: Hong Kong's Democratization under Chinese Sovereignty, 1997–2016." *Democratization*. Vol. 24, No. 4. 724–50.

Foucault, Michel, 1980. *Power/Knowledge: Selected Interviews and Other Writings*, ed. Colin Gordon. New York: Pantheon Books.

Frankel, J., 2012. "Internationalization of the RMB and Historical Precedents." *Journal of Economic Integration*. Vol. 27, No. 3. 329–65.

Freedman, Maurice, 1966. "Shifts of Power in the Hong Kong New Territories." *Journal of Asian and African Studies*. Vol. 1, No. 1. 3–12.

Fu, Hualing, Carole Petersen, and Simon Young, eds., 2005. *National Security and Fundamental Freedoms: Hong Kong's Article 23 under Scrutiny*. Hong Kong: University of Hong Kong Press.

Fung, Hung-gay, Ko Chi-wo Glenn, and Jot Yau, 2014. *Dim Sum Bonds: The Offshore Renminbi (RMB)-Denominated Bonds*. New York: Wiley.

García-Herrero, Alicia, 2011. "Hong Kong as an International Banking Center: Present and Future." *Journal of the Asia Pacific Economy*. Vol. 16, No. 3. 361–71.

Gettinger, Dan, 2016. "Drone Smuggling: Inside Illegal Exports." Center for the Study of the Drone, Bard College, June 13, 2016. At http://dronecen ter.bard.edu/drone-smuggling-inside-illegal-exports.

Goldstein, Melvyn C., 1973. "The Circulation of Estates in Tibet: Reincarnation, Land, and Politics." *Journal of Asian Studies*. Vol. 32, No. 3. 445–55.

Goldstein, Melvyn C., 1986. "Reexamining Choice, Dependency and Command in Tibetan Social System: 'Tax Appendages' and Other Landless Serfs." *Tibetan Journal*. Vol. 11, No. 4. 79–112.

Goldstein, Melvyn C., 1989. *A History of Modern Tibet, 1913–1951: The Demise of the Lamaist State*. Berkeley and Los Angeles: University of California Press.

Goldstein, Melvyn C., 1997. *The Snow Lion and the Dragon: China, Tibet, and the Dalai Lama*. Berkeley: University of California Press.

Goldstein, Melvyn C., 2007. *A History of Modern Tibet*. Vol. II. *The Calm before the Storm, 1951–1955*. Berkeley: University of California Press.

Goldstein, Melvyn C., 2014. *A History of Modern Tibet*. Vol. III. *The Storm Clouds Descend, 1955–1957*. Berkeley, CA: University of California Press.

Goldstein, Melvyn C., 2019. *A History of Modern Tibet*. Vol. IV. *In the Eye of the Storm, 1957–1959*. Berkeley: University of California Press.

Goodstadt, Leo F., 2000, "China and the Selection of Hong Kong's Post-colonial Political Elite." *China Quarterly*. Vol. 163, 721–41.

Grant, Charles J., 1962. *The Soils and Agriculture of Hong Kong*. Hong Kong: Government Printer.

Grimmer, Sarah, 2019. "Distinction and Connection: Hong Kong and Mainland China, a View from the HKIAC." *Global Arbitration Review*, May 24, 2019. At https://globalarbitrationreview.com/review/ the-asia-pacific-arbitration-review/2020/article/distinction-and-connec tion-hong-kong-and-mainland-china-view-the-hkiac.

Gross, Raphael, 2007. *Carl Schmitt and the Jews: The "Jewish Question," the Holocaust, and German Legal Theory*. Madison: University of Wisconsin Press.

Groves, R.G., 1964. "The Origins of Two Market Towns in the New Territories." Royal Asiatic Society, Hong Kong Branch, ed., *Aspects of Social Organization in the New Territories: Weekend Symposium*. Hong Kong: Cathay Press. 16–20.

Groves, R.G., 1969. "Militia, Market and Lineage: Chinese Resistance to the Occupation of Hong Kong's New Territories in 1899." *Journal of Hong Kong Branch of Royal Asiatic Society*. Vol. 9. 31–64.

Grunfeld, Tom A., 1987. *The Making of Modern Tibet*. Armonk, NY: M.E. Sharpe.

Guo, Guocan (郭國燦), 2009. *Chinese Conglomerates in Hong Kong* (香港中資財團). Hong Kong: Joint Publishing Co. Ltd (三聯書店 (香港) 有限公司).

Hamashita, Takeshi, 2008. *China, East Asia and the Global Economy*. London: Routledge.

Hamilton, Gary ed., 1999. *Cosmopolitan Capitalists: Hong Kong and the Chinese Diaspora at the End of the Twentieth Century*. Seattle: University of Washington Press.

Hamilton, Peter E., 2018. "Rethinking the Origins of China's Reform Era: Hong Kong and the 1970s Revival of Sino-US Trade." *Twentieth-Century China*. Vol. 43, No. 1. 67–88.

Han, Sunsheng, 1998. "Real Estate Development in China: A Regional Perspective." *Journal of Real Estate Literature*. Vol. 6, 121–133.

Hannum, Hurst, 1990. *Autonomy, Sovereignty, and Self-Determination*. Philadelphia: University of Pennsylvania Press.

Harris, Paul, 2008. "Is Tibet Entitled to Self Determination?" Center for Comparative and Public Law, Faculty of Law, Hong Kong University, Occasional Paper No. 18. At https://ccpl.law.hku.hk/content/uploads/2018/03/Pub/OP/OP%20No%2018%20Harris%20-%20Eng.pdf.

Hayes, James, 1977. *The Hong Kong Region 1850–1911: Institutions and Leaderships in Town and Countryside*. Hamden, CT: Archon Books.

He, Xi and David Faure, eds., 2016. *The Fisher Folk of Late Imperial and Modern China: An Historical Anthropology of Boat-and-Shed Living*. London: Routledge.

Head, John, 1998. "Selling Hong Kong to China: What Happened to the Right of Self-Determination?" *Kansas Law Review*. Vol. 46. 283–304.

Heaton, William, 1970. "Marxist Revolutionary Strategy and Modern Colonialism: The Cultural Revolution in Hong Kong." *Asian Survey*. Vol. 10, No. 9. 840–57.

Herman, John E., 1997. "Empire in the Southwest: Early Qing Reforms to the Native Chieftain System." *Journal of Asian Studies*. Vol. 56, No. 1. 47–74.

Himsworth, Chris, 2013. "The Autonomy of Devolved Scotland." In Yash Ghai and Sophia Woodman, eds., *Practising Self-Government: A Comparative Study of Autonomous Regions*. Cambridge: Cambridge University Press. 349–82.

HKFS (香港專上學生聯會), 1982. *Hong Kong Student Movement in Retrospect* (香港學生運動回顧). Hong Kong: Wide-Angle Lens Publishing (廣角鏡出版社).

Ho, Leung Mau (何良懋), 2019. "Recollecting the Past and Presents of the Maoist Faction [of the student movement]: They Are All Exposed in the Conflict over the Extradition Law Amendment" (細數香港國粹派前世今

生, 親共政府修例一役全露底), *News Lens* (關鍵評論), October 21, 2019. At www.thenewslens.com/article/126297.

Ho, Ming-sho, 2019. *Challenging Beijing's Mandate of Heaven: Taiwan's Sunflower Movement and Hong Kong's Umbrella Movement.* Philadelphia: Temple University Press.

Hong Kong Free Press, 2016. "CUHK Survey Finds Nearly 40% of Young Hongkongers Want Independence after 2047," July 25, 2016. At www.hongkongfp.com/2016/07/25/17-hongkongers-support-independence-2047-especially-youth-cuhk-survery.

Hong Kong Government, 1948. *Hong Kong Annual Report 1947.* Hong Kong: Government Printer.

Hong Kong Government, 1957. "Review: A Problem of People." In *Hong Kong Annual Report.* Hong Kong: Government Printer. Available at https://en.wikisource.org/wiki/Hong_Kong_Annual_Report,_1956/Chapter_1.

Hong Kong Journalists Association, 2007a. *Shrinking Margins: Freedom of Expression in Hong Kong since 1997.* Hong Kong: HKJA.

Hong Kong Journalists Association, 2007b. *Survey on Press Freedom in Hong Kong.* Hong Kong, HKJA.

Hong Kong Observer Society, 1982. *Observing Hong Kong* (觀察香港). Hong Kong: Baixing banyuekan (百姓半月刊).

Hong Kong University, 2016. "Categorical Ethnic Identity Poll, 1997–2016." At www.hkupop.hku.hk/english/popexpress/ethnic/eidentity/poll/eid_poll_chart.html.

Hu, Jiaheng (胡佳恒) 2007. "Can Shenzhen–Hong Kong Metropolitan Circle Attract Population Dividend?" (深港都會圈能否圈來人口紅利), *Sina News*, August 17, 2007. At http://finance.sina.com.cn/china/dfjj/20070817/23423894323.shtml.

Huang, Tianlei, 2019. "Why China Still Needs Hong Kong." Peterson Institute of International Economics, July 15, 2019. At www.piie.com/blogs/china-economic-watch/why-china-still-needs-hong-kong.

Hughes, Richard, 1968 *Borrowed Place, Borrowed Time: Hong Kong and Its Many Faces.* London: André Deutsch.

Hui, Victoria Tin-bor, 2015. "Hong Kong's Umbrella Movement: The Protests and Beyond." *Journal of Democracy.* Vol. 26, No. 2. 111–21.

Hung, Ho-fung. 1998. "Thousand-Year Oppression and Thousand-Year Resistance: The Tanka Fishersfolks in Tai O before and after Colonialism." *Chinese Sociology and Anthropology.* Vol. 30, No. 3. 75–99.

Hung, Ho-fung, 2001. "Identity Contested: Rural Ethnicities in the Making of Urban Hong Kong." In Lee Pui-tak, ed., *Hong Kong Reintegrating with*

China: Political, Economic and Cultural Dimensions. Hong Kong: Hong Kong University Press. 181–202.

Hung, Ho-fung, 2010. "Uncertainty in the Enclave." *New Left Review*, Series 2. Vol. 66. At https://newleftreview.org/issues/II66/articles/ho-fung-hung-uncertainty-in-the-enclave.

Hung, Ho-fung (孔誥烽), 2011a, "Discovering Yushan from Victoria Harbor: The Resonance between Hong Kong and Taiwan Local Consciousness" (從維港發現玉山—港台本土意識的共振). In Local Discourse Editorial Board (本土論述編輯委員會), ed., *Annal of Local Discourse 2010: New Class Struggle in Hong Kong* (本土論述 2010:香港新階級鬥爭). Taiwan: Voyager Books (漫遊者文化). 115–22.

Hung, Ho-fung, 2011b. *Protest with Chinese Characteristics: Demonstrations, Riots, and Petitions in the Mid-Qing Dynasty.* New York: Columbia University Press.

Hung, Ho-fung, 2015. *The China Boom: Why China Will Not Rule the World.* New York, NY: Columbia University Press.

Hung, Ho-fung, 2016. "From Qing Empire to the Chinese Nation: An Incomplete Project." *Nations and Nationalism.* Vol. 22, No. 4. 660–65.

Hung, Ho-fung, 2018. "The Tapestry of Chinese Capital in the Global South." *Palgrave Communications.* Vol. 4, Article 65. At www.nature.com/articles/s41599-018-0123-7.

Hung, Ho-fung, 2020a. "China and the Global South." In Thomas Fingar and Jean Oi ed. *Fateful Decisions: Choices That Will Shape China's Future.* Palo Alto, CA: Stanford University Press. 247–71.

Hung, Ho-fung, 2020b. "How Capitalist Is China?" *Socio-Economic Review.* Vol. 18, No. 3. 888–92.

Hung, Ho-fung, 2020c. "The US–China Rivalry Is about Capitalist Competition" *Jacobin* July 11, 2020. www.jacobinmag.com/2020/07/us-china-competition-capitalism-rivalry.

Hung, Ho-fung, 2021. "The Periphery in the Making of Globalization: The China Lobby and the Reversal of Clinton's China Trade Policy, 1993–1994," *Review of International Political Economy.* Vol. 28, No. 4. 1004–1027.

Hung, Ho-fung, forthcoming. *Clash of Empires: From "Chimerica" to the "New Cold War".* Cambridge: Cambridge University Press.

Hung, Ho-fung and Ip Iam-Chong, 2012. "Hong Kong's Democratic Movement and the Making of China's Offshore Civil Society." *Asian Survey.* Vol. 52, No. 3, 504–527.

Hung, Ho-fung and Kuo Huei-ying, 2010. "'One Country, Two Systems' and Its Antagonists in Tibet and Taiwan." *China Information.* Vol. 24, No. 3. 317–37.

Ip, Iam-Chong, 2015. "Politics of Belonging: A Study of the Campaign against Mainland Visitors in Hong Kong." *Inter-Asia Cultural Studies*. Vol. 16, No. 3, 410–21.

Ip, Iam-Chong, 2018. "State, Class and Capital: Gentrification and New Urban Developmentalism in Hong Kong." *Critical Sociology*. Vol. 44, No. 3. 547–62.

Ip, Iam-Chong, 2019. *Hong Kong's New Identity Politics: Longing for the Local in the Shadow of China*. London: Routledge.

Jao, Tsung-I 饒宗頤, 1959. *Historical Materials on Kowloon and Late Song* (九龍與宋季史料). Hong Kong: Wanyou (萬有出版社).

Jiang, Guansheng (江關生). 2012. *Chinese Communist Party in Hong Kong*. Vol. 2 (中國共產黨在香港). Hong Kong: Cosmos Books (天地圖書).

Jiang, Shigong (強世功), 2008. *Hong Kong, China: Cultural and Political Perspectives* (中國香港:政治與文化的視野). Hong Kong: Oxford University Press.

Jiang, Shigong (強世功), 2019. "The Internal Logic of Super-Sized Political Entities: 'Empire' and World Order" (超大型政治實體的內在邏輯:"帝國"與世界秩序) *Aisixiang*, April 6, 2019. At www.aisixiang.com/data/115799.html. English translation at www.readingthechinadream.com/jiang-shigong-empire-and-world-order.html.

Jing, Suzie, 2018. "The Mirror: Colonial Britain and China's Rationale for Hong Kong's Functional Constituency." Draft paper presented at the Seminar on Corporations and International Law, Duke University, January 29, 2018. At https://sites.duke.edu/corporations/2018/01/29/the-mirror-colonial-britain-and-chinas-rationale-for-hong-kongs-functional-constituency.

Jones, Carol, 2015. *Lost in China? Law, Culture and Identity in Post-1997 Hong Kong*. Cambridge: Cambridge University Press.

Kaeding, Malte Philipp, 2014. "Challenging Hongkongisation: The Role of Taiwan's Social Movements and Perceptions of Post-handover Hong Kong," *Taiwan in Comparative Perspective*. Vol. 5. 120–33.

Kaeding, Malte Philipp, 2017. "The Rise of 'Localism' in Hong Kong." *Journal of Democracy*. Vol. 28. No. 1. 157–71.

Kamm, J.T., 1977. "Two Essays on the Ch'ing Economy of Hsin-An, Kwangtung." *Journal of the Hong Kong Branch of the Royal Asiatic Society*. Vol. 17. 55–84.

Kani, H., 1967. *A General Survey of the Boat People in Hong Kong*. Hong Kong: Southeast Asia Studies Sections, New Asia Research Institute, Chinese University of Hong Kong.

Karreman, Bas and Bert van der Knaap, 2009. "The Financial Centres of Shanghai and Hong Kong: Competition or Complementarity?" *Environment and Planning A: Economy and Space*. Vol. 41, No. 3. 563–80.

Keating, Michael, 2013. "Nationalism, Unionism and Secession in Scotland." In Jean-Pierre Cabestan and Aleksandar Pavkovic, eds., *Secessionism and Separatism in Europe and Asia: To Have a State of One's Own*. London: Routledge. 127–44.

Keliher, Macabe, 2020. "Neoliberal Hong Kong Is Our Future, Too." *Boston Review*, September 9, 2020. At http://bostonreview.net/global-justice/macabe-keliher-neoliberal-hong-kong-our-future-too.

Kennedy, John James, 2002. "The Face of 'Grassroots Democracy' in Rural China: Real versus Cosmetic Elections." *Asian Survey*. Vol. 42, No. 3. 456–482.

Ku, Agnes Shuk-mei, 2004. "Immigration Policies, Discourses, and the Politics of Local Belonging in Hong Kong, 1950–1980." *Modern China*. No. 30. 326–60.

Ku, Agnes Shuk-mei, 2012, "Re-making Places and Fashioning an Opposition Discourse: Struggle over the Star Ferry Pier and the Queen's Pier in Hong Kong." *Environment and Planning D: Space and Society*. Vol. 30. No. 1. 5–22.

Ku, Agnes Shuk-mei, 2019. "In Search of a New Political Subjectivity in Hong Kong: The Umbrella Movement as a Street Theater of Generational Change." *China Journal*. Vol. 82. 111–32.

Ku, Agnes Shuk-mei and Pun Ngai, eds., 2004. *Remaking Citizenship in Hong Kong: Community, Nation and the Global City*. London: Routledge.

Kuo, Huei-ying, 2014. *Networks beyond Empires: Chinese Business and Nationalism in the Hong Kong–Singapore Corridor, 1914–1941*. Leiden: Brill.

Kwong, Bruce K., 2010. *Patron–Client Politics and Elections in Hong Kong*. London: Routledge.

Kwong, Ying-ho, 2016. "State–Society Conflict Radicalization in Hong Kong: The Rise of 'Anti-China' Sentiment and Radical Localism." *Asian Affairs*. Vol. 47. No. 3. 428–42.

Lam, Jermain T.M., 2010. "Party Institutionalization in Hong Kong." *Asian Perspective*. Vol. 34, No. 2. 53–82.

Lam, Nora, 2017. *Lost in the Fumes* (biographical documentary). Hong Kong: Ying e Chi.

Lam, T.W., 1985. *Essays on the Ancient History of Hong Kong*. Taipei: Taiwan Commercial Press.

Lam, Wai-man and Luke Cooper, 2018. *Citizenship, Identity and Social Movements in the New Hong Kong: Localism after the Umbrella Movement*. London: Routledge.

Lam, Wai-man and Kay Lam Chi-yan, 2013. "China's United Front Work in Civil Society: The Case of Hong Kong." *International Journal of China Studies*. Vol. 4. No. 3. 301–25.

Lardy, Nicholas, 2019. *The State Strikes Back: The End of Economic Reform in China?* Washington DC: Peterson Institute for International Economics.

Lau Siu-kai, 1984. *Society and Politics in Hong Kong.* Hong Kong: Chinese University of Hong Kong Press.

Lau, Siu-Kai and Hsien-Chi Kuan, 1988. *The Ethos of the Hong Kong Chinese.* Hong Kong: Chinese University Press.

Law, Wing-sang, 2009. *Collaborative Colonial Power: The Making of the Hong Kong Chinese.* Hong Kong: University of Hong Kong Press.

Lee, Ching-kwan and Ming Sing, eds., 2019. *Challenging Beijing's Mandate of Heaven: Taiwan's Sunflower Movement and Hong Kong's Umbrella Movement.* Ithaca, NY: Cornell University Press.

Lee, Eliza, 2020. "United Front, Clientelism, and Indirect Rule: Theorizing the Role of the 'Liaison Office' in Hong Kong." *Journal of Contemporary China.* Vol. 29 No. 125. 763–75.

Lee, Francis L.F. and Joseph M. Chan, 2008, "Professionalism, Political Orientation and Perceived Self-Censorship: A Survey Study of Hong Kong Journalists." *Issues and Studies.* Vol. 44, No. 1. 205–38.

Lee, Francis L.F. and Joseph M. Chan, 2011. *Media, Social Mobilisation and Mass Protests in Post-colonial Hong Kong: The Power of a Critical Event.* London: Routledge.

Lee, Francis L. F. and Joseph M. Chan, 2018. *Media and Protest Logics in the Digital Era: The Umbrella Movement in Hong Kong.* Oxford: Oxford University Press.

Lee, Kelvin, 2019. "Post-June-Fourth Hong Kong: Radical Organizations and the Culture of Abiding by the Law" (後六四香港:激進組織與守法文化). *Generational Redemption: Archaeological Note of Hong Kong's Future* (時代懺悔錄:香港前途考古扎記). At https://medium.com/recall-hk/p64-f4b7a31c62ea.

Lee, Martin, 1996. "The Fight for Democracy." In Sally Blyth and Ian Wotherspoon, eds., *Hong Kong Remembers.* Hong Kong: Oxford University Press. 233–43.

Lee, Martin, 2012, "Tibetization of Hong Kong" (香港西藏化). *Next Magazine*, September 27, 2012. Available at https://danscons.wordpress.com/2012/09/27/%E9%A6%99%E6%B8%AF%E8%A5%BF%E8%97%8F%E5%8C%96-%E3%80%8A%E5%A3%B9%E9%80%B1%E5%88%8A%E3%80%8B%EF%BC%8C27092012/.

Lee, Zardas Shuk-Man, Phoebe Y.H. Tang and Carol Tsang, 2013. "Searching for an Identity: Debates over Moral and National Education as an Independent Subject in Contemporary Hong Kong." *History Education Research Journal.* Vol. 11, No. 2. 88–97.

Leung, Benjamin K.P., 2000. "Student Movement in Hong Kong: Transition to a Democratizing Society." In Stephen W.K. Chiu and Tai-lok Lui, eds.,

Dynamics of Social Movement in Hong Kong. Hong Kong: Hong Kong University Press. 209–26.

Leung, Dennis K.K., 2015. "Alternative Internet Radio, Press Freedom and Contentious Politics in Hong Kong, 2004–2014." *Javnost: The Public.* Vol. 22, No. 2. 196–212.

Leung, Mo-han (梁慕嫻), 2012. *The Underground CCP and I* (我與香港地下黨). Hong Kong: Open Press (開放出版社).

Li, Hao-ran (李浩然), 2012. *An Overview of Hong Kong's Basic Law Drafting Process* (香港基本法起草過程概覽). Hong Kong: Joint Publishing Hong Kong (三聯書店 (香港) 有限公司).

Li, Hou (李後), 1997. *End of the Hundred-Year Humiliation: The Beginning and End of the Hong Kong Question* (百年屈辱史的终结—香港問題始末) Beijing: Central Document Press (中央文献出版社).

Lian, Yi-Cheng, 2017. "Red Capital in Hong Kong." *New York Times*, June 1, 2017. At www.nytimes.com/2017/06/01/opinion/red-capital-in-hong-kong-china-investment.html.

Lilla, Mark, 2010. "Reading Strauss in Beijing." *New Republic*, December 10, 2010. At https://newrepublic.com/article/79747/reading-leo-strauss-in-beijing-china-marx.

Lin, Gongqin 林貢欽, 2012. "Replacing National Education with Civic Education" (以公民教育取代國民教育). *BBC*, September 5, 2012. At www.bbc.com/zhongwen/trad/hong_kong_review/2012/08/120814_hkreview_education.

Lin, Tian-wei (林天蔚), 1985. "A Preliminary Analysis of the Thesis That Lantau Island Was a Yao Area in Southern Song" (南宋時大嶼山為瑤區之試證). In Lin Tian-wei (林天蔚) and Siu Kwok-kin (蕭國健), *Essays on Hong Kong Precolonial History* (香港前代史論集). Taipei: Commercial Press. 80–120.

Liu, Mingtang, 2020. "Two Faces of China's Statist Shift since the 2000s: A State-Led Counter-movement." Unpublished paper, Department of Sociology, Johns Hopkins University.

Liu, Xiaoyuan, 2003. *Frontier Passages: Ethnopolitics and the Rise of Chinese Communism, 1921–1945.* Palo Alto, CA: Stanford University Press.

Lo, Pui-Yin, 2014. *The Judicial Construction of Hong Kong's Basic Law: Courts, Politics and Society after 1997.* Hong Kong: Hong Kong University Press.

Lo, Sunny Shiu-Hing, 2013. "Democratization of China and Hong Kong: The Hong Kong Alliance in Support of Patriotic Democratic Movements of China." *Journal of Contemporary China.* Vol. 22, No. 84. 923–43.

Lo, Sonny Shiu-Hing, 2018. "Ideologies and Factionalism in Beijing–Hong Kong Relations." *Asian Survey.* Vol. 58 No. 3, 392–415.

Lo, Sonny Shiu-Hing, Steven Chung-fun Hung and Jeff Loo Hai-Chi Loo, 2019. *China's New United Front Work in Hong Kong: Penetrative Politics and Its Implications*. London: Palgrave Macmillan.

Lockhart, J.H.S., 1899. *Extracts from Papers Relating to the Extension of the Colony of Hong Kong*. Hong Kong: Hong Kong Government Printer.

Loh, Christine, 2010. *Underground Front: The Chinese Communist Party in Hong Kong*. Hong Kong: Hong Kong University Press.

Long, Zi-Wai (龍子為), 2011. "The Myth of Hong Kong's Cultural Preservation Movement" (香港文化保育運動迷思), *Sina News*, January 31, 2011. At http://news.sina.com.cn/c/sd/2011-01-31/12072190 4691.shtml.

Lotta, Moberg, 2017. *The Political Economy of Special Economic Zones: Concentrating Economic Development*. London: Routledge.

Louis, Wm. Roger, 1997. "Hong Kong: The Critical Phase, 1945–1949." *American Historical Review*. Vol. 102, No. 4. 1052–84.

Lowe, John and Eileen Yuk-ha Tsang, 2017. "Disunited in Ethnicity: The Racialization of Chinese Mainlanders in Hong Kong." *Patterns of Prejudice*. Vol. 51, No. 2. 137–58.

Lui, Tai-lok, 2017. "'Flying MPs' and Political Change in a Colonial Setting: Political Reform under MacLehose's Governorship of Hong Kong," In Michael H.K. Ng and John D. Wong, eds., *Civil Unrest and Governance in Hong Kong: Law and Order from Historical and Cultural Perspectives*. London: Routledge. 76–96.

Lui, Tai-lok and Stephen W. K. Chiu, 2009. *Hong Kong: Becoming China's Global City*. London: Routledge.

Lui, Tai-lok and Stephen W.K. Chiu, 1999. "Social Movements and Public Discourse on Politics." In Tak-wing Ngo, ed., *Hong Kong's History: State and Society under Colonial Rule*. New York: Routledge. 101–18.

Lui, Tai-lok and Thomas Wong, eds., 1998. Class *Analysis* and Hong Kong (階級分析與香港). Hong Kong: Youth Literary Book.

Ma, Jun (馬駿) and Xu Jiangang (徐劍剛). 2012. *The Road of Renminbi Internationalization: Offshore Markets Development and Capital Account Opening* (人民幣走出國門之路:離岸市場發展與資本項目開放). Hong Kong: Commercial Press (商務印書館).

Ma, Ngok, 1997. "The Sino-British Dispute over Hong Kong: A Game Theory Interpretation." *Asian Survey*. Vol. 37, No. 8. 738–51.

Ma, Ngok, 2005. "Civil Society in Self-Defense: The Struggle against National Security Legislation in Hong Kong." *Journal of Contemporary China*. Vol. 14, No. 44. 465–82.

Ma, Ngok, 2007. *Political Development in Hong Kong: State, Political Society, and Civil Society*. Hong Kong: Hong Kong University Press.

Ma Ngok, 2015. "The Making of a Corporatist State in Hong Kong: The Road to Sectoral Intervention." *Journal of Contemporary Asia*. Vol. 46, No. 2. 247–66.

Ma, Ngok, 2017. "The China Factor in Hong Kong Elections: 1991 to 2016." *China Perspectives*. No. 3. 17–26.

Machiavell, Niccolo, 1992 (1513). *The Prince*. New York: W.W. Norton.

Mark, Chi-kwan, 2004. *Hong Kong and the Cold War: Anglo-American Relations, 1949–57*. Oxford: Oxford University Press.

Mark, Chi-Kwan, 2007. "The 'Problem of People': British Colonials, Cold War Powers, and the Chinese Refugees in Hong Kong, 1949–62." *Modern Asian Studies*. Vol. 41, No. 6. 1145–81.

Marx, Karl, 1978 [1852] "The Eighteenth Brumaire of Louis Bonaparte." In Robert Tucker, ed., *The Marx–Engels Reader*. New York: W.W. Norton & Company. 436–525.

Mathews, Gordon, 2000. *Global Culture/Individual Identity: Searching for Home in the Cultural Supermarket*. London: Routledge.

Mathews, Gordon, Eric Ma, and Tai-Lok Lui, 2007. *Hong Kong, China: Learning to Belong to a Nation*. London: Routledge.

Meacham, William, 1984. "Coastal Landforms and Archaeology in the Hong Kong Archipelago." *World Archaeology*. Vol. 16, No. 1. 128–35.

Michael, Franz, 1986. "Traditional Tibetan Polity and Its Potential for Modernization." *Tibetan Journal*. Vol. 11, No. 4. 70–78.

Miners, Norman, 1986. *The Government and Politics of Hong Kong*. Hong Kong: University of Hong Kong Press.

Mingpao Editorial Office, ed., 2004. *The Patriotism Controversy* (愛國論爭). Hong Kong: Mingpao Press (明報出版社).

Minkins, Robert and Kelvin Lau, 2012. *The Offshore Renminbi: The Rise of the Chinese Currency and Its Global Future*. New York: Wiley.

Modongal, Shameer (with Zhouxiang Lu as reviewing editor), 2016. "Development of Nationalism in China." *Cogent Social Sciences*. Vol. 2, No. 1. DOI: 10.1080/23311886.2016.1235749.

Morris, Paul and Edward Vickers, 2015. "Schooling, Politics and the Construction of Identity in Hong Kong: The 2012 'Moral and National Education' Crisis in Historical Context." *Comparative Education*. Vol. 51, No. 3. 305–26.

Muizarajs, Mikes, 2019. "Timor-Leste: A Nation of Resistance." In Jon B. Alterman and Will Todman, eds., *Independence Movements and Their Aftermath: Self-Determination and the Struggle for Success*. Lanham, MD: CSIS/Rowman and Littlefield. 53–80.

Mullaney, Thomas, 2011. *Coming to Terms with the Nation: Ethnic Classification in Modern China*. Berkeley, CA: University of California Press.

Muller, Nicolas, 2019. "Nicaragua's Chinese-Financed Canal Project Still in Limbo" *The Diplomat*, August 20, 2019. At https://thediplomat.com /2019/08/nicaraguas-chinese-financed-canal-project-still-in-limbo.

Murphy, Melissa and Wen Jin Yuan, 2009. "Is China Ready to Challenge the Dollar? Internationalization of the Renminbi and Its Implications for the United States." CSIS Report, October 7, 2009. At https://csis-website-prod.s3.amazonaws.com/s3fs-public/legacy_files/files/publication/ 091007_Murphy_IsChinaReady_Web.pdf.

Murphy, Peter, Fergus Saurin, Edward Beeley, Sian Knight, and Holman Fenwik Willian, 2017. "Arbitration Procedures and Practice in Hong Kong: An Overview." Thomson Reuters Practical Law Q & A session script, December 1, 2017. At https://uk.practicallaw.thomsonreu ters.com/9-381-2657?__lrTS=20180917122905573&transitionType=Defa ult&contextData=(sc.Default)&firstPage=true.

Ng Chi Shum (吳志森). 2017. "Questioning Carrie Lam" (詰問林鄭). *Mingpao* (明報), August 20, 2017. At www.pentoy.hk/%E5%90% B3%E5%BF%97%E6%A3%AE%EF%BC%9A%E8%A9%B0%E5% 95%8F%E6%9E%97%E9%84%AD.

Ngo, Jeffrey, 2018. "Why the World Should Be Alarmed at Hong Kong's Expulsion of a Foreign Journalist," *Time*, October 16, 2018. At https:// time.com/5425653/victor-mallet-hong-kong-china-ft-media-freedom-fcc.

Ngo, Tak-wing, 1999. "Industrial History and the Artifice of *Laissez-faire* Colonialism." In Tak-wing Ngo, ed., *Hong Kong's History: State and Society under Colonial Rule*. New York: Routledge. 119–40.

Ngo, Tai-Wing, ed., 1999. *Hong Kong's History: State and Society under Colonial Rule*. London: Routledge.

Norbu, Dawa, 1979. "The 1959 Tibetan Rebellion: An Interpretation." *China Quarterly*. No. 77. 74–93.

Norbu, Dawa, 1991. "China's Dialogue with the Dalai Lama 1978–90: Prenegotiation Stage of Dead End?" *Pacific Affairs*. Vol. 64, No. 3. 351–72.

Ortmann, Stephan, 2016. "The Lack of Sovereignty, the Umbrella Movement, and Democratisation in Hong Kong." *Asia Pacific Law Review*. Vol. 24, No. 2. 108–22.

Palmer, Michael, 1987. "The Surface–Subsoil Form of Divided Ownership in Late Imperial China: Some Examples from the New Territories of Hong Kong." *Modern Asian Studies*. Vol. 21, No. 1. 1–119.

Pang, Ka Lam Eddie (彭嘉林), 2018. "Take What They Want: When Chinese Capital Occupies Hong Kong Construction"(予取予求: 當中資進佔香港 工程) *Mingpao*, February 2, 2018, at https://life.mingpao.com/general/ article?issue=20180202&nodeid=1517510008434&tag=hktoday.

Pang, Laik-wan, 2020. *The Appearing Demos: Hong Kong during and after the Umbrella Movement*. Ann Arbor: University of Michigan Press.

Pauly, Louis W., 2011. "Hong Kong's Financial Center in a Regional and Global Context," *Hong Kong Journal* (Carnegie Endowment for International Peace). No. 21, July 2011. At https://munkschool.utoronto.ca /pauly/selected_publications/Pauly%20Hong%20Kong%20Journal.pdf.

Pavkovic, Aleksandar, 2013. "Seceding by the Force of Arms: Chechnya and Kosovo." In Jean-Pierre Cabestan and Aleksandar Pavkovic, eds., *Secessionism and Separatism in Europe and Asia: To Have a State of One's Own*. London: Routledge. 99–109.

Perdue, Peter C., 2001. "Empire and Nation in Comparative Perspective: Frontier Administration in Eighteenth-Century China." *Journal of Early Modern History*. Vol. 5, No. 4. 283–304.

Perdue, Peter C., 2005. *China Marches West: The Qing Conquest of Central Eurasia*. Cambridge, MA: Harvard University Press.

Petech, Luciano, 1973. *Aristocracy and Government in Tibet, 1728–1959*. Rome: Istituto Italiano Per Il Medio Ed, Esremo Oriente.

Qi Pengfei (齊鵬飛), 2004. *Deng Xiaoping and the Return of Hong Kong* (鄧 小平與香港回歸). Beijing, China: Huaxia Press (華夏出版社).

Rowe, William T., 2002. "Social Stability and Social Change." In Willard J. Peterson, ed., *Cambridge History of China: Mid-Ching*. Cambridge: Cambridge University Press. 473–562.

Sassen, Saskia, 2001. *Global City: New York, London, Tokyo*. Princeton, NJ: Princeton University Press.

Schein, Louisa, 2000. *Minority Rules: The Miao and the Feminine in China's Cultural Politics*. Durham, NC: Duke University Press.

Schenk, Catherine, 2001. *Hong Kong as an International Financial Centre: Emergence and Development 1945–65*. London: Routledge.

Schenk, Catherine, 2011. "The Re-emergence of Hong Kong as an International Financial Centre 1960–78: Contested Internationalisation." In L. Quennouelle-Corre and Y. Cassis, eds., *Financial Centres and International Capital Flows in the Nineteenth and Twentieth Centuries*. Oxford: Oxford University Press. 199–253.

Schiffer, J.R., 1991. "State Policy and Economic Growth: A Note on the Hong Kong Model." *International Journal of Urban and Regional Research*. Vol. 15 No. 2. 180–96.

Scott, Ian, 1989. *Political Change and the Crisis of Legitimacy in Hong Kong*. Hong Kong: Oxford University Press.

Scott, James C., 2009. *The Art of Not Being Governed: An Anarchist History of Upland Southeast Asia*. New Haven, CT: Yale University Press.

Serwer, Daniel, 2019. "Kosovo: An Unlikely Success Still in the Making." In Jon B. Alterman and Will Todman, eds., *Independence Movements and Their Aftermath: Self-Determination and the Struggle for Success*. Lanham, MD: CSIS/Rowman and Littlefield. 81–99.

Sewell, William H., Jr., 1996. "Historical Events as Transformations of Structures: Inventing Revolution at the Bastille." *Theory and Society*. Vol. 25, No. 6. 841–81.

Shepherd, John, 1993. *Statecraft and Political Economy on the Taiwan Frontier, 1600–1800*. Palo Alto, CA: Stanford University Press.

Simeon, Richard and Luc Turgeon, 2013. "Seeking Autonomy in a Decentralized Federation: The Case of Quebec." In Yash Ghai and Sophia Woodman, eds., *Practising Self-Government: A Comparative Study of Autonomous Regions*. Cambridge: Cambridge University Press. 32–6.

Sing, Ming, 2004. *Hong Kong's Tortuous Democratization: A Comparative Analysis*. London: Routledge.

Sing, Ming, 2009. *Politics and Government in Hong Kong: Crisis under Chinese Sovereignty*. London: Routledge.

Sing, Ming, 2019. "How Students Took Leadership of the Umbrella Movement: Marginalization of Prodemocracy Parties." In Ching Kwan Lee and Ming Sing, eds., *Take Back Our Future: An Eventful Sociology of the Hong Kong Umbrella Movement*. Ithaca, NY: Cornell University Press. 144–66.

Sinn, Elizabeth, 2003. *Power and Charity: A Chinese Merchant Elite in Colonial Hong Kong*. Hong Kong: Hong Kong University Press.

Siroky, David S. and John Cuffe, 2015. "Lost Autonomy, Nationalism and Separatism." *Comparative Political Studies*. Vol. 48, No. 1. 3–34.

Siu, Helen F., 1996. "Remade in Hong Kong: Weaving into the Chinese Cultural Tapestry." In Tao Tao Liu and David Faure, eds., *Unity and Diversity: Local Cultures and Identities in China*. Hong Kong: Hong Kong University Press. 177–96.

Siu, Helen F. and Liu Zhiwei, 2006. "Lineage, Market, Pirate, and Dan: Ethnicity in the Pearl River Delta of South China." In Pamela Kyle Crossley, Helen Siu, and Donald Sutton, eds., *Empire at the Margins: Culture, Ethnicity, and Frontier in Early Modern China*. Berkeley: University of California Press. 285–310.

Siu, Kwok-kin (蕭國健), 1985a. "On Tuen Mun" (屯門考). In Lin Tian-wei (林天蔚) and Siu Kwok kin (蕭國健), *Essays on Hong Kong Precolonial History* (香港前代史論集). Taipei: Commercial Press. 73–9.

Siu, Kwok-kin, 1985b. "Social Change before and after the Coastal Evacuation Order in Early Qing" (清初遷界前後香港之社會變遷). In Lin Tian-wei (林天蔚) and Siu Kwok kin (蕭國健), *Essays on Hong Kong Precolonial History* (香港前代史論集). Taipei: Commercial Press. 206–33.

Smart, Alan, 1992. *Making Room: Squatter Clearance in Hong Kong*. Hong Kong: Center of Asian Studies, Hong Kong University.

Smith, Warren W., Jr., 1994. "The Nationalities Policy of the Chinese Communist Party and the Socialist Transformation of Tibet." In Robert Barnett, ed., *Resistance and Reform in Tibet*. Bloomington: Indiana University Press. 51–75.

Smith, Warren W., Jr., 1996. *Tibetan Nation: A History of Tibetan Nationalism and Sino-Tibetan Relations*. Boulder, CO: Westview Press.

Snow, Edgar, 1968. *Red Star over China*. New York: Grove Press.

Snow, Philip, 2004. *The Fall of Hong Kong: Britain, China, and the Japanese Occupation*. New Haven, CT: Yale University Press.

So, Alvin Y., 1999. *Hong Kong's Embattled Democracy: A Societal Analysis*. Baltimore: Johns Hopkins University Press.

So, Alvin Y., 2000. "Hong Kong's Problematic Democratic Transition: Power Dependency or Business Hegemony?" *Journal of Asian Studies*. Vol. 59, No. 2. 359–81.

Solheim, Wilhelm G., II, 2006. *Archaeology and Culture in Southeast Asia: Unraveling the Nusantao*. Diliman, Quezon City, Philippines: University of the Philippines Press.

Song, Wendy W., 2014. "U.S. Export Controls Update: Why Hong Kong Dominates the New Unverified List." *Corporate Compliance Insights*, July 30, 2014. At www.corporatecomplianceinsights.com/us-export-controls-update-why-hong-kong-dominates-the-new-unverified-list.

Spruyt, Hendrik, 1996. *The Sovereign State and Its Competitors: An Analysis of Systems Change*. Princeton, NJ: Princeton University Press.

Starr, Frederick S., 2004. *Xinjiang: China's Muslim Borderland*. Armonk, NY: M.E. Sharpe.

Stein, Rolf Alfred, 1972. *Tibetan Civilization*. Palo Alto, CA: Stanford University Press.

Steinhardt, H. Christoph, Linda Chelan Li, and Yihong Jiang, 2018. "The Identity Shift in Hong Kong since 1997: Measurement and Explanation." *Journal of Contemporary China*. Vol. 27, No. 110. 261–76.

Stoddard, Heather, 1986. "Tibet from Buddhism to Communism." *Government and Opposition*. Vol. 21, No. 1. 76–95.

Suksi, Markku, 2013. "Prosperity and Happiness through Autonomy: The Self-Government of the Åland Islands in Finland." In Yash Ghai and Sophia Woodman, eds., *Practising Self-Government: A Comparative Study of Autonomous Regions*. Cambridge: Cambridge University Press. 62–90.

Szeto, Wah (司徒華), 2011. *River Runs East* (大江東去). Hong Kong: Oxford University Press.

Tai, Benny, 2020a. "Pan-Democrats Legislative of More than 35 Seats Amounts to a Constitutional Weapon of Mass Destruction" (泛民逾35

席如大殺傷力憲制武器) *Apple Daily*, March 27, 2020. At https://hk.apple
daily.com/local/20200327/URW4QYY7U5B6TLRRUU3V47UP44.

Tai, Benny, 2020b. "We Go Up and Down Together Our Goal Is 35+" (齊上齊
落 目標35+). *Apple Daily*, March 10, 2020. At https://hk.appledaily.com
/local/20200310/HB36XAV5FGKYTM47D6NYRMMTSM.

Takla, T.N., 1969. "Notes on Some Early Tibetan Communists." *Tibetan
Review*. Vol. 2, No. 17. 7–10.

Tam, Wai-keung, 2012. *Legal Mobilization under Authoritarianism: The
Case of Post-colonial Hong Kong*. New York: Cambridge University
Press.

Taylor, Peter J. and Ben Derudder, 2015. *World City Network: A Global
Urban Analysis*. 2nd edn. New York and London: Routledge.

Tilly, Charles, 1989. *Big Structures, Large Processes, Huge Comparisons*.
New York: Russell Sage Foundation.

Tilly, Charles, 1993. *Coercion, Capital, and European States, AD 990–1990*.
Oxford: Blackwell.

Tilly, Charles and Wimp Blockmans, eds., 1994. *Cities and the Rise of States
in Europe, A.D. 1000 to 1800*. Boulder, CO: Westview.

Ting, Chun Chun, 2013. "The Star and the Queen: Heritage Conservation
and the Emergence of a New Hong Kong Subject." *Modern Chinese
Literature and Culture*. Vol. 25, No. 2. 80–129.

Topley, M., 1964. "Capital, Saving and Credit among Indigenous Rice
Farmers and Immigrant Vegetable Farmers in Hong Kong's New
Territories." In R. Firth and B.S. Yamey, eds., *Capital, Saving and
Credit in Peasant Societies*. London: George Allen and Unwin. 157–87.

Tsai, J.F., 1993. *Hong Kong in Chinese History: Community and Social
Unrest in the British Colony, 1842–1913*. New York: Columbia
University Press.

Tsang, Steve Yui-sang, 1988. *Democracy Shelved: Great Britain, China, and
Attempts at Constitutional Reform in Hong Kong, 1945–1952*. Oxford:
Oxford University Press.

Tsang, Steve Yui-sang, 2007. *A Modern History of Hong Kong*. London: I.B.
Tauris.

Tse, Kwun Tung (謝冠東) 2010. "This History of the Resistance against the
XRL: An Afterword of the January 16 Rally" (這段高鐵抗爭的歷史：1.16
反高鐵集會後記). *Inmedia* (獨立媒體), January 27, 2010. At www
.inmediahk.net/node/1005946.

Tse, Thomas Kwan-choi, 2004. "Civic Education and the Making of
Deformed Citizenry: From British Colony to Chinese SAR." In
Agnes S. Ku and Ngai Pun, eds., *Remaking Citizenship in
Hong Kong: Community, Nation, and the Global City*. London:
Routledge. 54–73.

Tsui, Eric (徐承恩), 2017. *Depressed and Agonized Home Nation: Local Views on Hong Kong Origins* (鬱躁的家邦: 本土觀點的香港源流史). Taipei: Rive Gauche Publishing House.

Undergrad Editorial Board, ed., 2014. *Hong Kong Nation, Self-Determination of Destiny* (香港民族 命運自決). Special issue of *Undergrad*, February 2014.

Veg, Sebastian, 2007. "Cultural Heritage in Hong Kong: The Rise of Activism and the Contradictions of Identity." *China Perspectives*. No. 2. 46–8.

Veg, Sebastian, 2017. "The Rise of 'Localism' and Civic Identity in Post-handover Hong Kong: Questioning the Chinese Nation-State." *China Quarterly*. Vol. 230. 323–47.

Walter, Carl E. and Fraser J.T. Howie, 2012. *Red Capitalism: The Fragile Financial Foundation of China's Extraordinary Rise*. New York: Wiley.

Wang Lixiong (王力雄). 1998. *Sky Burial: The Fate of Tibet* (天葬:西藏的命運). Hong Kong: Mirror Books (明鏡出版社).

Wang-Kaeding, Heidi and Malte Philipp, 2019, "Red Capital in Hong Kong." *Asian Education and Development Studies*. Vol. 8, No. 2. 149–60.

Wangye, Bapa Phuntso (with Melvyn C. Goldstein, Dawei Sherap, and William R. Siebenschuh), 2004. *A Tibetan Revolutionary: The Political Life and Times of Bapa Phuntso Wangye*. Berkeley: University of California Press.

Wasserstrom, Jeffrey, 2020. *Vigil: Hong Kong on the Brink*. New York: Columbia Global Reports.

Watson, James, 1975. *Emigration and the Chinese Lineage: The Mans in Hong Kong and London*. Berkeley, CA: University of California Press.

Watson, James, 1983. "Rural Society: Hong Kong's New Territories." *China Quarterly*. Vol. 95. 480–90.

Weber, Max, 1966 [1921]. *The City*. New York: Free Press.

Wong, Kevin Tse-wai (黃子為), Victor Wan-tai Zheng (鄭宏泰), and Po-san Wan (尹寶珊), 2020. "Are Mainland Immigrants Arriving after Handover More Affined to Establishment Parties?" (回歸後來港內地移民 更親建制派?). *Hong Kong Economic Times*, August 8, 2020. At https://paper.hket.com/article/2718596/%E5%9B%9E%E6%AD%B8%E5%BE%8C%E4%BE%86%E6%B8%AF%E5%85%A7%E5%9C%B0%E7%A7%BB%E6%B0%91%20%E6%9B%B4%E8%A6%AA%E5%BB%BA%E5%88%B6%E6%B4%BE%EF%BC%9F.

Wong, Stan Hok-Wui, 2014. "Resource Disparity and Multi-level Elections in Competitive Authoritarian Regimes: Regression Discontinuity Evidence from Hong Kong." *Electoral Studies*. Vol. 33. 200–19.

Wong, Stan Hok-Wui and Kin Man Wan, 2018. "The Housing Boom and the Rise of Localism in Hong Kong: Evidence from the Legislative Council Election in 2016." *China Perspectives*. No. 3. 31–40.

Wong, Thomas W.P., 1998. "Colonial Governance and the Hong Kong Story." Occasional paper, Hong Kong Institute of Asia–Pacific Studies, Chinese University of Hong Kong.

Wong, Thomas W.P. and Tai-Lok Lui, 1992. "From One Brand of Politics to One Brand of Political Culture." Occasional Paper No. 10, Hong Kong Institute of Asia–Pacific Studies, Chinese University of Hong Kong.

Wong, Thomas W.P. and Tai-Lok Lui, 1993. "Morality, Class and the Hong Kong Way of Life." Occasional Paper No. 30, Hong Kong Institute of Asia–Pacific Studies, Chinese University of Hong Kong.

Wong, S., 2015. "Real Estate Elite, Economic Development, and Political Conflicts in Postcolonial Hong Kong." *China Review*. Vol. 15, No. 1. 1–38.

Wong, S., Ngok Ma and W. Lam, 2018. "Immigrants as Voters in Electoral Autocracies: The Case of Mainland Chinese Immigrants in Hong Kong." *Journal of East Asian Studies*. Vol. 18, No. 1. 67–95.

Wong, Timothy Ka-ying, 1996. *Ethnic Identity and National Identity of the People in Hong Kong: A Liberal Explanation*. Hong Kong: Hong Kong Institute of Asia–Pacific Studies.

Wong, Wang-chi (王宏志), 2000. *The Weight of History: Viewing Hong Kong Historiography in China from Hong Kong* (歷史的沉重: 從香港看中國大陸的香港史論述). Hong Kong: Oxford University Press.

Wong, Yiu-chung, 2004. *One Country, Two Systems in Crisis: Hong Kong's Transformation since the Handover*. Lanham, MD: Lexington Books.

Woodman, Sophia and Yash Ghai, 2013. "Comparative Perspectives on Institutional Frameworks for Autonomy." In Yash Ghai and Sophia Woodman, eds., *Practising Self-Government: A Comparative Study of Autonomous Regions*. Cambridge: Cambridge University Press. 449–86.

Wu, Rwei-Ren, 2016. "The Lilliputian Dreams: Preliminary Observations of Nationalism in Okinawa, Taiwan and Hong Kong." *Nations and Nationalism*. Vol. 22, No. 4. 686–705.

Xia, Xueping (夏學平), 1997. "The Chinese Communist Party and Hong Kong" (中國共產黨與香港). Ph.D dissertation, School of Law, Northeast Normal University, Shenyang, Liaoning, China.

Xu, Jiatun (許家屯), 1993. *A Memoir of Xu Jiatun* (許家屯回憶錄). Taipei: Lianjing chubanshe (聯經出版社).

Yahuda, Michael, 1993. "Hong Kong's Future: Sino-British Negotiations, Perceptions, Organization and Political Culture." *International Affairs*. Vol. 69, No. 2. 245–66.

Yeh, Anthony G.O., Guanghan Chen, Victor Fung-Shuen Sit, and Yunyuan Zhou, 2006. *Developing a Competitive Pearl River Delta in South China under One Country–Two Systems*. Hong Kong: University of Hong Kong Press.

Yen, Ching-Hwang, 2013. *Ethnic Chinese Business in Asia: History, Culture and Business Enterprise*. Singapore: World Scientific.

Yep, Ray, ed., 2013. *Negotiating Autonomy in Greater China: Hong Kong and Its Sovereign before and after 1997*. Copenhagen: NIAS Press.

Yep, Ray and Tai-lok Lui, 2010. "Revisiting the Golden Era of MacLehose and the Dynamics of Social Reforms." *China Information*. Vol. 24, No. 3. 249–72.

Yew, Chiew-Ping and Kin-ming Kwong, 2014. "Hong Kong Identity on the Rise." *Asian Survey*. Vol. 54, No. 6, 1088–1112.

Yuan, Qiushi (袁求實), 1997. *Chronology of Hong Kong's Return, 1979–1997* (香港回歸大事記, 1979–1997). Hong Kong: Joint Publishing.

Yuen, Samson, 2019. "Transgressive Politics in Occupy Mongkok." In Ching Kwan Lee and Ming Sing, eds., *Take Back Our Future: An Eventful Sociology of the Hong Kong Umbrella Movement*. Ithaca, NY: Cornell University Press. 52–37.

Yuen, Samson, 2020. "Native-Place Networks and Political Mobilization: The Case of Post-handover Hong Kong." *Modern China*. Forthcoming (online first). At https://journals.sagepub.com/doi/abs/10.1177/0097700420934093.

Yuen, Samson and Chung San-ho, 2018. "Explaining Localism in Post-handover Hong Kong: An Eventful Approach." *China Perspectives*. No. 3. 19–29.

Zhao, Suisheng, 2004. *A Nation-State by Construction: Dynamics of Modern Chinese Nationalism*. Palo Alto, CA: Stanford University Press.

Zheng, Yongnian and Chiew Ping Yew, eds., 2013. *Hong Kong under Chinese Rule: Economic Integration and Political Gridlock*. Singapore: World Scientific.

Zhou, Xiaochuan, 2009. "Reform the International Monetary System." Bank of International Settlement, March 23, 2009. At www.bis.org/review/r090402c.pdf.

Zhou, Yi (周奕), 2002. *A History of the Struggle of Hong Kong Leftists* (香港左派鬥爭史). Hong Kong: Lee Man Publisher (利文出版社).

Zhou, Yi, 2009, *A History of Hong Kong's Labor Movements* (香港工運史) Hong Kong: Lee Sun Publisher (利訊出版社).

INDEX